THE GIRL FROM FOREIGN

THE GIRL FROM FOREIGN

A Search for Shipwrecked Ancestors,
Forgotten Histories, and a Sense of Home

SADIA SHEPARD

THE PENGUIN PRESS

New York

2008

THE PENGUIN PRESS
Published by the Penguin Group
Penguin Group (USA) Inc., 375 Hudson Street, New York, New York 10014, U.S.A. •
Penguin Group (Canada), 90 Eglinton Avenue East, Suite 700, Toronto, Ontario, Canada M4P 2Y3
(a division of Pearson Penguin Canada Inc.) • Penguin Books Ltd, 80 Strand, London WC2R 0RL,
England • Penguin Ireland, 25 St. Stephen's Green, Dublin 2, Ireland (a division of Penguin Books Ltd)
• Penguin Books Australia Ltd, 250 Camberwell Road, Camberwell, Victoria 3124, Australia (a division
of Pearson Australia Group Pty Ltd) • Penguin Books India Pvt Ltd, 11 Community Centre,
Panchsheel Park, New Delhi–110 017, India • Penguin Group (NZ), 67 Apollo Drive, Rosedale,
North Shore 0632, New Zealand (a division of Pearson New Zealand Ltd) • Penguin Books
(South Africa) (Pty) Ltd, 24 Sturdee Avenue, Rosebank, Johannesburg 2196, South Africa

Penguin Books Ltd, Registered Offices: 80 Strand, London WC2R 0RL, England

First published in 2008 by The Penguin Press,
a member of Penguin Group (USA) Inc.

Copyright © Sadia Shepard, 2008
All rights reserved

Photographs courtesy of the author

LIBRARY OF CONGRESS CATALOGING-IN-PUBLICATION DATA

Shepard, Sadia.
The girl from foreign : a search for shipwrecked ancestors, forgotten histories,
and a sense of home / Sadia Shepard.
p.   cm.
ISBN 978-1-59420-151-6
1. Jews—Identity—United States.   2. Shepard, Sadia.   3. Shepard Sadia—Family.   4. Jewish
women—United States—Biography.   5. Jewish women—India—Biography.   6. Muslim converts
from Judaism—United States—Biography.   7. Grandparent and child—Biography.   I. Title.
E184.36.E84S54   2008
973'.04924054092—dc22
2008003912

Printed in the United States of America
1   3   5   7   9   10   8   6   4   2

DESIGNED BY NICOLE LAROCHE
MAP BY MEIGHAN CAVANAUGH

For Nana

CONTENTS

PART THREE

DEPARTURES

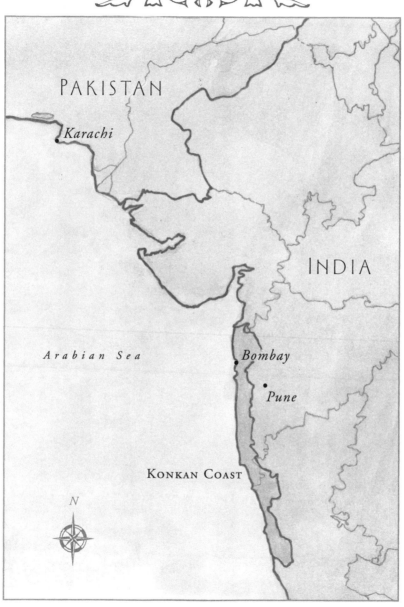

PAKISTAN

Karachi

INDIA

Arabian Sea

Bombay

Pune

KONKAN COAST

N

When I think of Bombay now, at this distance of time, I seem to have a kaleidoscope at my eye; and I hear the clash of the glass bits as the splendid figures change, and fall apart, and flash into new forms, figure after figure, and with the birth of each new form I feel my skin crinkle and my nerve-web tingle with a new thrill of wonder and delight. These remembered pictures float past me in a series of contrasts; following the same order always, and always whirling by and disappearing with the swiftness of a dream, leaving me with the sense that the actuality was the experience of an hour, at most, whereas it really covered days, I think.

—*Following the Equator*, MARK TWAIN

And might it not be, continued Austerlitz, that we also have appointments to keep in the past, in what has gone before and is for the most part extinguished, and must go there in search of places and people who have some connection with us on the far side of time, so to speak?

—*Austerlitz*, W. G. SEBALD

THE GIRL FROM FOREIGN

ARRIVAL

It is the sounds we hear as children that shape us.

It is the snap-crush of spices under the heel of my grandmother's hand. It is the slip-splash of her fingertips, sliding fish into turmeric water. It is the thwack of her palms, clapping chapattis into life on her flat stone, a perfect circle, every time. It is the swish of her sari, the click of her knitting needles, the tap-tap of the soles of her feet hitting the soles of her sandals. There lies my grandmother's Morse code.

Her voice is quiet and fierce as she braids my long hair, telling me fragments of stories, pieces of her life in India. In my child's ears she whispers her dreams—strange, frightening dreams that have come to her in sleep since she was a child, predicting every death in our family. She weaves these dreams and these stories into my braids. They are mine now, tied with red ribbons.

Listen carefully. These are the sounds of my house.

Downstairs my father is teaching my six-year-old brother, Cassim, to ride a bicycle in the driveway. Cassim is too small; he is falling off the bike and laughing; my father is calling out to him to look straight ahead, don't look down, there you have it. "Stay straight! Stay on the driveway!" My mother is in the kitchen, talking on the telephone to her brothers in Pakistan. It is afternoon in Boston, the middle of the night in Karachi; she is shouting in Urdu to be heard across the distance. "I'll be arriving on the sixteenth of next month! What do you need from here? Send the driver to the airport!"

YEARS LATER, I visit Bombay as an adult, and the city seems strangely familiar, like the end of an interrupted conversation. Its smell: burnt tea, freshly lit fire, fish splayed open and hung out to dry on long sticks, those pungent antennae. Its noise: the cacophony of car horns, the flight of birds overhead, the blaring pop song wailing ever present in the background. Its light: the haze of morning giving way to the splintering bright of noon, and then 5:30 p.m. high tea, when the city looks like a giant, writhing picture show, chaos bathed in a patina of dusty gold.

The stories my grandmother told me are outlines, marks in black ink on a page, the salient details. *Bombay was my birthplace. My mother had twelve children; six of them died.* Everything Nana told me about her life was a remnant, a piece of a phrase. Whenever Nana told me stories, I badgered her for details, as many as I could think to ask. I worried that someday, when I needed to tell these stories to explain who I am, I would wonder about the color of the dress she wore in a certain black-and-white photo and she would no longer be alive to tell me. The sum total of what I could imagine about India was contained in my grandmother's brown vinyl album, hundreds of tiny prints with scalloped edges. What comes in between these details is my own invention; the shape and shade are the work of a grandchild to embroider. I've spent years trying to paint the colors in.

A Fulbright Scholarship allowed me to quit my job, put my belongings in storage, and buy a one-way ticket to India. Now that I'm here, the possibilities are dizzying. I look at the new stamp in my passport, trace the embossed letters with my fingertips, curious about what the next year will bring. In the upper left-hand corner of my visa is an "R," for "Research." So much of what I want to know about my grandmother and my ancestors is a mystery, a well-guarded secret. I am here as an amateur detective on that most American of journeys: a search for the roots of my own particular tree. This is a reverse migration. I have returned to the land that nurtured my grandmother and my mother, to walk where they walked, to make my own map within their maps. In my shoulder bag I'm carrying a curious collection of objects: a crumbling mimeograph of family names, five yellowing books with beloved cracked spines, a handful of sepia photographs of unfamiliar faces.

I feel very far from Chestnut Hill, from the white clapboard house where I was raised, the tiny eyes of Mughal miniature paintings, the watchful, gilded gaze of my father's great-great-grandmother's portrait. The presence of that house stays with me, the happy disorder of holidays unfolding in the embrace of its deep, wide doorways and dark wood. It was a solid kind of place, anchored by my three parents: my father, my mother, and my maternal grandmother, Nana. As a child I thought of our home as a miniature kingdom, ruled by a fierce and benevolent triumvirate. It's the prospect of adulthood that has brought me here, seeking Bombay, the backdrop of the stories I grew up with. I want to know if it exists, the mythic home my mother and my grandmother spun in their stories. I want this city to fill the gaps in my understanding and make me whole.

As my taxi speeds through Bombay traffic, a memory of Nana's voice, its quality of hushed electricity, rings in my ears:

"Your grandfather built me a house in Bombay, facing the ocean. You could hear the sound of the waves as you slept, as if you were sleeping in a ship. . . ."

WHAT I KNOW ARE FRAGMENTS. I am here to weave them together, to create a new story, a story uniquely my own.

PART ONE

STORYTELLING

1

THE PAINTED CITY

CHESTNUT HILL, 1985 / BOMBAY, SEPTEMBER 2001

I n the upstairs front hallway of my childhood home near Boston there hung a large, vivid portrait of my mother. It was painted by Bombay cinema painters, those billboard romantics, homesick for undivided India. I remember when the painting first arrived, a sticky evening in 1985, my brother, Cassim, my father, my grandmother, and I impatiently waiting at Logan Airport among a throng of expatriates from the Subcontinent—a sea of brown faces and my tall white father, forming a ring outside of International Arrivals, there to meet the night flight from Karachi. The double doors swung open with a mechanical snap and thud; the passengers began to pour through. Signs with handwritten names went up like a flock of birds, flap-flap, higher! Higher! And cries of "Over here! Over here!" And "There she is!"

Mama emerged with the portrait under one arm and a look of happy triumph on her face. We soon saw why. She had asked the painters to right the hand that fate dealt her—in the portrait she's fairer, thinner, and richer. Her dark hair is lit with shades of gold, and her right hand cups her slim

cheek, as if she is lost in thought. A pair of shoulder-length diamond earrings graze her collar. It's a remarkable likeness; there's something unmistakably familiar about the heart-shaped face, the mischievous angle of the chin.
And yet to accept it as an accurate representation of my mother is to accept
a double reality, the Indian shake of the head, back and forth, right to left,
yes and no both.

The city in the background of the painting—blue, tented, the skyline
punctured with minarets—I have always assumed to be Bombay, the city she
and my grandmother left behind during Partition, the city my grandmother
missed deeply. There's no doubt that it's a dreamlike, hazy rendition of pre-
Partition India, a likeness of my family's remembered home. This mythic city
is the stage set of the stories I was told in childhood, a place frozen in time.
It cannot, by necessity, be the India I walk through as an adult.

I ARRIVE IN BOMBAY on a sweltering day in September 2001, fifteen
months after my grandmother's death. I have received a Fulbright Scholarship to study in India for a year. The contents of my New York apartment
are now packed into a storage space; with me I have five cameras and two
suitcases stuffed with supplies. I'm hoping to use the time here to discover
how to navigate the places of my grandmother's childhood and to fulfill a
promise that I made to her before she died, to learn about her ancestors. For
the beginning of my scholarship, I will be based in Pune, a city 170 kilometers to the southeast, but my first destination is Bombay, my grandmother's
hometown.

I decide to spend the night in Colaba, a part of Bombay frequented by
Western travelers. It is only a few days after the World Trade Center attacks,
and I push thoughts of the chaos back home into a corner of my mind as I
walk along the Causeway, a roofed path where hawkers sell cheap clothing
and knickknacks. I pass stacks of newspapers in English, Marathi, and
Hindi, all running the same images of smoke and debris.

I find a room in an old guesthouse. I set my bags down and shower,
dressing in a worn cotton salwar kameez left over from one of my trips to

Pakistan. Around my neck is something I found among my grandmother's papers—a tiny, bent copper key on a long gold chain. I have no idea what it's for, but I've been wearing it as a sort of talisman, a reminder of her, since she died. I like the idea that something of hers will make the journey back, with me.

I walk into the bright heat of the day, hail a taxi, and tell the driver to go to Worli Sea Face—a mostly residential part of the city that faces the ocean. As we drive the crowded streets, fragments of my grandmother's stories come back to me. I remember a conversation we had—how many times?—as we stood by the stove, peeling buds of garlic and ginger and mashing them to make a paste, that sharp concoction that formed the basis of everything we ate. The story always began the same way; I always asked the same questions.

"Your grandfather built me a house facing the ocean on Worli Sea Face. It was a beautiful white house with three stories and two gardens, one front and one back. You could hear the waves crashing on the shore. It was like sleeping in a ship. A big ship. On the front was the name of the house, Rahat Villa."

"Named for you, Nana?"

"*Haan,* named for me. My husband named the house for me. Your mother was born there, and we lived there until we had to go to Pakistan. My mother and my brothers lived with me, and I was independent then, it was my own home. It was not like in Karachi, with so many wives, so many children."

"Nana, why did you marry Grandfather if you knew he was already married?"

"That's not a story for a young girl."

I have told the taxi driver everything I know: Worli Sea Face, a big white house, Rahat Villa, facing the ocean. As we drive beside the shore, I see now that there are precious few private homes left; they have been replaced with high-rises. I have a sinking feeling. Perhaps it's not here; perhaps it's been torn down. We reach the end of the buildings facing the water, and I ask the driver to go back the way we came, slower this time. I see an Art Deco bungalow, white stucco, but it's two stories, not three. Is that it? No, she said three, with a garden in front and a garden in back. And a shrine. I remember that there was a tiny Sufi shrine, a small alcove built into the wall, which my grandfather had restored.

And then suddenly I see it. The house looks familiar, as if I have seen it a million times, and I realize that I must have seen photographs of it, pasted into my grandmother's album. Where it should say "Rahat Villa" it now reads "Shandilya Villa," but it is unmistakably the same house. I ask the driver to stop and I send him away, before realizing that I don't know where I will find a taxi back.

But I'm here. I walk up the driveway, toward the house, with the sea at my back. There's the carved gazebo on the front lawn, ringed with knotty trees, and the grand front door, dark wood with a brass knob. There's the wall where my mother peered into the neighbor's yard, crying out for her *ayah,* her nurse Lucy, who was offered more money to work for the family next door. There's the covered veranda where my great-grandmother grated coconut.

A watchman approaches me slowly, curious about my purpose.

"Mr. Shandilya hain?" I ask. "Is Mr. Shandilya here?" I guess that the new owner has named the house after himself.

He waves me ahead, and I approach the side entrance. It occurs to me after I have rung the bell that I have no idea what I will say. A houseboy opens the door, and I repeat my question: *"Mr. Shandilya hain?"*

There is some confusion. There are, apparently, two Mr. Shandilyas, one elder and one younger. Asked to clarify, I request to see the elder Mr. Shandilya. I am ushered into the hallway, and I am surprised again by how familiar it all seems. There is something in the heft of the white marble and the intricate pattern of the lattice that is Nana all around me. She chose these walls, these mantels and fixtures, and these choices were gestures of permanence—strong, heavy, timeless materials. The six years she lived in this house with her first two children, her mother, and her brothers was the only time she ever had a place of her own, something she would try to replicate for the rest of her life but would never find again. Her husband, the provider, was a rare visitor to Rahat Villa in those days. He would arrive unannounced, then leave with little warning, for his other homes, his other wives and children. When Nana left Bombay for Karachi after the Partition of India, she left behind her birthplace and her community for a new life; she became the third wife in a joint Muslim household, all three families under one roof.

My heart is pounding. I feel as if I have come to take back this house.

I am led through the front hall and into the main parlor, still furnished in the Art Deco style popular when my grandmother completed the house in the late 1930s: dark, carved wooden furniture with stylized forms, scalloped edges. The furniture is arranged in conversational groups, and it reminds me powerfully of my grandmother's room in Boston. I realize what she was trying to re-create. It is all here; I see it.

We walk up a central staircase, and my breath catches when I recognize a low set of drawers in one of the rooms; it has the same inlaid ivory pattern and carving as an armoire my grandmother had in our family home in Karachi, where she kept her jewelry and important papers. I motion to the houseboy to ask him if I may enter the room, and he nods. I imagine this could have been her bedroom. I post imaginary telegrams to her in my mind: "I am sitting on your bed in Rahat Villa, Nana. I am imagining you here."

Mr. Shandilya is resting on the upstairs veranda of the house, in a chair facing the lawn, smoking a pipe. He appears to be in his mid-eighties, the age my grandmother would be now if she were alive. He is dressed in white and looks as if he is made of paper, as if he may blow away if the wind gets any stronger. I explain that I am Rahat's granddaughter, from America, and it's clear that he finds this news perplexing. He smiles an apologetic, befuddled smile and busies himself with his pipe while I speak all of the Hindi I know. When I come to the end of my speech I begin again, this time in English. "I am from New York. My name is Sadia. My grandmother was Rahat." And this time, I tell him other things.

"My grandmother spoke of this house. She used to wake up sometimes thinking that she was here, in the upstairs bedroom facing the ocean. She used to sit on the rocks facing the water. There, across the street."

Mr. Shandilya begins gently thumping his cane on the floor, and the houseboy comes running. Tea is produced, and I am grateful for it. I know that he probably doesn't understand me. But it feels important to speak of Nana here, in the one place that was ever really hers. We sit in a benevolent, awkward silence. Sweat trickles down my side.

Something she often said comes back to me. For each of us, there is a time in our lives that we return to again and again in our thoughts, a place we walk through silently. Mine is the spring before Nana died. When I sleep, I am locked in April and May of my grandmother's last year, when I could still see Nana and talk to her. For Nana, it was the years she spent in Rahat Villa. For the rest of her life, when she woke up disoriented in the middle of the night, it was this house that she was stumbling back from.

Mr. Shandilya turns his cane between his thumb and forefinger, back and forth, back and forth. A bird begins its afternoon call.

"I wanted to see it with my own eyes," I tell him.

He nods, gravely, as if it were all perfectly clear. He is either too polite or too deaf to respond. He refills his pipe. A young man arrives and exchanges a few words with Mr. Shandilya. He is Vitin, Mr. Shandilya's grandson. I explain who I am, and he nods quickly. He offers to take me on a tour of the rest of the house. I want most of all to see the roof: Nana spoke so often of watching the water crash on the shore from the top of the house. Vitin leads me through the rooms upstairs, and while he does I ask him about his family and his studies. He responds to my questions shyly and quickly. He is a little younger than I am, and is studying computer science. He takes me up the stairs to the roof, and we walk across the wide, flat space, ringed with a parapet wall, looking down on the waves crashing below.

"Does your grandfather know who I am?" I ask.

There is a pause, and then he says, thoughtfully, "Actually, it's a remarkable thing. I believe he thinks you are Rahat, the original owner of the house."

"She was my grandmother," I say, as I watch a washerwoman on the edge of the shore hold a piece of wet laundry high above her head and bring it down, like a cracking whip, against the black rocks, again and again. "Before she died, she asked me to come here. She wanted me to see her house. It's just the way she described it."

We stand, looking at the water and watching the cars zoom by on the road, far below. Nana always said Rahat Villa felt like a tall ship, and I understand what she meant for the first time.

"It was good of you to come," Vitin says.

2

SHIPWRECKED ANCESTORS

CHESTNUT HILL, 1988

One Saturday, when I was thirteen years old, I found myself lurking at the door to my grandmother's room. My mother was sitting at my grandmother's feet, her head between my grandmother's knees, and Nana was rubbing coconut oil into Mama's scalp. They were speaking in Urdu, their private language, and I wished that I could understand what they were talking about.

In the shelves by the door, Nana kept her precious china and strange odds and ends from her journeys abroad: a teacup from Sweden that read "Farmor = Grandma," a tiny egg in a ceramic nest, a miniature guard from Buckingham Palace. There was a radio on in the background, a woman singing a Hindi pop song. I wanted to enter the room, but I wasn't sure I was welcome.

Nana's giant, dark wood four-poster bed occupied the center of the room. The windows were hung with English-style chintz, large red roses that matched her rose-colored quilt. On the right side was a fireplace, the mantel lined with family photographs. There were pictures of Nana's children: my mother and her brothers, growing up in Pakistan; my mother at fifteen, the day she left for America, proud, garlanded with strings of marigolds, her long black hair in a thick braid almost reaching her waist; my uncles in their twenties at each of their weddings. Then there were color photographs of my immediate family: my parents' wedding at my father's family home in the Rocky Mountains of Colorado; my younger brother, Cassim, and I as babies; then the two of us as toddlers; then us at thirteen and ten.

Nana never spoke to me the way she did with Mama. With me she spoke English, quietly and haltingly. With Mama she spoke quickly, in Urdu, and often seemed to be angry. That day, I guessed that they were talking about the property disputes surrounding Siddiqi House, our family home in Karachi, shared among my grandfather's three widows and ten children. Nana's sons, my mother's four younger brothers, were scattered across Europe and the United States. Often we would not see them for long periods, and then they would arrive with presents, driving fancy cars and wearing nice clothing. My grandmother seemed happiest then, when her children were in one place. It's not the custom for a woman to live with her daughter and son-in-law, and Nana often talked about wanting to move in with one of her sons. She spent part of every year traveling to see them, carting her large, carefully packed suitcases to their homes, places as far as Pakistan, England, and Sweden and as close as New Jersey. The rest of the year, she was with us, the eyes and ears of our household. Her room was at the top of the stairs, and from her four-poster bed she watched the comings and goings of our family.

I edged myself into the room. The pungent smell of coconut oil, a heady combination of candy and musk, filled the room. I knew better than to interrupt, and so I walked quietly to my grandmother's bureau and rested my hands on the double handles. I said that I was looking for a safety pin and asked if I could open the bureau.

Mama and Nana were barely listening. Nana poured oil from a small, dark bottle onto Mama's scalp and used her right hand to distribute it, pulling her fingers together and massaging. Mama had her eyes closed with pleasure, and she murmured to me that I could do what I wanted.

I sifted through the contents of Nana's top drawer, looking for an excuse to listen to them talk. I felt I was intruding into a private space, the way I did when I entered Nana's room and found her with her head covered, performing her afternoon prayers.

I found spools of thread and small wooden boxes with coins and scraps of paper tucked inside. I opened up a small box, padded with dark blue velvet. Inside was a small, round metal pin inscribed with an image of Florence Nightingale and a motto that read:

You are required to be sober, honest, truthful, trustworthy, punctual, quiet, orderly, clean and neat.

On the pin was a shiny plate brushed clean for a name to fit, and in that space it read:

Awarded to: Rachel Jacobs

"Nana, who is Rachel Jacobs?" I asked, interrupting her.

"That was my name before I was married," she said quietly.

A silence settled into the room, and in my memory of this moment the radio pop star saw fit to pause briefly in her song.

I was confused. I had always known Nana as Rahat, not Rachel. "But it sounds like an American name."

My mother opened her eyes and turned around to look at her mother, smiling slightly, as if to see what she was going to say.

"That was my Jewish name, before I was married."

"What do you mean, your Jewish name?" I knew that my grandmother was Muslim, because she had a Qur'an that she prayed with and she got very angry if she found my father with bacon in the house.

She poured oil into the palm of her right hand and paused for a moment, looking at the small pool. Then she began a story, one that I had never heard before.

"A very long time ago, your ancestors left Israel in a ship—a big, wide wooden ship—and they were shipwrecked, in India. They were Jews, but they settled in India. In the shipwreck they lost their Torahs, and they forgot their religion."

"They didn't remember who they were?"

"They remembered, but they remembered only one prayer, and they continued to believe in only one God, Allah, but they had a different name for him. They stayed in India and they lived there for generations, until it came time to return to Israel. When your mother was your age, my family went to Israel, except for my brother Nissim, who stayed behind in India."

I nodded. I asked why, if her family went to Israel, she didn't want to go, too.

Nana smiled, looking down. "I was already married, and I had already become a Muslim to marry your grandfather. I couldn't go."

Nana said this with some regret; I wondered why.

"So are you Muslim or are you Jewish?" I wanted Nana to pick a side, and I wanted her to pick us.

"Now I'm a Muslim, but God is the same in both religions."

My mind reeled with new information. I stared at a picture on the mantel: Nana and her mother wearing shiny silk saris. I tried to imagine Nana going to Temple Emanuel in Newton, where I had attended my friends' bar and bat mitzvahs, and it seemed impossible. I turned around with a new thought. My mother was silent; she seemed far away.

"This means you're Jewish, too," I told her. I had learned in social studies that you are Jewish if your mother is Jewish.

"According to Jewish law I am Jewish," Mama said. "But when I was small I was taught the Arabic prayers. That's what I know."

"Can I choose?" I asked, trying to put together the fact that my mother was Muslim, my father was Christian, and my grandmother was Jewish. I had been to mosque and to church and to synagogue. Did I have a choice?

"Of course," Mama said. "We can show you all about each one, and you can make the decision."

"Are you sad to not be Jewish anymore?" I asked Nana.

She didn't say anything, and after a few moments she said something to my mother in Urdu. It was clear that the window into her world had shut. Their adults-only conversation began again.

I put the pin back in the drawer and walked down the stairs and into the bright sun of our driveway, blinking. The name rattled around my head like the name of a new girl in school. Rachel Jacobs. I tried to imagine Nana as a girl like me, named Rachel, but I couldn't do it. I couldn't imagine her ever being anything but Nana.

THAT NIGHT, I had trouble falling asleep. I wandered into the hall that separated my bedroom from my younger brother's room and lingered in the bedroom doorway, listening to the sound of my father's voice telling a bedtime story, deep and low and even. My father always fell asleep before Cassim did, and his bedtime stories became a list of architecture-related words from his latest project—"hanging beam," "bay window"—and strings of numbers: 18 by 24, 36, 42. Cassim tapped him lightly on the arm. "Abba, what happened next? What happened after that?"

My father jerked awake and continued. That night, my father was weaving another fantastical tale, making it up as he went—a long, rambling saga of King Ludwig and his green-eyed queen, Lucinda, and their son, Prince Humphrey. Cassim watched him eagerly, following the plotline closely, his eyes two large moons in the half-light.

"Prince Humphrey had decided to undertake a long and arduous journey to the kingdom of Princess Tristianna, to bring her sweets and delicacies, and to compete in the royal poetry festival. Hello, Sadu," he said as he noticed me. "You want to come sit down?"

I nodded, and he moved over, making room on the bed.

"Prince Humphrey was hoping to impress the Princess Tristianna, so he scoured the countryside for rare treasures that she might enjoy and composed beautiful poems to perform in her honor at the festival. . . ."

"Did he want to marry the princess?"

"Yes, Casu, very much. But she was already engaged to an evil count, who hailed from the faraway kingdom of Monchubeestan and had quite a temper. . . ."

As he spoke, I saw Cassim's eyelids fluttering, though he was trying very hard to stay awake to hear the rest of the story. Finally, he succumbed to sleep, and my father and I both heard his breathing deepen. We listened in silence to the soft, raggedy sound.

"Abba, Nana is *Jewish*," I announced. I let this information permeate the room. I wasn't sure what my father would say.

"That's right," he said, looking over at me. "That's true."

"What does that make me and Cassim?" I asked him.

"Well, it makes you whatever you want to be, really."

"You're Christian," I said, needing to verify this.

"I am."

"But you converted religions to marry Mama. I thought that made you Muslim."

"That's true, I did. My parents raised me in the Episcopalian Church. But when I married your mama, I learned about her religion. What I believe is that when I embraced Islam I didn't give up my own religion, that it's still part of me."

"That's why we celebrate Christmas."

"That's right, that's why we celebrate Christmas. And we celebrate Ramadan and Eid for your mom."

"But we don't celebrate Hanukkah or Passover."

"True, we don't."

"If Nana is Jewish, we should celebrate her holidays. Maybe she feels left out."

"I hadn't thought of that. That's a good idea, sweetheart."

In my own room, I quickly got dressed in my nightgown and got under the covers, thinking about Nana. I said her old name over and over. Rachel Jacobs. I felt as if a puppet string had just been lifted, and my head was rising up, up, connecting me to a web of people I never knew existed.

I could choose. Which one would I choose?

3

THE GIRL FROM FOREIGN

PUNE, SEPTEMBER 2001

The day after my trip to Rahat Villa, I board an express train to Pune. In Pune Station I find a surly man holding a placard that reads "SHEPARD, SADIA MISS, Film and TV Institute of India." I guess my telegrams to the Institute have gone through after all. I am relieved and excited. I have been "met," as my mother would say.

The Film and TV Institute of India, or FTII, is the host institution for my Fulbright Scholarship, and it is where I plan to base myself for the next several months. When I was applying for the Fulbright, a former professor of mine suggested that I contact the director of the Institute, and I arranged to come here through a series of letters. Did I plan to take classes at the Institute? the director wanted to know. I told him that mostly what I was looking for was a library, a place to stay, and the chance to interact with other young filmmakers. "Young filmmakers we have plenty of," came the reply, "when they're not on strike, that is."

The Institute is a public government institution based on the grounds of a former film studio. Students from all over India take a rigorous exam for

the chance to secure one of the coveted spots in the program. A degree from
FTII means access to the competitive world of the Indian film industry, and
its students become leaders in paths as varied as the Indian avant-garde and
the highly lucrative Bollywood blockbuster. When he was first appointed
two years ago, the director had tried to introduce some unpopular changes,
among them a hike in the annual fees, and the students had rebelled.

The details of my Fulbright project, as outlined in my proposal, are
vague: I've told the United States Educational Foundation in India that I
intend to study the Bene Israel community, which my maternal grandmother was descended from—a tiny community, mostly in Bombay, who
believe they are one of the lost tribes of Israel. I plan to document the Bene
Israel in a series of still photographs and a documentary film. I have with me
too many cameras: a video camera, a 16mm Bolex, a Super 8mm camera, a
medium-format still camera, a 35mm camera, and, last but not least, a point-
and-shoot, which I carry at all times, afraid of missing something. At customs in the Bombay airport, I aroused a certain amount of curiosity: what
did I plan to do with all of this equipment? The officer saw the title of my
research project on my visa: *The Jews of India.* How many Jews are there in
Bombay? he quizzed me. Thirty-five hundred, I replied. I don't know much
more than that, but the answer granted me access to the throng of the airport and the teeming city outside it.

Pune has one of the larger Bene Israel populations outside of Bombay,
and it seemed a more manageable place to begin my research. I have confidently told the Fulbright's administrators that I am in close contact with
Bene Israel community leaders, who are eager for me to interact with them
and tell their story. But the truth is that all I have is a list of hastily scribbled
phone numbers from my grandmother's old telephone diaries, the name of
an elderly cousin by marriage, and two ethnographies written by anthro-
pologists in the late 1980s. There is very little information about the Bene
Israel in print, and almost no record of what they look like.

I had half expected to arrive in this strange city and muddle my way to
the campus in a prepaid black-and-yellow taxicab. My mother is terrified by

the idea of my taking a taxi by myself in India. As I collect my bags in the claim area, I can hear my mother's voice: ⟨

"If you were going to *Pakistan,* I'd have you fetched. But here you are going to *India. . . .*"

I say, "But we're from India, Mama. We were from India before we were from Pakistan."

"True," she relents. "But, still, we don't *know* anyone there."

I chose India to fulfill my promise to Nana, but there's another reason, one I feel almost guilty about. I have a mobility here that I will never have in Pakistan. In Pakistan I am Samina's daughter, I am Rahat's granddaughter, I am the American cousin, the unmarried oddity, the occasional visitor. When we arrive in Karachi, we are met by my mother's friend Nariman's head servant, Sajjad, no matter what kind of ungodly not-morning-not-night it is. As we drive to Uncle Nariman's house, I always look out the window and marvel at the new buildings that have sprung up since my last visit. On my last trip I was astonished to find a gleaming McDonald's as we left the airport, surrounded by huddles of small children begging for change. I do not walk in Karachi; if I need toothpaste or saline solution, I go with a driver or a relative to find it. This is a stifling kind of luxury, knowing that in an unsafe city you will always be safe.

In India I have a sense that I will have the freedom of anonymity, something I have not experienced in Pakistan. The danger and the potentials keep me alert. As we load my bags into the back of the FTII minivan, I notice a woman about my age nimbly get on a motorcycle and speed out of the parking lot. So much looks the same about the two countries: the Pepsi ads, the crush of people, the dust. But I have the palpable sense that things are different here, that I am different here.

The driver takes me through the city, and I look out the low windows of the van at Pune. Nana spent part of her childhood here, and she was tremendously fond of the place. She used the British spelling, Poona, and she pronounced it "Pooh-nah," not the modern Marathi spelling, Pune, which some people pronounce "Pooh-nay." I know how she spelled it from writing addresses on her letters toward the end of her life, when her eyesight worsened and her handwriting disintegrated. Until a few years ago, she had a first cousin who lived here named Lily. I make a mental note to look up Lily's husband, who is still alive. I stick my hand out of the window and feel the air, somehow thicker than New York. There are trees, more of them than I would have expected. It is a low city, with no tall buildings in sight.

When we reach the Institute gate, the watchman gives me an envelope with my name on it and a key inside. He gestures down a slight, sloping hill with his flashlight and follows us on foot as the driver goes slowly down a long driveway of red earth. I see a group of concrete apartment buildings set in a kind of hollow, surrounding one small, undernourished tree with a rope swing. He drives me straight to one of the many doors. There is a flash of white cotton on the step, a form that shifts into the shape of three small, grimy, beautiful little girls. Two of them flee when they see the car, but one of them sits fixed in the beam of the headlights. She has a pixie's grin and impossibly long eyelashes. She looks up into the light and cocks her head to one side, daring the watchman to shoo her away. The watchman blinks his flashlight and mutters something, and the little girl disappears as fast as she appeared, a sprite.

A long bolt opens my door. There is a fluorescent-tube light and the smell of camphor. I open the heavy padlock to my cement-block room and crawl onto the cot provided for me, fully dressed. That night, I dream of Nana.

In the dream, I am in the house I grew up in, in Chestnut Hill. There is a party going on; the house is filled with people in suits and brightly colored salwar kameezes. Someone, a messenger, comes to tell me that I can talk to Nana, and I shake my head no, I didn't make it to the hospital in time to see her. But the messenger insists that she's there, she's up in her room—I can go and talk to her, but I must hurry. I walk up the spiral staircase to the second floor. I push the door open, and Nana is sitting upright in her bed, her bearing almost regal, dressed in a blue silk sari. Her long silver hair is gathered in a bun— the way she wore it when I was small—and she has a curious smile on her face. She gestures for me to sit down.

"Listen. There is something I need you to do for me."

I sit, and she begins speaking, slowly.

We have a conversation that is based on something that happened the last time I saw her, three months before she died. At the time, Nana appeared diminished, weakened by age and illness. We were sitting side by side on the sofa, talking about my plans for the future, when she placed a hand on my arm.

"Promise me one thing," she said, her voice suddenly serious. "Go to India, learn about your ancestors."

I looked at her, blinking quickly, trying to hold back tears. I knew what she meant—that this was something she wanted me to do after she was gone. Nana had never asked me for anything before.

"Of course, Nana," I said. "I promise."

"Then all of this will be worth it," she said, leaning her head back. "If you tell my story."

I WAKE UP DISORIENTED, the cloud of heat settled on me like a film. The room is very dark, with heavy brown curtains blocking the light; when I draw them to see what is outside, dust covers me and I instantly start sneezing. I see the room now for the first time. It contains a long, narrow cot, a wooden desk, a chair, and a derelict, moss-colored couch. By the door there is a bathroom, and I peer inside it, only to move away from the smell as quickly as I find it. I move the desk and see its imprint marked on the floor; this room has not been inhabited for some time. There is a knock at the door, and I answer it. A small man in dirty blue shorts, with a bucket of black water and a scraggly hand broom, gives me an apologetic look. He motions to ask if he can come inside. I hesitate, and then I let him in. I watch as he sloshes the black water around the bathroom, swirling it with the broom. The floor looks worse when he has completed this task, and I try to tell him so, but he doesn't understand. I shake my head to say, "Never mind."

He leaves, and I dress carefully, draping the dupatta shawl of my outfit over my right shoulder and patting my unruly hair down in the bathroom mirror. I am tall, at least a head taller than most Indians. My hair is curly and loose. I play a game I have played since I was a child. Would I fit in better here if my hair were stick-straight? If I were shorter? If my skin were darker? Or is it something else, something less tangible?

I walk into the courtyard and see now what I could only partially make out last night. I am staying in a compound, with perhaps a hundred pale blue stucco rooms and apartments facing a small driveway that leads to the main road. I walk up the driveway and look at the impenetrable traffic of Law College Road, with the imposing Institute gate straight ahead of me. Motorbikes, rickshaws, and cars whiz by me at alarming speeds. I see two male students about my age walk unperturbed into the street and stop at the yellow line, letting bikes and cars dodge them by inches on either side. They wait about a minute and then zip across the street, nearly colliding with a man on a motorcycle, his four tiny children huddled behind him. The young men reach my side of the street, and one of them looks at me with a mixture of pity and contempt.

"It's not a river. You won't drown, you know," he says, waving his right hand dismissively.

The young men brush past me and enter the compound. I stand there feeling stupid for a few moments. I know how alien I look. I am paler and taller than anyone on the street, and in my outdated salwar kameez, I can be pegged for an outsider right away. I hate that. At home, in New York, I am invisible. Here I am foreign, or, as I will come to be known, *the girl from Foreign*. I brace myself and dash across the street, panting from the effort when I reach the other side.

I try to enter the gate of the Institute and am stopped by an officious guard in a khaki uniform demanding to know who I am. I produce my scholarship letters, explaining that I am the recipient of a research fellowship and will be a visiting student at the university for one year.

"Madam, you are not in the register."

"Could you check again, sir? I am here for a meeting with the director of the Institute. I have been invited here."

I show him my sheaf of papers, which he waves away.

"You come tomorrow. There is no record of you."

"But I was fetched at the airport. I am on a fellowship. To study here. I am a student."

"You are from Foreign?"

I nod. He disappears inside an interior office.

I sit on the bench near the gate, watching the students spill into the street. They come in pairs and threes and fours, some laughing, some holding hands. Everyone reminds me of someone, and I feel homesick.

Pune is in the western state of Maharashtra and is dominated by remnants of British order. It came under British rule in 1817, and it was here that officers created a large military cantonment and set up residence in the summers to escape the heat and crush of Bombay. Wide verandas pour into the street, covered in romantic-looking vines. Though the main avenues look like those in most Indian towns—painted billboards, new fast-food restaurants—the side streets still retain a sense of what Pune might have been like when it was a retreat, lined with green trees and flowering bushes. I wonder how it looked when my grandmother visited relatives here as a child. I pick out a stone house with a date over its front door: 1917, the year Nana was born.

The guard returns and tells me that the director has gone for a meeting in Delhi and will not return for five days.

"May I stay where I am until the director comes back?"

"This is not a matter for me to decide."

"Does that mean yes?"

The guard shakes his head back and forth, yes and no both, and disappears into the office again.

I stumble back to the street and walk against the traffic, the way my parents taught me when I was a child. The rickshaws are producing a fog of carbon monoxide fumes, and my throat itches with the taste of exhaust. Two ragpickers amble alongside the street, hauling their bundles on their backs and picking up stray bits and pieces of color. Mothers are doing their day's shopping with their children in tow, tugging at the fall of their saris, asking for candy. I am not sure where I am heading, but I want to find a newspaper and some food.

I come upon a vegetable seller, her meager wares laid out before her on a patterned bedsheet. Four cucumbers, a handful of small red onions, bunches of coriander, bunches of limes, and a handful of tangerines. I gesture to the tangerines and ask how much they are.

She looks up at me. She is probably not much older than I am, but her history is written in lines upon her forehead and rings her eyes with red. She looks at me curiously, her head cocked to one side to take in my face, my unfashionable salwar kameez. And then she stretches her arms on either side of her as if she is an airplane, and she makes strange mechanical noises, tilting her body to one side and then to the other, listing right and then left, making louder and louder sounds, a kind of growl coming up in her throat. Then she mimics hitting a tall tower, forming the shape of the tower with her hands, showing me how tall, how long. I realize, with a mixture of horror and surprise, that she is performing an imitation of the World Trade Center attacks. Boom! She pauses and becomes a second plane, hitting the second tower. Boom! She's smashed into a million pieces twice over. She laughs, looking at my sickened reaction. She throws her head back and laughs wildly and points at me.

"Amreeka! Amreeka!" She laughs, and starts making the plane noises again, trying to establish a connection.

I nod at her, trying to tell her that I understand what she is trying to say, asking her to stop. I start to cry.

"Amreeka," I repeat, nodding. "Amreekan," I say, pointing to my chest.

And then she looks at me anew, with a question mark on her face. She puts one hand on her heart, and the other in front of her, as if to say, Stop, enough. She shakes her head back and forth, the unknowable shake, everything at once. She is trying to have a conversation with me. She is trying to tell me that she is sorry.

I nod, thanking her, and wander farther down the street, in the direction of a phone booth, a rickety stall by the side of the road.

It's not only that Mama didn't teach me her language. She might also have taught me the hand gestures, the head toss, the way to walk in leather sandals, picking up the sole of the shoe a little bit each time with a small squeeze of your first and second toes. Whenever I ask her about why she didn't teach me these things, she says the same thing, "I didn't want you to be different from the other children in your school." But of course I am different. I am different at home and I am different here. At home it is unusual, interesting to be different, a cultural curiosity. Here it is merely uncomfortable.

I take a seat in the phone booth and look up the phone number of one of the two Pune synagogues in my notebook; I dial the number of its director. I explain who I am and why I have come to India, and ask if I can make an appointment to come and see the synagogue the following day. I hear him put the phone to one side and say to someone else in the room: "It's a Muslim name. 'Sadia' is a Muslim name."

Someone else says something muffled that I can't hear. He returns to the line, polite and firm: "I'm afraid it won't be possible. You will please call back in one week's time."

And the line goes dead, abruptly. I sit, unsure of what to do next.

Reflexively, I think of calling my old boyfriend Tony, tracing the familiar numbers on the keypad, calculating what time it must be in San Francisco. I think of him waking up in his attic apartment, the corner desk covered with his dissertation, sheets of mathematical equations. It must be early on a Sunday morning, about the time we would be planning our afternoon. I think of the day we might have spent stretching out before us, those endless possibilities of sun and hills. But now we are separated by more than living on separate coasts. I left him and all of that when I decided to come to India, something that I felt I had to do alone.

There's a knocking on the window, insistent and getting louder. At first I don't notice, staring through the glass into the traffic. The door opens and a young man peers inside.

"Are you finished?"

I gather my change and my handbag.

"Sorry, sorry," I say, emerging from the booth. "What do I owe you?"

"Perhaps you should ask the phone attendant."

I realize that he is one of the students that I watched cross the street earlier today, the one who told me that I wouldn't drown. I notice now that he has a shock of black hair that hangs into his eyes. He is wearing a blue woolen vest over a blue-and-white-checked oxford shirt and is carrying a small canvas army satchel. On one of the fingers of his left hand is an unusual ring, a ruby and emerald sitting next to each other, mismatched twins set in yellow 22-karat gold. He has a studious air, and there's something comfortable and musty about him, as if he just stepped out of a library. That's what it is; he smells like books.

He gestures in the direction of the desk next to the phone booth, where a young girl is sitting with a tally book of the day's calls and the numbers dialed.

"Oh, I'm so sorry," I mutter, counting my change. "I'm Sadia," I say, extending my hand, trying to make amends. "I'm here on a fellowship, but no one knows who I am, and the director is out of town, and I don't know what to do."

"I know who you are," he says matter-of-factly, shaking my hand quickly. "You're the American filmmaker. From New York."

He ducks into the booth to make his call, and I am left standing there, perplexed. I watch the telephone girl entering in her book the number I called.

He shouts something into the phone, in a rapid Hindi that I don't understand. When he leaves the booth he looks at me quickly, surprised I'm still there.

"How did you know I was from New York?"

"Rumor," he says, and walks past me.

I feel strangely emboldened by how alone I am. "Do you know where I can find something to eat?" I ask after him.

He looks back at me over one shoulder and nods. "I'll take you to my favorite place."

He walks down the main road ahead of me and then down a small lane. It's difficult to keep up with him, and I'm worried that I might lose him. It occurs to me after we've been walking for twenty minutes that I don't know his name to call out to him.

He ducks underneath a low overpass, a dark, dank space with women crouched on each side, sitting on crossed legs, sewing small, fragrant white jasmine flowers into long strands, which their female customers will wind into their chignons. On the other side of the overpass we enter a narrow alleyway, lined with tiny shops that sell hundreds and hundreds of bright-colored glass bangles and plastic jewelry. Children dart beside me on either side, threading their way through the steady flow of people haggling over prices. I overhear an exasperated shopkeeper scold a customer: "This is a *fixed-price shop!*" The young man I'm following turns to me halfway through the alleyway and gives me a pointed look tinged with frustration.

"I wish you spoke Hindi."

And I reply, "Me too."

After several more minutes, we arrive at a place called Lucky, a small basement-level canteen with fluorescent-tube lights.

"All the great Indian filmmakers spent time in this café," the young man says, introducing me to the dingy room with a small sweep of his hand.

This place holds some kind of magic for him, and I look around, trying to see it.

"Is that what you study? Filmmaking?"

He nods, noncommittal. "Direction. Among other things. What kind of films do you make?"

"Documentaries."

I have forgotten how much more comfortable people are here with silence than I am. I ring a table bell for the waiter, who emerges from the kitchen awaiting direction, looking as though I have woken him up from a nap, his dishcloth stained a dark gray and hanging limply on his arm.

"Cold drink?" he asks.

I ask for some biscuits and a Coke. The student orders one for himself, and then stops the waiter as he leaves our table.

"No, you should have Thums Up. Indian cola. Two."

The waiter nods, shuffles into the back of the canteen, and emerges carrying a plastic tray with a packet of cookies and two cold Thums Up bottles, wrapped in wet napkins and bearing long straws.

"What's your name?" I ask, once we have our sodas.

"Rekhev. What are you doing in India, exactly?"

"I am studying a community called the Bene Israel, or Children of Israel, which my maternal grandmother was descended from."

Rekhev nods, sipping his Thums Up.

"You want to make a film about them?"

"I want to make a series of pictures, then perhaps a film, once I know them and understand what their story is."

"Do you like it?" he asks, gesturing to the soda.

"It's more interesting than Coke," I say.

"Many of these Muslim café owners are starting a ban on American products, so they don't like to sell Coke. But the funny thing is that Coke owns Thums Up, and no one knows it. India is very funny that way. What do you think of the attack on your country?"

"The world feels like a different place now. I wonder if I should stay here or go home."

"Do you want to go home?"

"No."

"Then stay." Rekhev looks me in the eyes for the first time. He lights a cigarette. "You should form an opinion about the American response to the attacks. People will ask you."

"I never said that I didn't have an opinion," I say, feeling defensive.

We sit in silence for a few moments. "May I have one?" I ask, pointing to his cigarette. I don't smoke. The Indian cigarette makes me cough, and Rekhev smiles.

"What do you make films about?" I ask.

"Actually, I'm writing a novel, set along the border with Pakistan, the area where I grew up. How much do you know about Indian mythology?"

"Not much."

"That's too bad. You won't understand my book. There are a few essential texts you should read while you're here, just to begin to contextualize what you are seeing. Don't bother with anything contemporary; just get yourself a decent translation of *The Ramayana*."

"What do you mean?"

"Westerners make this mistake—they think that India can be 'understood,' that with diligent study it's somehow going to make sense. But they never go back to these early texts to see the foundation of what they are looking at. There's a story that I heard in Jammu, that two scientists—one from Austria and one from Japan—are collecting samples of dirt alongside a road, and two villagers pass by. One villager says to the other: 'How sad, they have no jobs in their own country so they have to come here and collect our dirt?'"

I smile at this thought. I am a dirt collector.

"I'm not used to speaking so much English," he says, pulling out another cigarette.

"You speak it well."

"Only because I read it all day. But I don't usually speak so much of it at once. Perhaps you'll be good for me in this way."

He lights his cigarette and we fall into silence. I don't fully recognize it yet, but Rekhev has volunteered, in his terse way, to keep an eye on me. The next day, I pass a used-book stall and buy a copy of *The Ramayana*.

4

LUCKY CHILD

CASTLE ROCK, 1917

achel Jacobs. Once I had discovered it, the name opened up new doors, new curiosities in my mind. I began to pester Nana for details. What did it mean to be Jewish, growing up in India? How did her ancestors practice their religion without a Torah? When Nana was in the mood to tell me about her childhood, she always began with the same story: the tale of her first prophetic dream. She told it quietly and urgently, to reaffirm for herself that it had happened, to warn me to be careful. The first time I heard it, the story kept me up all night. Usually, Nana's stories were a series of simple facts; she told them sparingly, as though words cost money. But the stories of her dreams were haunting—filled with evocative, metaphorical images, images whose meanings weren't always clear.

"Don't worry," she liked to tell me. "I will always send you messages, even after I'm gone. While you are sleeping, we will visit."

RACHEL'S EARLY CHILDHOOD was spent in a rural mining outpost called Castle Rock, a two-day journey from Bombay. Her father, Ralph, ran a manganese-ore mine. Before she was born, Ralph and Segulla-bai, Rachel's mother, had lived for years in temporary housing, moving between Bombay, its outskirts, and various mining sites throughout the region. One season they found a two-story stone bungalow, a four-kilometer walk from the train station in Castle Rock. The house was set back from the road, with a small duck pond in the front and a river on its left, framed by a footbridge. Ralph inquired after the house and was told that it was vacant; in fact, it had been empty for several months. There was a rumor in the village that it was haunted, and no one in the community wanted to rent it. Ralph and Segulla-bai decided that they would stay there and moved their possessions in—a stream of trunks, two tables, and one double bed.

In the course of six years, Segulla-bai gave birth to six children. When two of her children died in infancy, some Bene Israel women in other towns whispered that Segulla-bai was unlucky, that she should not be so pious, and should pray to the local Hindu deities as they did, to ward off the threat of smallpox, to be safe.

"After all, our God is so far away, *na?* We should be protected here also," the women whispered behind their fans.

But Ralph would not hear of it, and took Segulla-bai and his children the three-day journey to his family synagogue for the Jewish High Holidays. There were four children: a strong, dark-haired girl named Lizzie and three boys, Eliezer, George, and Benjamin, who had the light coloring and lithe frame of their father, Ralph.

On Saturdays the Jacobses observed the Sabbath at home, resting and eating foods Segulla-bai had prepared the day before. Their Hindu neighbors asked why the Jacobses rested all day on Saturday, and they explained that this was their tradition, passed down from generation to generation, to honor their God. The neighbors nodded and agreed to take care of their livestock on that day. As a sign of respect for their friends, the Jacobses abstained from eating beef. Once a week, a Hebrew tutor visited the house to teach the boys how to read Torah, and when they mastered the basic lessons, he brought them a small ram's horn, to practice blowing the shofar. The children were inseparable. As they moved from town to town, they formed an invincible circle, a tiny army. They were self-sufficient and strong, and took care of their mother, whose constant pregnancies left her weak.

When Segulla-bai was pregnant with Rachel, she visited her family synagogue so that she could perform the traditional *malida* offering, asking the Prophet Elijah to keep this baby safe. She prepared a deep *thali* dish with mashed rice and coconut. Up the path from the bazaar came the women of the community, their satchels filled with fruit from the market. They sat in the shady grove of the synagogue courtyard, set out a sheet, and begin to work in a neat assembly line, dipping dates, bananas, figs, oranges, and *chiku* fruit in bowls of water, peeling skins, and grating coconut as they talked. It was said that a wish made in the synagogue would come true, and when a person made that wish he or she should make an offering to the Prophet Elijah, beloved Eliyahoo Hanabee.

Segulla-bai's husband, Ralph, said prayers over their offering, and asked that his business might prosper, so that he could provide for his growing family. They rested easier that night, encouraged that they had performed all of the possible precautions and blessings to prepare for their child's arrival.

Rachel's birth was an easy one. The labor pains began in the morning, and by the time the midwife arrived at the house, Segulla-bai was ready to begin. That day, while Segulla-bai pushed Rachel into the world, Ralph received word that his company had been given a new large government contract, and that his business would triple in size in the next year. It meant almost certain wealth.

That evening, Ralph returned from the mine to find his wife and mother-in-law and children gathered in the bedroom around the new child, a beautiful baby girl.

"This child is lucky," he proclaimed.

He smiled, looking at Segulla-bai, exhausted but happy, resting on her pallet. She looked weakly up at him while he told her about the contract.

"*Haan*, I knew something was different today."

From then on, Rachel was considered a lucky child, and her father gave special instructions that she was to be given the utmost care. They called her their Lakshmi, after the Hindu goddess of wealth. He brought miniature gold bangles from Bombay for her to wear, tiny gold rings for her ears. Her grandmother Sara bathed her in rose water, and massaged her tiny limbs with almond oil. At night, she slept in her grandmother's double bed, and her grandmother stroked her back long into the night with her right hand, while she fanned her small, fragrant body with her left hand. This greatly annoyed Rachel's elder sister, Lizzie, who ran the house as second-in-command to her mother and had never received such lavish attentions. Rachel had clothes made of silk and was not allowed to get dirty. As she grew, she watched her brothers and sister in the yard below her balcony playing games at twilight and wished that she could play, too, to no avail. Her grandmother explained to her that when she grew up she was going to marry a rich man and live in a fine house, and provide for her siblings. With beauty and luck such as she had, she could not afford to darken in the sun.

"Nanijan, tell me a story," asked Rachel. Then her grandmother would begin the story of their ancestors, how seven couples survived the great journey from Israel, and how they made their houses with their hands, and learned how to crush local seeds to make lamp oil.

In this way, Rachel and her grandmother passed their afternoons, the afternoons of nine years.

ONE NIGHT, her grandmother was missing. Rachel woke up Lizzie, curled around Benjamin, sleeping peacefully in the crook of her arm.

"Where's Nanijan?" she cried.

"She's gone," replied Lizzie sleepily.

"Gone to where?" cried Rachel in a panic.

"She died. Sleep now, we'll talk in the morning."

Rachel couldn't sleep. She missed her grandmother's hand on her back, the coolness of her fan. The loss was too sudden, too hard to understand. Rachel lay in bed that night, listening to the sounds of the crickets, the sounds of breathing, her entire nine-year old world packed into this two-tiered house, with her grandmother, its center, suddenly gone.

It was during these nights without her grandmother that Rachel began to dream. The first dream she had was terrifying; in it, she saw three heads in a row in the sand. The three heads belonged to her brothers, two of whom had died before she was born—David and Menahim—and the third was her brother Eliezer. Eliezer's head was in the middle, and bright orange flames lapped his face, surrounded it. Rachel awoke early that morning to her mother's cry, like that of a wild animal being shot. She ran into her brother's bedroom and saw her mother cradling Eliezer's body, rocking back and forth. He had died in his sleep. The doctor was sent for, and even he could not explain why God had taken Eliezer. He was fourteen.

When Segulla-bai returned to her bed, she did not move for weeks. Her meals were brought to her in her bedroom, and she spent hours looking out the window at the pond below, where ducks dipped their long beaks into the water to feed, in and out, in a rhythmic pattern. Rachel tried to keep her company, sitting at the foot of her pallet and pressing her feet. Sometimes she could coerce a smile out of her mother. Most days Segulla-bai just looked back at her, mourning her children. Her arms ached with missing them.

Segulla-bai began to withdraw, relying more and more heavily on Lizzie. When her son Nissim was born, the midwife placed him in his mother's arms; she gave him one hard look. She counted his tiny fingers and toes: five, five, five, five. Then she turned her head away toward her pillow and said: "Give him to his sister."

The sadness of losing children hung on Segulla-bai like a cloak. Lizzie, now fifteen, took Nissim and raised him as if he were her own child. Rachel watched these activities in her parents' room with curiosity. She was pleased that Nissim had been born; now she hoped she would have somone to play with.

Rachel never told her mother about her dream. She kept her secret to herself, where she thought about it only in the safety of Lizzie's bed. One night, five months later, she had another dream. This time, she saw four heads in a row in the sand. As before, she saw the heads of David, Menahim, and Eliezer, but this time, little Benjamin's head was in the middle, and bright orange flames surrounded it. Rachel awoke early that morning, her nightdress wet with fear. She ran into her brother's bedroom and saw that everything was normal; nothing seemed out of the ordinary. Her father got ready to go to work at the mine, kissing all of his children on the tops of their heads. Rachel began to play in the nursery, watching her brothers down below in the yard. Benjamin called up to his mother and Rachel, watching him from the balcony above.

"Mumma, Mumma! Look at the ducks!" he cried, pointing, noting how fast they dipped their heads in the water to catch his scraps of bread.

Segulla-bai smiled.

"I see them, I see them," she called down softly.

Two hours later, Benjamin walked into his mother's bedroom. His eyes were red, and he was sweating.

"Mumma, the ducks are on fire. The ducks are burning!" he cried.

Rachel and her mother leapt to the window, but there the ducks swam, as peacefully as before. Benjamin was hallucinating, trying to jump out of the window.

"I can fly! I can fly, Mumma, let me go!" he cried, wriggling out of her grasp.

Segulla-bai called to George and Lizzie to come quickly.

"What have you done? What happened to him by the pond?" she asked.

But George had been playing cricket with his friends behind the house, and had not seen anything unusual happen to Benjamin. Lizzie had been in the kitchen. Segulla-bai sent George to bring the doctor, and he began the four-kilometer walk to the town center. She and Lizzie took turns applying cool cloths to Benjamin's forehead and taking his temperature with a thermometer. His temperature was 104 degrees, and rising steadily—104, 105, 107. Segulla-bai was in a panic. Rachel hovered by the bed, watching her brother writhe under her mother's and sister's grips.

Behjamin called out, "Mumma! Eliezer is standing in a garden. He's surrounded by roses. He's calling me to come play—let me go!"

Segulla-bai sat on one side of the bed and Lizzie sat on the other. They joined hands across Benjamin's body, clutching each other, trying to keep him from leaping out of the bed, up toward the garden he alone could see.

And then, as suddenly as it had begun, it was over. The doctor arrived to find Segulla-bai and Lizzie still clasping hands across Benjamin's limp body, and Rachel, her eyes wide with terror, one hand on the bedpost.

When Ralph arrived home from work at the end of the day, it was to a changed household. Benjamin had died at 7:15 p.m., within the cruel span of six hours. Ralph had been gone for eight. There was no explanation for Benjamin's sickness; his brothers searched the pond, running back and forth across the footbridge in their grief. There was nothing to point to—no vial of poison, no mysterious visitor.

People in town said again that the house was haunted, and a local sage was sent for to perform a purifying ritual. He called out his chants, swinging a censer as he walked from room to room, and around the water, seven times. Ralph woke up one morning and fired seventeen shots into the duck pond. Each one a spark of white, then a burst of red; the squawk of fear, a collapse.

In the years after Benjamin died and before she left her parents' house, Rachel had two more prophetic dreams. Two more children died, a daughter and a son. These times, she warned her mother. Her gift gave Rachel a sadness that was hard to place, just under the surface, which she carried with her throughout her life.

As an adult, Nana would be able to predict the deaths of her father, her mother, her sister, her husband, and both of his other wives.

ONE MORNING WHEN I was fourteen years old, we received a long-distance phone call from Pakistan at six o'clock. I heard the sound of my mother shouting in Urdu, then silence. A bird outside. One of our shutters banging shut in the wind. Bari Amma, my grandfather's eldest wife, was dead. Mama and I went to wake Nana, but she was already dressed; she already knew. She had had a dream.

Mama and I crawled into bed with Nana. She held Mama's head in the curve of one arm and stroked my hair with her other hand.

The darkness of the night was lifting, and the day was starting. I wanted to make it stop, to make it still night, to keep this moment in my pocket. I wanted to run all over the house and close all the shutters and stay here in the quiet of Nana's room.

"Amma, when it's your time, you have to promise me that you will warn me," my mother said. "Promise me."

"I promise, *beti*. Hush, hush. Sleep now."

5

M. Ibrahim, Professional Photographer

PUNE, OCTOBER 2001

One evening, after I have been in Pune about a month, I am having trouble crossing the street from the library back to my room in the guest hostel. A young man helps me cross, motioning a careening rickshaw out of my way so that I can pass. When we reach the other side, I thank him, and he replies enthusiastically, "No problemo!" Curiously, the young man is wearing a pair of jeans fastened tightly above his navel with a black patent-leather belt, and matching patent-leather shoes. He reminds me of a grown-up Mouseketeer. He walks me to my door and, as he drops me off, offers brightly: "In fact, I have been wanting to meet you for some time. You see, I am not a student. My father works at the university. I am a *professional* photographer. I would like to talk *camera* with you."

He raises his eyebrows for emphasis, as if he is surprised. I reply casually that we should meet sometime, and shake his hand goodbye. I unbolt my door and walk inside my room, sighing with relief to be in a quiet place, and lie down on my cot. When I get up to go to dinner in the ladies' hostel an hour later, I find a note that has been slipped underneath my door.

Miss Sadia
Respected Mam, hi!

> *Remember me? We just met this afternoon.*
> *I would like to invite you to tea with my family at 9 a.m., 10 a.m., 11 a.m., or 12 noon tomorrow. You may decide and just come. I hope you will accept this invitation. Do not disappoint us.*
> *Respectfully,*

M. Ibrahim, Professional Photographer
Flat No. 2218

The next morning, I walk upstairs with some trepidation, carrying the note in one hand. My mother has warned me to be careful of being too friendly with young men in India. But tea with an entire family of neighbors seems innocent enough. *Do not disappoint us.* It would be rude not to go.

When I knock on the door to No. 2218, everyone in the family except for Ibrahim scatters instantly, like birds. I learn that M. Ibrahim lives in a two-room flat with his parents, who are staff at the university, and his younger brother, who is six years old. When I enter, the elder Mr. Ibrahim nods at me stiffly and leaves the apartment. Mrs. Ibrahim peeks out from the kitchen at me from behind her dupatta.

Ibrahim and I talk camera. He shows me his color enlargements of flowers, taken in the Botanical Garden, and we inspect an unironic series of self-portraits—Ibrahim wearing ripped blue jeans and leaning on a motorcycle. Silently, Mrs. Ibrahim brings tea and toast from the kitchen, and I stand up, thanking her quickly and profusely before she retreats to the kitchen. Though my visit is clearly an event that is out of the ordinary, Ibrahim behaves as if he invites American women to tea on a regular basis, so I try to follow suit. Ibrahim's brother points at me and does an impression of an owl: "Hoot! Hoot!"

Ibrahim is horrified that I don't have a lens brush and insists that I borrow his, a standard small gray blower with a small brush attached on one end, used to blow away dust particles. I ask him where I can purchase camera supplies, and he replies enthusiastically that he will take me the following day to meet his "Sir," the man who taught him photography. I want to be polite, but I am reluctant to take help from Ibrahim, for fear of how my neighbors might interpret my entering and exiting the compound on Ibrahim's motorcycle.

After tea, I thank Ibrahim and his mother and retreat to the library, where I notice Rekhev sitting across from me in the reading room. I want to tell him about my morning, but I don't want to disturb him. I decide to write him a note, which I slide across the table, feeling as if I am back in grade school. He slips the note over his book, turning it over to read it without looking up. I can see him frowning. When he's finished reading, he writes something on the paper and passes it back to me. At the bottom of the page he has written: *This is a strange story.*

FOUR DAYS LATER, I wake up to a knock. It is Ibrahim, sporting a newly fashioned handlebar mustache. In his hand is a plate from his mother, and on it, a *dosa* pancake. How can I refuse a hot breakfast? I thank him for his mother's kindness.

When I go upstairs to return the plate, I make the mistake of mentioning that my camera is malfunctioning. Ibrahim jumps, in his twitchy, nervous way.

"Why you didn't tell me earlier! Come on, man. I am professional photographer! This is my field! My *city!*"

Ibrahim is jumping up and down and yelling at me. He has a habit of jumping as if he has stuck his finger in an electric socket, and he does it after many things that I say. It's a comic reflex—he jumps and then looks at me expectantly—but it's also a fearful gesture, as if I have alarmed him in some way.

"Ibrahim, why on earth do you jump like that when I talk?" I ask him. It is an incredibly grating habit.

"You see, my hearing in one of my ears is better than my hearing in the other one." He points at his ears and wiggles them for emphasis, raising his eyebrows as he does so. I worry that I might laugh. "The sound travels from my good ear to my bad ear very slowly, and then with a *bang*."

"Bang!" echoes his brother, clapping his hands.

"Ibrahim, if we're going to be friends, you have to try and stop jumping like that. It makes me very nervous."

"Okay, boss!" Ibrahim replies pleasantly.

"Do you know where I could get a six-volt camera battery?" I ask.

"Come on! I am working in this photography field, am I not? Why you didn't tell me? Why?"

Ibrahim and I take a trip to visit his "Sir," who runs a photo shop on the other side of Pune. Unfortunately, a new battery doesn't fix the problem with my camera. Sir sits behind his desk, placing my camera on a kind of lazy Susan, spinning it around and around, and looking at it intently. I watch the camera turn useless circles for several minutes until, exasperated, I begin to explain my theories of what is wrong with the camera.

"Sir, the problem seems to be that the interior mirror is locked. . . ." I say.

Sir refuses to acknowledge my presence. After a few minutes, he begins to take the viewfinder off and put it back on, repeatedly and for no apparent reason.

Ibrahim starts snapping at me in a jovial way. "Stop looking sad! You have too much of tension! It doesn't matter!"

We sit in silence for several minutes. The shop is quiet except for the clicking sound of Sir tapping my camera with a small stick. I start to ask about how I might be able to buy another camera in India. No, no, Ibrahim says, that will not be necessary.

And then, miraculously, I hear the click and whir of the shutter. Sir looks at me for the first time and smiles. The camera is fixed. I am suddenly relieved and utterly grateful. I feel terrible for misjudging the brilliance of Sir.

"See! I told you Sir would fix it! I told you! Now your tension is gone! Sir has fixed your tension!" Ibrahim starts jumping up and down.

I am indebted to Ibrahim, and I endeavor to be nothing but patient and kind with him from now on. But I also feel beholden to him. He insists on dropping off my film for me. When I need another battery, he procures one instantly. I am grateful, and Ibrahim seems to get things much cheaper than I can, but I want to do these things myself.

I often find Ibrahim revving up his motorcycle in the morning outside my door. I ask him about his latest photography projects before heading to the library. He begins to follow behind me to the cafeteria at dinnertime, and I try to strike the right mix of politeness and distance. One morning, I mention gently that I am very grateful for his help but I'd like to start doing my own camera-related errands. Where would he recommend that I have my film developed?

"Why do you want to do this yourself? Ibrahim is here!"

"Thank you, Ibrahim. But I'm here to learn. I have to find out how to do these things by myself. Please understand."

The next evening I find a note underneath my door.

Dear Miss Sadia,

You say you want to do these camera things yourself. I am always at your service here in my home city, Pune. I get special rates. After all, I have been specially cultivating these rates for years. But if I help you, you must never ever EVER ask me where I get things or how much things cost. These are SECRETS.
Yours respectfully,

Your friend,
M. Ibrahim, Professional Photographer
Flat No. 2218

The next day, I see Rekhev sitting on a wall smoking a cigarette. He's with some other students, and one of them is telling a long story in Hindi; the rest are laughing at some kind of private joke. I don't know whether I should bother him. I linger for a few minutes, until I can catch his eye, and then I show him the note.

"He's a bit mad, no?" he says, shaking his head. "Best to stay away from this one, I think."

THE NEXT NIGHT, I can't sleep. What was it that Nana wanted me to do here? I wonder. I look in the books I brought with me for answers, rereading passages of history and making notes. I look at my contact sheets. I have made two trips to Succath Shelomo, the Bene Israel synagogue in Pune, but none of their photographs seem worth enlarging. When I finally feel sleep approaching, at 2 a.m., I remember with a jolt that I should collect my laundry from the back porch, knowing it will be dew soaked if I leave it until morning. My porch is a small strip of space below my back window demarcated by a railing, where I hang the wet clothes I've washed in a bucket, a little embarrassed that my brassieres and underwear are there on the back porch for all to see. Lately I've been attempting to dry them underneath my other clothing, which is not the most effective method.

Exhausted, I begin to grab the loose pieces of clothing and bunch them underneath my arm when I see a dark shape moving behind the railing. It is Ibrahim, dressed entirely in black clothing.

"Ibrahim! What are you doing here?"

He jumps up with a start.

"I was planning to surprise you!"

It occurs to me that he could have been out here any number of times, peering at me through my back window. The thought makes me shudder. Then I get angry.

"Ibrahim, go home. And please leave me alone. You really scared me. Please go now."

"Miss Sadia . . ."

"No, really, it's late. Good night, Ibrahim."

I go inside and shut the door.

THE NEXT MORNING there is a note underneath my door.

Dear Miss Sadia,

Last night I played a funny joke on you that I thought was funny and now I see that it was WRONG. I told my girlfriend (I have a girlfriend) and she said that I should have not done that. Please accept my apology. I should not have scared you. You looked scared! Ha-Ha. Ha. Your friend,

M. Ibrahim, Professional Photographer
Flat No. 2218

On campus, I find Rekhev sitting underneath a large, knotty tree outside the auditorium, a meeting place known as the Wisdom Tree. I sit down and tell him what happened, and he listens carefully, staring at a point in the distance. When I have finished, I ask him what he thinks I should do. After a minute or so, he lights a cigarette.

"Sometimes it might be better for you to distance yourself from people. Fewer complications."

THE ONLY REMAINING FAMILY I have left in India is my grandmother's brother Nissim, who lives in Hyderabad, India, and a cousin by marriage, Uncle Moses, who lives in Pune. My hope is that Uncle Moses may be able to introduce me to other people in the Jewish communities of Pune and Bombay.

I call him and explain who I am to the woman who answers the phone. May I come to visit? She gives me a series of convoluted directions, and the next day I bundle myself and my camera equipment into an auto-rickshaw with my dupatta tied around my head and over my mouth, the way I see other women do in Pune, to try to filter the thick, soot-filled exhaust hanging over the road like fog.

A woman greets me at the door of a large concrete apartment building. She is attractive, about fifty years of age, with her hair cropped in a short, modern style and an open, friendly face. She explains that she is Moses's daughter Nina and warns me that her father is not in the best of health, that his moods can be unpredictable. She leads me into the living room, which is decorated with two couches wrapped in protective plastic, and offers me tea, which I gratefully accept. Then she disappears to another room to boil water, and I am left by myself in the living room, a large room with one wall covered in plants, the other walls decorated with an occasional picture and a series of hanging plates.

A few minutes later, Uncle Moses enters the room with the help of a cane. I stand to greet him, and he says: "You're Rachel's granddaughter. From America."

I nod and say yes.

"So you want to know about Jews!" he bellows at me, sitting down and fixing a piercing look at me.

"I do."

"Well, you're not pointing those things at me, I can tell you that!" he shouts, motioning toward my camera bags.

Nina calls to him from the other room, a note of warning in her voice: "Daddy . . ."

"It's a terrible topic, Jews. Terrible topic," he mutters, shaking his head.

Nina comes into the living room with tea and a plate of sliced pink cake. "Daddy, be nice."

"You should change your topic!" he says, and thumps his cane on the floor.

"Why do you say that?" I ask.

"It's a small community. Most people have gone to Israel; the ones who are left fight with each other. 'Who owns this?' 'I want this'—all that sort of thing. They are all in each other's business. I used to see these people regularly, but I'm too old for all of that. My religion is in here"—he points at his heart—"and in here!" He points at his head. "I'm through with all of this nonsense. Everybody is old now. All the Jews are old."

"That's why I want to do this project, Uncle Moses," I begin. "Twenty or fifty years from now, these communities won't exist the way they do now. Are there Jewish people in Pune that you think I should meet? That I might be able to interview for my project?" I ask, sounding hopeful.

"You have paper? Write this down!"

I take out my black notebook and a pen.

"I called the synagogue and told them about you." He shakes his head. "They said: '"Sadia" is a Muslim name! Why does she want to come here and take pictures of our synagogue?' They're sensitive because of the attacks on New York. I told them about your grandmother. I said she was my wife's cousin, what's wrong with you? Better you go to Bombay. Many synagogues are there. And I have something for you. This is everything you need to know. A cousin of your grandmother's wrote it. Read this."

He hands me a copy of a small book from his side table, entitled *The History of the Bene-Israel of India,* by H. S. Kehimkar, written in 1897 and published in 1937.

"Kehimkar didn't make any of this up! He wrote down our history, it's all there."

"Thank you, Uncle Moses. I'm grateful for your help."

Uncle Moses grumbles and nods. "Yes, yes."

"Is there anyone in Bombay that you think I could meet? I've read that there's a Jewish vocational school, a place where people go to learn Hebrew. Do you know anyone who works there?"

"My son's the head of it! Benny Isaacs is his name. Tell him you're his mother's cousin's granddaughter. Mother's cousin's granddaughter, you hear me? Everyone in Bombay is leaving for Israel. Who's left? I don't know why you bother with it."

He gets up and goes to his room to lie down. Nina smiles, apologetically.

"Daddy has a mind of his own," she says to me.

6

THREE PARENTS

CHESTNUT HILL, 1992

Nana ran our house. Its movements and cycles chimed according to her schedule, to the meals that she prepared, to the buzz and drone and constancy of her washer and dryer. Her kitchen, a windowed perch, overlooked the long L-shaped driveway in our backyard, pointing toward the carriage-house building where my parents kept their office. There my mother and father tended to a young staff of architects and designers who sat bent over building plans and annual reports; they met with clients, and pasted images onto white boards for an endless series of presentations. In the evenings, after the other adults went home, Cassim and I liked to hang around there, drawing houses on rolls of newsprint paper, making collages out of old magazines. But the real center of our house was Nana's kitchen, where she coordinated the comings and goings of our household, fed us, and kept us well. This was her life's work.

Three parents. Three religions. It sounds fantastic and unusual to me now. As a child, it was merely our topic sentence. Whereas other children we knew had two parents, perhaps two pairs, Cassim and I had three: a grand-

mother, a mother, and a father. Two related by blood—my grandmother and mother; two related by temperament—my grandmother and father; and two related by devotion—my mother and father. An idea to explain our private world grew like an insatiable, invisible beanstalk in the spiral staircase of our house. This idea became so central that, to my amazement, I cannot trace its beginnings. Throughout our childhood, my brother and I repeated it back to one another.

"Judaism is the law, Christianity is compassion, Islam is the law *and* compassion."

For me, over time, Nana became synonymous with the law; Abba, with compassion; and Mama, with the law and compassion combined.

Nana was the ruler of the morning, the keeper of the kitchen, the protector of the rules of the house. On her watch, my brother and I woke up at 6:30 a.m., showered, and dressed for school, then rapidly ate a few morsels of a meal she had carefully designed to help us fulfill our highest mission, *to study well.* "Car's here!" came my father's booming cry, which always meant that I had dallied too long upstairs, as usual, trying to decide what to wear. As we tumbled out the front door and into the carpool van, Nana stood at the front door, holding plates of our half-eaten breakfast in her hands—

Cream of Wheat, fried bananas with brown sugar, baked eggs with cream—pleading with us to eat only one more bite. "Have-have, take-take," she would say as she watched our passage down the long driveway. I knew, as I watched her figure receding through the back window of the van, her arms still holding two white plates, those half-moons of regret, that I had violated my part of the bargain once more.

On those mornings, I promised God that I wouldn't disappoint Nana again. She didn't know much of what went on once we were outside her purview, but she knew that my mother and father worked very hard to put Cassim and me in *the best school,* and that in *the best school* tremendous learning took place, and from learning would come great opportunity. She kept every school trophy either of us ever won, dusted and polished, in a proud line on one of her bedroom shelves. She had little idea what they meant; what mattered to her was their height, shine, and the fact that her grandchildren had received praise. The spectrum of possibility open to us was beyond her grasp or expertise, but this she left to my mother and father to oversee.

My father's dominion was the early evening, when we returned from school, dragging piles of workbooks, confounded by problem sets and term papers. Abba had an uncanny ability to right confusion, to lay out a plan to tackle the tasks that overwhelmed us, to make outlines, and to reacquaint himself with high school subjects so that he could guide us. I was a fast learner in English and history, and a terribly slow one in math and science. I was resentful of having to do something that I was so clearly bad at; I insisted that I would not need these skills as an adult. My father, the architect, showed me patiently how he needed math to practice his art.

Later, I would recognize that feeling of resentment as the same powerlessness and discontent that accompany losing a job or a lover. In college, I would curse my childhood reluctance to wage war with these tiny demons as I struggled with the figures and physics so integral to comprehending cameras. I would be too quick to accept the mystery of light refracting off mirrors to make an image, even though I knew it was an evasion. "It just *works,*" I would say out loud in empty classrooms, not trying harder to understand.

My brother, younger and quicker than I was, would run up the staircase when we entered the house to sequester himself in his third-floor bedroom, insistent that he needed no help. He would emerge several hours later. Some days he entered the dining room enthusiastically, settling himself in his seat and piling his plate high with food. "Done!" he would say, grinning. Other times he would sheepishly reveal that he had been staging elaborate battles with his action figures and had accomplished nothing at all.

On those nights, Abba would look at him and say gently, "But, Casu, you're making life harder for yourself." I would look away, hoping that Abba wasn't going to ask me how I had spent my afternoon. I am three and a half years older than Cassim, a big enough difference that my father let me police my own time. As a gesture of faith, he no longer checked in on me before dinner to make sure that I was not simply staring out my second-floor window. After our meal, if he sensed that I was avoiding a particularly terrible task, he would amble into my room.

"How's your math going, Sadu?" he would ask.

"Fine," I would say, attempting to sound unfazed.

He would casually look over my shoulder at the blank page in front of me and nod, stoically accepting my lie.

One night he said: "You have a little of what I have, you know, Sadu."

"What's that, Abba?"

"I see you expend a great deal of energy avoiding what you don't want to do. But I think you'll find in life that if you first tackle the thing you want to do least, you will give it the most energy you have. The things that come easier for you will happen quite naturally."

It was one of the truest things my father ever told me, and of course I was not ready to hear it, not yet. I didn't know how to admit that the very act of trying to solve these problems on my own gave me a feeling of distinct and irrational terror.

"Shall we try and tackle this together?" he asked, sitting down. "I'll get you started."

I knew that after he left my room my father would return to his office to work on drawing plans and balancing his accounts until midnight. He would then sleep for four hours and return to his office to put in two hours of work before he started to help Nana with breakfast at 6 a.m. I felt guilty for delaying him, and, simultaneously, giddy with relief.

My mother was the queen of our house, the mistress of the day and the night. She had the ability to make everything feel special, as if instead of a mundane family meal we had entered a magical dinner party, created just for brilliant children. My job was to lay the table, and I carefully counted out the silverware—one, two, three, four, five—and pulled out five place mats, alternating English roses one day with printed Pakistani squares of cloth the next day. "Fantastic!" she would exclaim, looking at the finished table with pride.

When we sat down, my mother said grace.

"Dear Lord," she began, "of *all* nations and *all* peoples . . ."

Mama's blessing was a reference to my father's grandmother, who was called Pie. A devout Episcopalian, she began every meal with a prayer, and when my mother joined the family, Pie amended her grace with the hope of making Mama feel more included. Mama loved telling us about Pie, about how, after she and my father were married, Pie and Nana became fast friends, partners in crime even. In one of my mother's favorite stories, one day my father received a call from the Denver Botanic Gardens. Pie and Nana had been caught whacking leaves off the trees with Pie's cane, so that Nana could make baked fish in banana leaves for Sunday lunch. When my father went to pick the two ladies up, he found Pie giving the security guard a piece of her mind. "I'm on the board of the Botanic Gardens, young man!" she said. "And my friend here needs banana leaves for her recipe!"

It was at the dinner table that we had a kind of family meeting. My mother asked each of us about our day, and we entertained her with stories of our friends, teachers, and auditions for the school play. Nothing could dissuade her from the idea that Cassim and I were the most perfect, well-behaved, intelligent children our school had ever seen. If someone—a rival, a peer, an unpleasant teacher—had upset us, she was never without a plan of attack. We spent the dinner hour devising strategies. Mama almost always had a solution. And if she didn't have one, she had spells.

"I will put a spell on that person," she said, in response to a vexing disagreement I was having with my drama teacher. "We must be kind to her, poor thing." It was in these moments that I learned the great strength of high-mindedness.

Cassim and I had moved beyond the age of belief in Mama's spells, but we never shook the notion that she wielded the tremendous power of impeccable instincts. When she was excited, she illuminated the room. She would tell us stories of her days at the office—days spent mired in conflict with surly employees and fussy clients—which made us laugh. To our delight, she was always victorious. When she had recently returned from a trip to New York or Karachi or London, she was filled with tales of her adventures, of nearly missed planes, of lunches with politicians, of visits to village workshops where folk artists shared their stories with her. Mama was working on a series of books about Pakistan—big, beautiful illustrated books. In them, she showed *her* Pakistan, a side she was frustrated that no one in America knew existed. It was one of majestic mosques and palaces, vast and stunning landscapes, and winding lanes crammed with the curious wares of the marketplace. Once a year we accompanied our mother and father to Pakistan, where they took rolls and rolls of pictures for the books.

"My books are my real work," she said seriously one evening, punctuating one of her stories. I knew that she wished she could work on them all the time. "In Pakistan, I would never have worked, I would only have made art." When she said this, I know that she was testing the idea out loud, imagining the life she might have lived had she stayed in Karachi, had she not married my father.

"Green beans are on sale at Star Market," Nana said, apropos of nothing at all. "I have a coupon from the newspaper."

My mother and brother and I all laughed at the incongruity of her comment. Nana's hearing was getting weaker with age, and she seemed increasingly to hover near our conversations, without always connecting. My father looked pointedly, kindly in her direction, as if they were sharing a secret.

"I'll take you tomorrow, Nana. We'll go first thing in the morning," he said.

"Thank you, sweetheart," she replied, at peace. "I don't want to miss it."

TO UNDERSTAND NANA I had only to stand beside her while she cooked. She didn't particularly want my help; she always preferred that I do my schoolwork. "Do your studies, don't bother here," she would say, as I picked up a spoon and tried to stir one of her pots after school. Sometimes I watched as she expertly sliced ten onions in quick succession; deboned a chicken; turned white cauliflower yellow; sifted through rice, removing tiny rocks and imperfections. She kept her spices in a round metal tin with tiny compartments; each one was a fragrant parcel of seeds. She ground these seeds with her mother's mortar and pestle, the mortar marble and white and rounded from years of work. When she was finished, I would marvel at this object, holding it in my hand. Its surface was hard and smooth, like an unbreakable egg. From among all the things she left behind in India, she chose to bring this with her. I tried to imagine its other homes, its other lives. "It was Mumma's," she said by way of explanation, the name she called her mother, Segulla-bai. As she browned the onions, I stood in the path of the sloping white column of steam, inhaling the smell of the onions binding with the spices. "Don't stand there, *beti!* Mind your hair!" It was the kind of smell that clung to you long after you left a place, reminding you where you had come from.

She made *puran poli, sandan*s, mutton curry with tamarind, and fish curry with coconut milk. These dishes I used to think of as food from Pakistan. Years later, I would realize that my grandmother was feeding us traditional Bene Israel recipes from the Konkan Coast. They were handed down to her by her mother, and her mother before her. In those recipes there was sweetness, grated coconut to temper the chili; and there was tartness, fresh tamarind, which she soaked and pulverized, for balance. Coconut milk replaced cow's milk in Nana's curries, the legacy of keeping kosher. She learned, in the years of her marriage, to make popular Muslim dishes like *biryani,* but the dishes I most closely associate with my grandmother are her preparations of fish—fried in chickpea flour with red chili; served in a light-green broth over rice; thick slices of pomfret stewed with tomatoes. Nana was a transplant from a series of seashores—from Bombay to Karachi to Boston. She was a coastal creature.

Cooking required hours of standing, and at the end of most days, Nana's back ached. She barely admitted to the pain. She knew from experience that when she did so we wouldn't let her cook the next day. Sometimes after dinner I went to her room and rubbed her back for her. She didn't like to accept my help. She worried that this was time I was not spending on my homework. I usually found her reading *Family Circle* and *Reader's Digest,* trolling for cookie recipes and storing up ideas. Lately, however, I found her reading about Judaism. She had recently joined Hadassah, a Jewish women's organization, and I noticed how eagerly she devoured its monthly journal within an hour of its arrival.

"What are you doing, Nana?" I asked, sitting on the edge of her bed.

"I am learning about the Jews," she would reply, simply, looking at me.

I looked at the book cover and wondered what was inside. "How did your people come to India, Nana?"

"I've told you, *beti.*"

"Tell me again."

Her ancestors were a puzzle to her that she was trying to solve. She moved forward and backward in her search, in pieces and paragraphs, a little more each year of her life, inching toward its end. Her sons didn't understand why she wanted to learn about her Jewish ancestry; they told her to leave it be. "What's past is past," they would say. I suppose it was awkward for them, to present themselves as Muslim Pakistanis in the U.S. and then have to explain the mystery of how their mother came to be Jewish. My mother was more supportive. We lived in Chestnut Hill, a neighborhood of Newton, which, like the rest of the western suburbs of Boston, had a large Jewish population. Our doctor was Jewish, and we had a smattering of supportive friends who were curious and interested in Nana's background. "There are Jews in India?" they would ask, their eyes growing wide. "Really?"

I asked Nana to lie on her stomach while I coated my hands with homeopathic oil. She raised her handmade nightdress above her shoulders, and tucked her small arms beside her. I had the distinct feeling as I touched Nana's skin that I was not existing in present time, that I was storing up memories for the long winter of my adulthood, one she might not be present for. I knew that later I would play this memory back for myself, like a well-worn tape.

Afterward, I would wash my hands and dry them off with a tea towel near her bookshelves, looking at the titles. On one wall of her room, hidden from first glance, she had created a kind of personal reference library, four rows of books that covered her areas of interest. Here she kept her collection of cooking magazines—organized by date and neatly arranged in sequence—an entire shelf of books about knitting, a shelf of her nursing-school manuals from the 1930s, a Marathi-English dictionary, and, on the highest shelf, a Qur'an, a Torah, selections from the Talmud, *101 Christmas Cookie Recipes,* a picture book of Israel, and three books about the Bene Israel community. "Don't worry, finish your schoolwork," she would say as I picked up one of the books about the Bene Israel. Nana reminded me of a story I read about Venus flytraps when I was a child: if you asked the wrong question, she would close and would not reopen, no matter how much cajoling you did.

Every time she gave me the opportunity, I tried to piece together the different chapters of her adulthood, from her marriage to my grandfather, to nursing school, to her life in Bombay, and to her migration to Pakistan after the Partition of India. I knew the barest sketches of her life story, but none of the details. She hid these stories from view, like her books, to protect them.

"Were you in love with my grandfather, Nana?" I asked one evening.

This kind of question embarrassed her, and she waved it off with a small sweep of her hand.

"Never mind about me, *beti,*" she said, picking up her knitting. "When you find someone someday, you must make sure he loves you above all else. More than you love him, even. He must be someone who looks after you, who gives you comfort when you are sad. You'll only know this if you know different people before you make your decision."

I assumed she was making reference to her own marriage. My mother had told me that Nana married my grandfather when she was very young, a fact that embarrassed her now.

"How old were you when you got married, Nana?"

"Too young," she said. She would never give me an exact date or age. "I didn't know any better."

"What did you wear?" I asked her, trying to picture her as a bride.

"Wear?" she said, squinting slightly. "I don't remember."

I found her response odd. What woman doesn't remember what she wore on her wedding day?

"Was it a big wedding?"

"No, no," she said hurriedly. "Nothing like that. It was just myself and my husband, two witnesses. We signed a paper. It was very quick."

"How old were you when you had Mama?"

"Oh, that came much later. I was twenty-six."

"Twenty-six . . ." I said. "So you were married for several years before you had a baby. . . ."

She nodded, unwinding a ball of yarn.

"Why did you wait so long?" I asked.

"It was a secret," she said softly. "I kept my marriage a secret for ten years."

WHENEVER MY GRANDMOTHER discussed her marriage, the secret she kept, the sharpness of her guilt was evident. Her father died without ever knowing the truth about her relationship with my grandfather. Her mother found out about her marriage only when Nana became pregnant with my mother. Though a Jewish or Christian woman who marries a Muslim man is not required to convert, Nana lived as a practicing Muslim for most of her adult life. When she prayed, she prayed in Arabic, as she was taught in the years of her marriage. But now, toward the end of her life, she felt different, conflicted. Now she worried endlessly about the decision she had made to marry outside of her faith, about whether her life as a Muslim meant that she could not die as a Jew. Her husband had always promised her a Jewish funeral.

"Do you consider yourself Jewish or Muslim, Nana?" I asked her, and she waited a few moments before answering.

"I don't know," she said finally. "One is the religion of my forefathers, and the other is the religion of my children."

"All paths lead to God, Nana," I told her, and kissed her good night, reminding her, wanting her to feel comforted.

"All paths lead to God," she repeated.

THE STORY OF MY GRANDMOTHER'S MARRIAGE, as I finally understand it, starts in 1934. Nana is a seventeen-year-old girl. She has fallen in love with my grandfather, Ali, and married him in secret. He is ten years older than she is, a friend and business partner of her father's. She knows that there will be a scandal in the Bene Israel community when her mother and brothers find out, and she hates to think of it.

She convinces her husband to let her study at Cama Hospital, in Bombay. She moves from her mother's home into the ladies' hostel of the nursing school and works in the hospital for extra money. She sends money to her mother and brothers every two weeks and goes to see them on Sundays, happy, chaotic days when she slips back into her old role, Lakshmi, the lucky one. She sees her husband twice a year, when he visits Bombay on business from Gujarat. Each day, her husband's servant brings her meals to her in a metal tiffin-carrier. Other than this daily reminder, it is possible to pretend otherwise, even to forget that she is married.

At Cama Hospital there is a Sikh doctor in her ward, Dr. Singh. He is a quiet man and keeps to himself, but he always looks out for Rachel, making sure that she has enough supplies, asking her if she needs any water, or if she needs to sit down after she has seen something unpleasant. He is a good

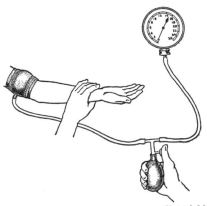

[Newton & Co]

96. *How Blood Pressure is Recorded.—Air is pumped
into a rubber sleeve placed round the upper arm until
the pressure is sufficient to block the arm artery. The
dial registers this pressure with precision.*

doctor, much admired by his patients. Rachel looks forward to assisting him in his rounds.

One day, an English doctor comes to Cama Hospital to give a lecture on rare tropical diseases. Dr. Singh asks Nana if she would like to attend the lecture, and she says yes. The English doctor shows slides, and Nana is fascinated. Afterward, Dr. Singh and Rachel go to the hospital cafeteria and drink tea. They discuss the lecture, and Rachel asks the doctor questions about things she does not understand.

"You ask very good questions, Rachel!" he says, smiling. "You should have been a doctor yourself!"

This delights Rachel; it makes her feel shy. She says softly that as a girl she had hoped to become a doctor.

"And why didn't you?" he asks.

She can't tell him the truth—that she is married, that her husband decided for her.

She looks at her lap and lets silence be her answer.

The next time there is a lecture, Dr. Singh invites her to attend, and she goes. After the lecture they linger in the courtyard between the hospital and the hostel.

"How about dinner?" he suggests casually.

She considers it for a moment. Certainly many people in the restaurant would assume that she was the Sikh doctor's wife. She is lonely in the hostel; she misses her brothers and sister. It would be nice to have a conversation. But her husband's servant will report back to his master if she doesn't eat her evening meal. Perhaps it isn't the correct thing to do.

"I can't," Nana stammers. "You see, my dinner is *sent*."

Dr. Singh looks disappointed.

"I see," he says, and nods to her. "Good night, then."

He leaves with a small wave.

Nana is too shy to speak to him unprovoked after that. She continues to assist him on his rounds, but they never speak of personal things again. They work side by side in silence for another six months, until she is transferred to another ward and promoted to head matron. A year later, she hears that he has married a Sikh girl.

One evening, Nana is turning a corner when she sees his wife, leaning out of a car in the turnabout of the hospital. The young woman is dressed like a new bride, wearing a red silk sari, with red *sindoor* in the part of her hair. She calls Dr. Singh's name as he leaves the building. "Gurudev!" she cries out, brightly. Nana watches him smile in response, that same smile she saw once in the cafeteria. She hadn't known his first name before she heard his wife speak it. "Gurudev," she repeats, testing out the syllables with her tongue.

Nana stands there for a moment and thinks about the Sikh doctor's wife.

Mrs. Singh. A proper married girl. Married for all the world to see.

"WERE YOU IN LOVE with the Sikh doctor?" I asked, feeling bold.

"No, of course not," she said. "I was in love with my husband."

I picked up an embroidered pillow from her bed and ran my fingers across her careful cross-stitching. Nana had taught me the cross-stitch a few years before. It was the only stitch I knew.

"It's just that I married so young," she said. "Love like that, it causes a *tamasha*. Too much fuss."

I nodded, pretending I understood what she meant.

BENE ISRAEL BOYS, her brother's friends, sometimes ask after Rachel. She always refuses to speak of marriage. She tells everyone she wants to finish her studies. She is the only one who knows the truth. It feels as if the knowledge is burning a hole in her stomach.

Then, one morning, she realizes that she has an option, a solution: she can vanish.

In front of Cama Hospital, two English nurses from the Women's Army Auxiliary Corps set up a table. Before them is a tall stack of papers. Applications. Nana looks out the corner of her eye at their colorful signs: "Join the War Effort" and "Be a Hero!" Nana has been hearing for weeks on the radio about the need for trained nurses abroad, how many wounded soldiers there are, and that there is never enough care. She has a brother named Jacques who is in the army, stationed in Burma. Her brother George serves in Bombay. She thinks to herself how either one of her brothers could be on the front lines at any moment.

On the fourth morning she passes the table, she lingers, listening to one of the nurses explain the application to a potential recruit. "There are two kinds of duty, active duty and nonactive duty. In nonactive duty you are stationed at a hospital; in active duty you are working in camps at the front. . . ."

"What if I were to join?" Rachel wonders. She imagines how angry her husband, Ali, would be if he knew she was contemplating it, and just the thought makes her shudder. She asks for an application and quickly stuffs it inside her handbag. She heads to her ward and resolves to think about it later.

That night she takes out the application and looks at it carefully.

"I could forget that I was ever married," she thinks. "I would never be a burden to anyone again."

She pauses for a moment and wonders if she should choose active duty or nonactive duty, and selects active duty. "If I die," she thinks to herself, "I will have died for a good cause."

She takes out a pen and begins to fill in her name and address. She writes the information quickly, printing her name in black ink. She will complete the application tonight and write two letters, she decides, one to her husband and one to her family. In the letters she will explain that she has joined the army. Her family will be proud of her. And her husband? She will tell her husband's servant that she is going out of station for a wedding and won't be back for two weeks. Her husband won't find out until she is already gone. It will be too late for him to do anything.

"My dear Ali Sahib," she begins. How should she say it? She looks out the window of her second-floor room at the courtyard below and watches the sweeper sitting on his heels, making rhythmic strokes with his long broom—right to left, left to right, and back—inching backward, erasing steps.

She doesn't hear the door to her hostel room open. Ali has the footfall of a cat. In three quick strides her husband is behind her chair, silent, watching the tentative strokes of her pen.

He snatches her letter and her application in one hand. "What is this?" he demands, waving the papers out of her reach.

Nana looks up at him, frightened, trying to grasp them back. She doesn't have any words.

"Is this what you think of me?" he asks. "To leave without telling me?" He crumples the application and her letter and sits on her bed, folding her into his arms and crying. He holds her face in both of his hands, covering her mouth with his. "*Meri jaan,* what if you died? I would die, too."

Nana looks up at him, her eyes filling with tears. She loves him too much for her own good, she thinks. It's a trap.

"Forget all this," he says. "I will bring you to stay near me, in Jamnagar, where I can see you."

Her husband is at the time the customs collector of Jamnagar, Nawanagar State, in Gujarat. The Jam Sahib of Nawanagar is his good friend, and they have a very good hospital there. Almost immediately, plans are put in motion for Rachel to go to Jamnagar and study nursing. Ali tells her mother that he has decided to sponsor Rachel's education in honor of her late father, his friend. Rachel's mother is grateful.

Ali watches her attentively now, looking for signs of flight. She takes in his attention like water.

RACHEL IS MISERABLE in Jamnagar. The nursing classes are in Gujarati, and she speaks only English and her mother tongue, Marathi. She misses Cama Hospital and Bombay. She misses her family. She studies hard but can't keep up. She fails her exams that year. I try to imagine my grandmother as a girl, staying up all night to prepare for an exam. I cannot produce the image in my mind.

One afternoon, the Jam Sahib's car arrives for her. "Rachel Bibi, you come to the palace," says the driver. Rachel does as she is told. She ducks her head and slips inside. It is a beautiful imported car, with real leather seats. The driver tells her that the Jam Sahib's wife, the Maharani, has sent for her. The Maharani is having a baby, and she wants a lady nurse to help her. Until that moment, Rachel thinks that her husband has sent the car to the nursing school. Now she wonders to herself what he will think of her going to the palace alone. There are very few motorcars in Jamnagar. As they drive to the palace, she recognizes her husband's car coming toward her in the opposite lane. He sees Rachel when the two cars pass one another and looks her dead in the eyes. She is frightened. He asks his driver to pull to the side of the road and waves to the Jam Sahib's driver to halt his vehicle. He gets out and raps his knuckles on the glass, asking Rachel to roll down the window. He immediately demands to know what she is doing inside of the Jam Sahib's car, and she tells him that the Maharani sent for her and she is on her way to the palace. He forbids her to go.

Her husband sends her back to the school in his car to find another nurse, and goes himself to the palace to explain.

· · ·

NANA TOLD THESE STORIES often enough that I began to play the alternate scenarios in my mind, thinking back upon these moments when her fate swung arbitrarily, turned like a hinge. What if my grandfather had not entered her room while she was writing him the letter? Minutes later, she would have been able to conceal it, and could have turned in the application the next morning, as she'd planned. She might have served in World War II, pretended she was never married, and returned to marry someone from her own community. What if her husband had not been passing the Jam Sahib's car at that exact moment? I imagine how she could have delivered the Maharani's baby and easily become the family's private nurse. Would she have met a young man in the court and lived an entirely different life?

"The Jam Sahibs in those days, they used to be fond of giving favors," Nana explained. "I think he was worried, what if the Maharani took a liking to me, then she'd be always sending the car, I would be over at the palace all the time. He was very jealous, my husband. He didn't like other men to see me."

Nana picked up a ball of wool and two knitting needles from her bedside table.

"If he hadn't been passing right at that time, I would have gone. . . ."

WITHIN A YEAR, Rachel is back in Bombay, back at Cama Hospital, where she will work for the next several years. Now her husband's visits are more frequent. They are always unpredictable, catching her unaware. Sometimes he brings a new pair of earrings for her in his front coat pocket. His visits leave her feeling thrilled and guilty. The stones in her ears catch the light, refracting it across her ceiling like stars. She turns her head and watches the lights moving, winking at her.

In 1943, when my grandmother is twenty-six, she becomes the head matron of Cama Hospital, her highest professional achievement. Rachel spends night shifts alone in the maternity ward, visiting with women, checking their charts. She thinks of how many babies her mother lost without the benefit of doctors and nurses, and she feels good about her work. One morning, as she does her rounds, one of her patients motions to her.

"You were so kind to me last night. Thank you for rubbing my back," she says.

Rachel nods and moves on. How odd, she thinks, I didn't rub her back last night. As she takes another woman's pulse, the patient smiles at her, patting her hand.

"Thank you for the water, dear."

Rachel begins to realize that many of her patients in the maternity ward mistake her for another nurse. Several people describe a beautiful young Anglo-Indian woman with wavy brown hair, dressed in a nurse's three-cornered white hat with matching white dress. Her name is Rose.

Rachel cannot understand who the other nurse could be. She checks the schedule again. There is no mention of a nurse named Rose. From time to time it happens once more: patients thank her in the morning for something she didn't do, or ask for Rose by name. Rachel asks the older nurses and learns that Rose had been a nurse in Cama Hospital in the 1920s. Her death was mysterious, something people talked about quietly. After she died, an army officer came to pick up her belongings from the ladies' hostel. People said that Rose had been pregnant with his baby and when he refused to marry her she had an abortion. She didn't survive the operation. People say that her ghost haunts the maternity ward, looking after pregnant women. Only pregnant patients see her.

Rose begins to appear to Rachel, late at night. Rachel feels a presence and looks up and sees Rose there, working diligently, always just out of reach. When Rachel tries to speak to her, she turns a corner, vanishes. Rachel begins to worry that she is sleep-deprived, seeing things that are not there. She begins to feel weak, strange, not herself. She cannot place what it is. One evening she looks up and sees Rose looking at her. Rose places her hand low on her abdomen and smiles, a slow, peaceful smile. Rachel wakes up the next morning and stares at the beams of the high ceiling. She speaks out loud, with only the walls of her room to hear her: "I am having a child."

She surprises herself, feeling, instead of dread, a welling up of relief. The waiting is over. She can no longer conceal her marriage. She is going to have a baby.

She enlists her sister, Lizzie, to help her tell her mother about her marriage. When Mumma hears the news, she weeps. Hot tears wet the lap of her sari.

She says, "It is good that you will have a child."

My grandfather builds Nana a house by the ocean, on Worli Sea Face in Bombay. He names it Rahat Villa, in honor of her new name.

Rachel becomes Rahat. Jew becomes Muslim. New eclipses old. Things will be different now.

"GO TO SLEEP, *beti,* it's late now."

Nana and I were sitting in the dark. There was no sound but the snow-wind, whipping around our old house.

"I'll go."

"Sleep, sleep."

I waited to hear Nana's breathing, to make sure she was still here.

"You too."

7

INFLUENCES

PUNE, NOVEMBER 2001

I cannot remember a time when I felt more alone.

In the evenings, the sameness of my room becomes suffocating, and I walk to the end of Law College Road. In a tiny, dusty cybercafé with three working computers, I read the news from home and assure my friends and family that I am fine. They write asking what kind of impact the World Trade Center attacks have made in India. Tony wants to know if it means that I'll come home sooner. I'm not sure what to say in reponse. Here life goes on as before, I tell them. People casually recount endless stories of floods and epidemics that have wiped out entire populations, bombs exploding on trains. The numbers are staggering, and then life moves on. My friends from home find these ideas odd. They tell me how New York feels different now, and I try to imagine it. So much has happened in the world in the two months since I left everything familiar. I have the incongruous feeling that I have stepped through a trapdoor in the universe into a parallel world.

Outside the cybercafé, I watch groups of young men wander down Law College Road, walking toward what seems to be an outdoor café, a three-sided wooden stall with a low bench in front for sitting. It reminds me of a puppet-show stage. They sit in various configurations around the stall, drinking from tiny tin cups, leaning on one another casually, two or three sitting on a motorbike. They are always deep in conversation, and I wonder what they are talking about. I wish I could join them, but it seems too forward, and I feel shy. In the daytime, I approach the café and look inside. Inside the stall, constructed like a simple wooden crate, are three large empty black cauldrons, too heavy to steal. Curiously, the proprietor is not there. His business seems to operate only after 11 p.m.

One night, my curiosity gets the better of me, and I wander past the stall. I try to introduce myself to a group of the male film students, who refuse to shake my hand and merely nod in my direction. I stand next to two girls sulking to one side, and try to make small talk with them, to little effect. I notice that when the students are speaking to one another informally, teasing each other and slapping each other on the back, they speak Hindi, but when they start a conversation they do so in English. One of the boys mutters, "Yes, the American," and the others laugh. Another approaches me with his hand extended. "I must apologize for my friends; they are being rude. I know better; I have a brother in Connecticut."

What looks like a tea stall is in fact a coffee stall, selling milky, sweet Nescafé, which the students sip out of small, chipped cups while complaining about the stacks of books in their rooms that they should be reading. At midnight, the female students grumble about their curfew, but I realize, feeling somewhat pleased, that I am not confined by the same rules. I notice Rekhev sitting on one side of the coffee stall, explaining the concept for a short film he is going to direct to three fellow male students, who listen with rapt attention.

"You see, a boy—who is also an old man—tries to tell a story. The film will be in two parts, and the first part will deal with the ritual of the boy going to school; the second part will be a visual storybook. We will use mythological references as riddles, some of them from Somdev's book *Kathasaritsagar,* and some from Milorad Pavić's *Dictionary of the Khazars.*"

"Your ideas are so damn complicated," I hear one of them say, shaking his head with admiration. "We're not all geniuses like you, *yaar.* . . ."

I sit down, and the young men return to an earlier thread of conversation in Hindi that I can't understand. Rekhev opens a large green notebook and writes something in it with a fountain pen while I sip my coffee. Then he closes his notebook and fixes me with a stare.

"Do you know the work of Robert Bresson?"

I feel grateful that someone has asked me a question, grateful at the prospect of having a conversation with someone. I say I remember seeing his films in college but don't remember them vividly at the moment. Rekhev frowns at me.

"Have you read his book, *Notes on the Cinematographer*?"

I shake my head to say no.

"We're very influenced by this book here. What are your influences?"

"Influences?" I repeat dumbly.

"Who are the artists and writers whom you most admire?" he asks me, looking serious.

I am embarrassed that I don't have a ready answer.

"Tell me something. Have you heard the music of John Cage?"

I have. I tell him so and see something flicker across his face.

"I have read his book *Silence.* I have read another book by him also. I am very fascinated by him. But I have not been able to hear his music. Tell me what it's like."

Rekhev is familiar with Cage's famous piece *4 ′ 33 ″,* where Cage sat in front of his piano for four and a half minutes of silence, but is most taken with Cage's experiments with the notion of chance and how they might apply to filmmaking. I'm not sure how to describe the music. I try for a few minutes, and then remember a story that a professor of mine once told me, about a performance that Cage gave at a small New England college in the middle of the woods. I describe how the professor was walking through the forest when he happened upon the artist standing quietly with a group of four or five people and recognized him. "Cage! My God, this is fantastic!" he said. "What are you doing here?" John Cage turned to him slowly and said: "I'm working, Tim. I'm in the middle of a performance." And the professor realized that he had walked into the middle of one of Cage's pieces.

The story makes Rekhev smile. I realize how much I miss New York.

I SPEND MY DAYS in the Institute library making notes on the book that Uncle Moses gave me about the Bene Israel. Before I return to Bombay and try to introduce myself to the community, I want to feel grounded in their history. Only a few other books have been written, some of which I brought with me from Nana's bookshelf. Each book begins with the same story, the story of a shipwreck, the Bene Israel leaving the ancient land of Israel in a boat that crashed on the beaches of Navgaon, a tiny village 160 kilometers south of Bombay. There are very few pictures, almost no contemporary ones.

"When did it happen, Nana?" I can hear myself asking.

"Two thousand years ago, *beti*," she says.

Two thousand years. I try to picture it now, spreading both palms over my books, one finger for every two centuries. I can do it no more easily now than I could as a child.

The twelve tribes of Israel, the original Jewish people—ten of them lost, imagined, and sought after, even still. The Bene Israel believe that they are one of those lost tribes, cast out to wander the earth in search of a new home. I can no longer recall where the stories my grandmother told me blend with what I have read; nor can I distinguish the history of the lost tribes from the dissemination of their legend.

According to their oral tradition, the Bene Israel who survived the ship-wreck settled into life along the Konkan Coast of India and lived there peacefully for generations. Separated from their religious texts, they practiced only what they remembered of their religion, observing the Sabbath, abstaining from eating fish without fins and scales, and circumcising their male infants on the eighth day after their birth. Over time they forgot the language of Hebrew and adopted the local language of Marathi. But they remembered the opening sentence of the *Shema* prayer—the central tenet of the Jewish religion—which they recited during rites of passage, times of trouble, and celebrations: "Hear, O Israel, the Lord our God is one Lord."

In the early nineteenth century, Christian missionaries from the Church of England, Scottish Presbyterian, and American Congregational missions working in Bombay and in Raigad District heard mention of the Bene Israel. They were intrigued to hear that the community members observed the Sabbath and knew a few words of Hebrew. When the missionaries came in contact with the Bene Israel, the community told them that their ancestors came from a country to the north. They described the shipwreck that had brought them to India, as the story had been passed down to them. They explained how the seven surviving couples buried those who did not survive in two large mounds and settled into nearby villages, and how for centuries they lived in isolation from other Jews.

The missionaries established primary schools in Bombay and in the Konkan, several of which employed Bene Israel men as teachers, and many of which taught Bene Israel children. These schools taught the Bene Israel English as well as the Old Testament, and in the stories of the Bible the Bene Israel recognized strains of their own oral histories. Instead of providing an impetus for large-scale conversion to Christianity, contact with missionaries served as a catalyst for the Bene Israel's increased communication with other Jewish communities, in India and in other parts of the world.

By the late nineteenth century, most of the community had relocated to the urban center of Bombay. In fewer than a hundred years, the Bene Israel had transformed themselves from a largely rural, Marathi-speaking, agricultural population to a Marathi- and English-speaking, middle-class, urban one. I realize, poring over census reports from the 1930s, that Nana's family would have been typical of their time. Her parents and grandparents may have been raised in villages, whereas Nana and her siblings grew up as urban children, attending weddings and community festivals at synagogues packed full of parishioners in Pune and Bombay. Nana reached adulthood at the height of the Bene Israel community, when it numbered over thirty thousand members and enjoyed the cosmopolitan, secular nature of pre-Partition Bombay. Her father's friends included Hindus, Christians, Jains, Sikhs. One of his closest friends and business associates was a Muslim, Ali Siddiqi. That man would become Nana's husband, my grandfather.

EVERYTHING I READ describes the migration of the Bene Israel from India to Israel in the same way. A Zionist federation from Israel made its first trip to India to recruit Indian Jews in the 1940s, as Indian independence and the creation of Israel were both becoming a reality. The Bene Israel considered its offer and, for the moment, decided to stay where they were.

In 1947, the story began to change. The British were preparing to end 240 years of colonial rule in India, to hand power back to Indians and create a new, independent nation. Amid rising tension and fighting between its Hindu and Muslim populations, there was increasing talk of dividing the country in two, of creating a new country, Pakistan, for India's Muslims. As the English spoke of leaving for England, the Muslims for Pakistan, and the Hindu majority was forming a new government, the Bene Israel began to re-examine their future in Bombay. They started to think more seriously about joining the world's Jews in Israel.

Nana told me that her older brother George was one of the first Bene Israel to leave India for Israel, settling on land reserved for champions of the Zionist cause. He was joined in a slow, steady trickle two decades long by the rest of his family—except for Nana and her younger brother, Nissim, who never emigrated to Israel. When Nana went to Pakistan, Nissim stayed in India.

I write in my notebook: "What about the other Bene Israel who stayed here?" There is very little record of their imprint, their tangled comings and goings, their holidays, their sites of worship, the places and people that have defined them. This is what I want to record, to preserve. I am interested in what remains. Is it possible, I wonder, for me to walk backward, to find the paths my grandmother didn't choose?

I NOTICE REKHEV sitting across from me in the library and wave in his direction. He looks up at me and slides a book across the table. It is a book about Amrita Sher-Gil, a half-Hungarian, half-Indian painter. I read about her early years as an art student in Italy and France in the 1930s. I look at her paintings, which seem like copies of other artists. Then a change. She comes to India in 1934 and begins to study Indian art. She incorporates elements of Mughal miniatures, the Ajanta paintings. She marries her first cousin, a doctor, and they move to her family home in Uttar Pradesh, later to Lahore. She is famous for her wit, and for her affairs. She sleeps with both men and women. At twenty-eight, she dies mysteriously. Some say of complications as a result of an abortion, others of syphilis. The lesson stops there. I look at her picture, tracing her Hungarian parent in her face, then her Indian one. A half-half person. Like me.

I get up from my chair at about 5 p.m., curious whether Rekhev will walk out at the same time. When he does, we walk in silence, a two-person procession out of the library.

There is a special-day feeling, a school's-out feeling. I'm not sure where we're walking to. We pass a small cigarette stand, and Rekhev buys a half-pack of cigarettes and matches. I have heard that there is a temple down the road, past the teahouse, but I have not been there. I ask him if it's far.

Rekhev shakes his head solemnly as if to say, No, it's not far.

"Are you busy?" I ask.

"I thought perhaps I would take you to where I buy books, a man on Karve Road."

"Oh, I see," I say, flattered that someone wants to take me somewhere.

"But first, if you like, the temple," he adds.

"Let's go," I say.

It is quickly apparent that we are not wearing appropriate shoes; we're both in sandals. It is a steep hill, and the sun has not gone down yet, making the trip hot.

"We should have waited," Rekhev says.

We make our way up the path to a small clearing with some rocks and take in the wide panoramic view of green and brown hills that surrounds us.

"Come, let's sit," he says, and sits down, taking out a cigarette. I laugh at the idea of getting exercise and smoking at the same time, but he doesn't see the humor.

"What are you learning about these Jews?" he asks me after a few moments, looking at the valley below.

"They believe they were shipwrecked here, two thousand years ago," I say. "Seven men and seven women survived the shipwreck; they believe the entire community is descended from those seven couples."

"Is it truth?"

"I don't know. But they believe it."

Rekhev looks up. "That's a very Indian idea, you know, to believe you're from somewhere else."

"How so?" I say.

"We're a mixture, none of us are really from here. Naipaul wrote about this. People cling to these ideas about coming from somewhere else, there are all kinds of folktales about it—coming here by sea, descending from Greeks. There's a community here in Maharashtra, the Chitpawan Brahmins, who also believe they came here by shipwreck. What did you think of Amrita Sher-Gil?"

"She seems like she was terribly confused."

Rekhev relights his cigarette, which has blown out in the wind. "Perhaps you will find the analogy too obvious, but I had this thought—half-Indian girl, coming here to find out who she is. When I was in school in Delhi, I used to visit her paintings on Sundays. There's a room in the art museum there devoted to them. Before that, I had only ever seen them in a book. I was so amazed to see them up close. I think, if you like, you can take Amrita as a kind of guide."

Rekhev smokes his cigarettes in quick succession, one after another. I realize on his fifth cigarette that he is not really smoking, just puffing through them without inhaling. I ask Rekhev about his family. His mother is a teacher. His father is in government service. He has not been home in a year and a half.

"Don't they want you to visit?" I ask.

"They know I don't travel much," he says.

Rekhev is curious about Pakistan. I tell him about Siddiqi House, the house in Karachi my mother grew up in with her mother, her father, her nine siblings, and her father's two other wives. Ten children in total, five of which were Nana's.

"They all lived there together?" he asks.

"My grandfather Siddiqi was eccentric," I reply.

Rekhev's family was originally from a village near Rawalpindi, in what is now Pakistan, and settled in Jammu after Partition.

"How do you find it different from here?" he asks me. The big differences seem too obvious to mention: The call to prayer. Guards with automatic rifles at the house gates. Gardens strung with roses for elaborate wedding celebrations. My strongest memories of Pakistan are set in the crowded corridors of my mother's family home.

"You don't walk in Karachi," I say.

"It's important to you to be on your own, isn't it?" he observes.

"I suppose so."

"A kind of test."

I nod and look out at the hills below, following the path of an ox and its owner as they make their way along a distant route.

"My father's mother told me our family had a beautiful garden, in what's now Pakistan. They say it's been razed to the ground," he says, putting out his cigarette on a rock.

I ask him about Jammu and Kashmir. He tells me about commuting to the army school he attended as a child; the quick dip-down reflex before he sat down, checking for bombs. He was four feet tall for most of his childhood and adolescence.

"This high," he says, placing his hand below his shoulder. I counter with the confession that I was five foot nine and a half inches, as tall as I am now, when I was thirteen.

"I like people with complexes," he says, and smiles.

8

SIDDIQI HOUSE

KARACHI, 1983

It is hard to say which side is the front of Siddiqi House; both sides have equal and opposite driveways and neatly trimmed grass lawns, facing parallel streets. This design, conceived by my grandfather, gives the home the feeling of two people with their backs against each other, arms crossed, each refusing to acknowledge what the other one sees. At both entrances, the words "Siddiqi House" appear, white plaster letters laid atop a background of pale yellow, with the date when the house was built inscribed into each set of gates: 1948. It's a large, imposing structure built with the rounded edges of the Art Deco style, and looks more like an apartment building than a house for a single family.

Siddiqi House was built on the foundations of an old bungalow that belonged to a former British officer. My grandfather bought the house after Partition and began to expand it immediately, step by step, for his family to settle in. His plan was that, by the time he was finished building the house, each branch of his family, each of his three wives and their children, would have their own separate apartment, their own entrance, and a piece of property in their own name. But while my grandfather was alive, the entire family lived together in one large flat, spilling on top of each other, trying to stay out of each other's way. The construction was built upward, stories on top of stories, creating an orbit around my grandfather, who called out orders, wearing his trademark white sharkskin suit, bright red fez, and black-and-white spats. My mother describes how in those early years the Siddiqis lived surrounded by the noise and traffic of workmen, just as they lived with the call of the sugarcane-juice *wallah,* the fruit seller, and the barking of dogs at dusk, and how that feeling of chaos never left the family.

WHEN I WAS eight years old and Cassim was five, my mother's youngest brother, Salman, was engaged to be married. Nana's other children had married people of their own choosing, but she wanted to do things right for her fifth and last child. She arranged a match for him with a Pakistani girl named Shehzadi from a family of Mohajirs like us, Muslims originally from India. Though Uncle Salman lived near us in Newton and his fiancée was from Pakistan, Nana wanted to host the wedding at Siddiqi House. She wanted to preside over this last of her children's marriages in a style that her husband would have appreciated, with receptions at the homes of his important Parsi friends and parties in the gardens of five-star hotels.

None of us could have known it then, but this would be the last wedding of our immediate family that we would celebrate in Pakistan. After Uncle Salman's wedding, the family would be too widely dispersed, our connections to Karachi too tenuous for us to travel such a long way.

Like everything to do with our family in Pakistan, the wedding preparations had a life of their own, an internal disordered logic. The planning was made more challenging by the fact that there were three factions of the family living inside Siddiqi House, two of which were in the midst of a long-standing feud, the origin of which few remembered. As the date grew closer, Nana's set of Samsonite suitcases became progressively more filled with requests from Karachi: a Casio synchronizer, Betty Crocker cake mix, Chanel N° 5.

The trip to Karachi from Boston was a series of journeys compounded into one: Boston to New York, New York to Frankfurt, Frankfurt to Cairo, Cairo to Karachi. My teacher had given me an assignment, to record my trip in a bright blue spiral notebook. I kept it tucked under one arm as Cassim and I followed Mama through the maze of security checks at Boston's Logan Airport. Mama was petrified of airport security—too many questions about how long she had lived in the U.S., why she was going back to Pakistan, who her husband was. She shuddered when she saw Indian, Pakistani, and Bangladeshi families—in sweater vests crammed over their saris—carrying bulging parcels tied with string, the fastidious block-lettered addresses of their destinations taped to the sides of their suitcases; Mama believed we would be treated better if we were well dressed. I was in a plaid pinafore dress and tights with Mary Jane shoes. Cassim was tucked into a new blue sweater and matching pants. Mama was in a dark green salwar kameez, and had ten gold bangles on her left wrist. She was too superstitious to remove them, and so we traveled through the airport setting off security buzzers along the way.

When we got to Frankfurt Airport, we quickly went to find the long black couches, the ones where we could stretch out our whole bodies and lie down almost flat. For the duration of our eight-hour layover we would make these couches our base camp. Mama and Nana laid out a blanket for us to lie on. Among all of the airports we had been to, I had decided, the chocolate here was best. Mama and Nana always bought three or four bags of sweets to give to my uncles and aunts and cousins, purple tins of Nestlé Quality Street, Roundtree Fruit Gums, tubes of Smarties, and Crunchie bars wrapped in gold foil. Cassim and I each chose a chocolate bar to eat on the plane. I did so with great deliberation, finally settling on a long milk chocolate rectangle in a gorgeous lavender-colored wrapper. Cassim clasped a Flake bar to his chest, smiling. His new shirt would be covered in its melted threads before long.

I was allowed to walk alone in the airport if I told Mama and Nana exactly where I was going and came right back. I was fascinated with the clock shop, where cuckoo clocks covered every surface. I liked to make sure that I was in the shop at the change of the hour, so I could see all of the clocks go off at once. I settled on the one that I wished I could take home, small, with a green A-line roof and three short gold-colored chains hanging down from what looked like a porch. On the stroke of the hour, a thumb-sized ballerina-like doll in a cloth skirt would emerge and twirl around to a tiny, tinny song, one plastic arm outstretched in a wave. Then, as quickly as she had appeared, she would retreat to the inside of the clock, and the little door would snap shut. I wondered if she ever felt sad that she couldn't leave her mountain. "Goodbye!" I whispered as I saw her retreat the last time. "I am going to Pakistan!" I returned to the couches by way of the electronic walkway, gliding past people on foot on my left and right, giddy with the rush of motion.

I had heard my mother's friends in Karachi joke to one another about PIA's many nicknames. Instead of "Pakistan International Airlines" they called it "Please Inform Allah," or "Perhaps I Arrive." Nothing connected to PIA ever seemed to run on time. The aging aircraft and everyone on board seemed to exist in a transitional space between the West and the East, not quite here or there. Businessmen—some who had emigrated to New York or London, some returning home from a trip—looked uncomfortable as they settled in for the all-night journey in their dark wool suits. The other mothers and children slipped us sidelong glances, sizing up my mother and us, her American-born *firangi* children. The lady stewardesses wore a uniform adapted from a traditional salwar kameez to look something like a short tunic and pants with a pre-folded miniature shawl pinned in place. After they pantomimed the safety procedures, they turned on the movie projectors to display an image of Mecca. Mama instructed us to close our eyes as the Traveler's Prayer boomed over the loudspeaker.

Mama had taught us the opening lines of the first sura of the Qur'an to say to ourselves as our plane took off, and I had been practicing it at night in preparation for this journey. As I heard the first rumbles of the jets, I held Mama's hand, shutting my eyes tight. I repeated:

La ill ah ha ill lil lah, Mohamedur Rasul-illah
In the name of Allah, the merciful and compassionate God.
Praise belongs to God, the Lord of the worlds,
He the merciful, the compassionate,
He, the ruler of the day of judgment
Thee we serve and Thee we ask for help
Guide us in the right path,
The path of those Thou hast blessed
Not of those Thou art wroth with; nor of those who err.

Sixteen hours later, we arrived in Pakistan in the hazy light of dawn. The crew burst open the doors of our 747 to receive those heady scents of arrival: jasmine flowers, gasoline, burning trash, and cow dung. The heat, even at this early hour, seeped into the cabin almost instantly. On subsequent trips I would come to think of these first sensations of touching down in Pakistan as one united feeling, the pungent smell of difference, the awareness that I had entered a new world, one with a separate set of laws. Nana handed us kurtas to change into, tucking our Western clothes into her carry-on luggage, and our transformation from half-Pakistani American children to half-American Pakistani children was complete.

Outside the airport, I held Cassim's hand to lead him through the throng of child beggars, many our age or younger. As our uncles supervised the loading of our luggage into a minivan, a little girl about my size looked at me through the glass window that separated us, tapping her hand against the glass. I had been told that we were not supposed to give children money, because it went right back into the pockets of the brokers who ran the begging operation. Instead, we were instructed to give to people we knew, or to donate to a local charity before we left the country. But I had in my miniature purse the Pakistani rupees I had collected from my parents' dressing table, and my hand itched to give them to the girl. Furtively, I rolled down my window and slipped her a few coins, trying to do so unnoticed by Mama and Nana in the front seat. When I watched the girl run away and hide behind another car to count the money, I thought suddenly of my classroom back home, the clean lines and order of my school hallways. I thought about how on my trips to Pakistan I had seen and experienced things that my classmates never had, things that they would barely understand or appreciate. This realization gave me a feeling of separation. I thought to myself, "Since half of me is from here, from Karachi, does this mean half of me is not from there, from Chestnut Hill?" After we drove out of the airport, I watched the city skid by my window and felt dizzy with the rush of images: huts, scooters, billboards, Technicolor trucks. This moment—the flash of white cotton as the girl disappeared, colliding with the image of my third-grade classroom—stays with me, even now, a shard of mirror under my feet, refracting light between the years that separate me and that day.

When we reached Siddiqi House, I had the same thought that I did every time we entered the driveway: This is Mama's house, from when she was a little girl like me. The house was impossibly tall, a soft yellow, with "Siddiqi House" emblazoned across the top and "1948," the year my grandfather built it, inscribed on the gate. When we passed through its front doors, Mama ceased to be just our mother and became so many other things— older sister, younger sister, superstar, foreign-returned, rebel, and entertainer. It seemed at these times as if Mama were really on loan to us in America, a kind of special vacation from her real home, in Pakistan. Once inside Siddiqi House, Nana slipped into the fabric of the place and seemed to disappear within it; whereas in our house in Chestnut Hill she had authority, here she was one quiet part of a large dysfunctional unit.

I tried desperately to stay awake. I wanted to see my cousins, whom I hadn't seen in the two years since I was last here. They must be so tall now, I thought. But I couldn't seem to stay up. Before I could protest, Mama and Nana were tucking Cassim and me into low cots, windows hung with dark cloth, jet lag settling on us like a heavy weight we couldn't bring ourselves to lift.

I woke up at five the next morning, startled by the call to prayer and disoriented. I ran to the edge of the room and looked out the window, staring at two large sand-colored dogs wrestling in the garden. I'm in Siddiqi

House, I reminded myself. We are ten and a half hours ahead of home, in a place with different rules. The dogs belonged to Farida Khala, my mother's half sister. Her babies, she called them, because she didn't have any of her own. *"Bechari,"* people said under their breath about Farida Khala, "poor thing." I recall a thick sadness to her that I didn't understand; I remember that the rolls of her stomach smelled like talc and sour milk. Her older husband, Uncle Hameed, spent the afternoons worrying a well-worn path between the television set and his prayer mat on the veranda. Last time we were here, when Cassim was three and I was six, Farida Khala took care of my brother the whole time, carrying him everywhere on her hip. This delighted Mama and Nana, who were happy to have free hands. Two days before we were due to leave, Farida Khala asked my mother to leave Cassim behind. "You're young," I heard her say in the sitting room while Uncle Hameed napped nearby. "You can have another child. I can't."

Through the curtain that separated our beds, I heard my mother and father talking all that night: "It's the custom if one sister can't have a child," she explained, "but I can't do it." I heard my mother crying, telling my father, over and over, "I can't bear to leave him."

I don't remember the words my father used to comfort her. I imagine now that he might have told her that we were going home the next day, home to Boston. Perhaps Mama comforted herself with the idea that she was leaving one home, its customs suddenly, cruelly unfamiliar to her, for another one, where her children and her mother and her husband were hers alone. But this is the invention of adulthood.

THE COMING DAYS were a rush of unfamiliar aunts and uncles, kissing strange cheeks, trying to remember to say *"As-salaam aleikum"* (God be with you) when we greeted someone new, and *"Walaikum asalaam"* (and also with you) when the person greeted us back.

We went to see Mama's childhood tailor, Master Sahib. His shop was on the other side of town, a closet-sized room down a winding alleyway hung with brightly colored plastic buckets. My mother presented me to him—a tiny, white-haired man dressed in white cotton with a measuring tape hung loosely around his neck—pushing me in front of her to show me off.

"*As-salaam aleikum,* Master Sahib," I said.

He threw his hands in the air and exclaimed, "*Mashallah!*" and I saw tears welling up in his eyes.

"Why is he crying, Mama?" I asked.

"Master Sahib has made all of my clothes all my life, from when I was small like you. Now he'll make yours, too."

She told me that Master Sahib was one of the people my grandfather helped to bring from India during Partition. The tailor, the cooks, the drivers, the wedding photographer, the jeweler—in the course of a week it seemed that everyone we met had some kind of connection to my grandfather.

"Did your father have a lot of friends?" I asked Mama.

"My father," she said, grandly, "was friends with everyone in Karachi."

BARI AMMA AND CHOTI AMMA were my other two grandmothers, my grandfather's elder wives. Bari Amma, my grandfather's first wife, spent all day in a tiny dark room, with a white dupatta on her head, praying. She was a tiny, bowed creature, the strands of her white hair pulled tight into a bun, and her pointed beak of a nose holding up a pair of wire-rimmed spectacles. She seemed perpetually disgusted with the commotion of Siddiqi House and preferred to spend her remaining days in the solemn cool of her private chambers. "Nonsense," I heard her muttering under her breath while we watched television. "All nonsense."

For years later, whenever I saw a picture of Gandhi, I thought to myself, He looks like Bari Amma. Mama told me that Bari Amma was the first lady doctor in all of Gujarat, and that the prince of Jamnagar had arranged her marriage to my grandfather; the prince had thought that Grandfather should have an educated wife. Bari Amma had two sons, Waris and Salik. Her elder son ran my grandfather's English-language bookstore, Campbell and Company, and her second son was settled in England. Bari Amma knew the entire Qur'an by heart and could recite it from start to finish. The only thing I ever saw her do other than pray was make small cloth pouches out of silk scraps, where she kept jewelry or anise seeds. I was fascinated by the pouches, and wanted desperately to bring them back to give to my third-grade class. Some afternoons, I wandered throughout Siddiqi House until I reached her room, where I would peek inside and see her sitting on her knees, her eyes closed, her hands counting a set of small prayer beads. One afternoon, I slipped and fell as I was watching her and tore the cloth of my pajama pants on a nail.

"Who's there?" she called out.

"Only me, Bari Amma," I replied, feeling apologetic.

"Is that you, Sadia?"

"Yes."

"Come here, child," she said, and I tiptoed into the dark space.

"Is there something you are looking for?" she asked me.

I told her that I was hoping she might have some extra silk pouches that I could take back with me to America. She considered this for a moment.

"How many?" she asked.

I was tentative. "I was thinking . . . ten?"

"I will give you *two,*" she said judiciously, and opened up a cupboard with a long key carried on a chain around her neck. I looked up at her shelves and saw rows and rows of books, mostly English books. She busied herself in her cupboard and fished out two bright pouches, one a brilliant purple and the other a dusky pink.

"You are like your mother," she said, shaking her head and handing me the pouches.

"Thank you, Bari Amma," I stammered and ran out.

Choti Amma, my grandfather's second wife, had three children settled in Pakistan: Irfan, Farida, and Sadik. She spent all day in her son Irfan's apartment, gossiping with her son's wife, Zaitoon, and supervising the cooks. Choti Amma was as talkative as Bari Amma was quiet, and as round as Bari Amma was thin. Choti Amma always smelled like the kitchen, a mixture of cumin and cooking grease. She spoke in a shrill voice, which became high-pitched when she was upset about something. She went out of her way to make me English porridge every morning, thinking that this might be something that a Western child would like. It was delicious, but unlike any breakfast I had had at home; this was covered in a layer of dark, sweet treacle. When I entered the kitchen, she would present it to me silently, and when I finished the whole bowl and returned it to her, she would place her hand on my head. *"Acchi beti,"* she said—"good girl." I never saw her read a book, or leave Siddiqi House. I thought of Bari Amma and Choti Amma as a pair of opposites, and wondered where my grandmother fit into the equation. The story went that when my grandfather's mother learned that her son had married a Gujarati lady doctor at the suggestion of the prince, she was furious, reminding him that in fact he had been engaged to Choti Amma since he was a child. She demanded that he return home to Ajmer and arranged for a wedding between Choti Amma and Ali. That's how my grandfather came to have two wives. The first was a professional arrangement, the second a familial obligation. Nana, I was always told, he married for love.

WHITE SHEETS WERE laid out on the floor of Siddiqi House. The ladies of our family sat and decorated twenty-one trays with red cellophane and ribbons to hold the twenty-one brightly colored silk salwar suits of the bride's trousseau. Two of my older cousins, Saima and Farah, were already at work, and they cleared a space for me to sit next to them. Only a year apart in age, they seemed to me almost like twins. I liked to be near them, with their soft, lilting voices and their skin smelling of sandalwood soap. I could never decide which one was my favorite. They teased me about one of my earliest trips to Pakistan, for Saima's wedding, when I was three years old and sat obediently at her feet during her *mehndi* ceremony, watching my aunts circle her head three times with shiny silver rupees and drop them in her lap, to be distributed to the poor at the end of the evening. As I watched the coins gather, I began to think what good gifts they would make for the ten other members of my nursery school class. Unable to resist the temptation, I began to slip each one silently into my pajamas. At the end of the evening, no one could figure out where the money had gone. I dutifully made a show of searching high and low for the rupees, squeezing underneath chairs and skirts, never letting on that I had stolen them. When Farah stooped to pick me up at the end of the ceremony, she could tell that I was unusually heavy and chuckled to find the coins in my pants.

"You had them all along!" they remembered, teasing me. "Some day, Sadu, you will have your own *mehndi,* and your own *nikaah.* You will be a beautiful bride."

I tried to imagine getting married in Pakistan, what I would wear, what my groom would look like. I had an equally strong image of myself in a white dress, getting married in America. The two pictures competed for attention in my mind's eye.

A lady came to the house to apply henna paste to our hands and feet for decoration. I could sit still through only one hand's worth of decoration without squirming, which made Saima Apa and Farah Apa laugh.

"Is Auntie Shehzadi getting henna put on her hands?" I asked Farah. I was intensely curious about my uncle's bride. Since she was not yet a member of our family, she did her preparations at her home, not ours. She and Uncle Salman were not allowed to see each other until the night of their marriage. Mama told me that Shehzadi was in the period of Manjah, during which she was to wear only yellow clothing and spend time with her sisters, cousins, and female friends, enjoying her last few days in her parents' home. Each day, they smoothed her body with a mixture of chickpea flour and sandalwood paste to make her skin glow, and at night, they sang songs. Mama said that by wearing yellow Shehzadi could avoid the evil eye that might fall on her otherwise. When she emerged on her wedding night in bright colors, the contrast would be stunning.

"Oh yes, she'll be having a very ornate design on her hands and feet," Farah told me. "You'll see when we go for her *mehndi* ceremony."

I bothered Mama about Shehzadi until she agreed to take me to her house to meet her. While Mama sat with the Nawab family and had tea, I waited impatiently in the hallway for Shehzadi to come downstairs. I heard her parents tell Mama that she was studying for her final exams. She wanted to finish her degree before she left for America.

Shehzadi was smaller than I expected. In her yellow cotton salwar kameez she looked more like a girl than an aunt, but she had the confidence of an aunt. She took me to the backyard, and we stood there looking at one another.

"You wanted to meet me?" she asked me gently, and I felt instantly embarrassed.

"You are coming to live with us, in America," I said, stating the obvious.

"Yes," she said, nodding.

"I can show you around, show you how things work. I can take you shopping and show you what we eat."

"Thank you," she said, smiling. "That would be nice."

"Do you like horses?" I asked.

"I don't know much about them, but, yes, I like them."

"Uncle Salman loves horses."

"Yes."

THE NIGHT OF the *nikaah* ceremony, I was allowed to wear my mother's jewelry from when she was my age, a necklace made of amethysts and small diamonds that her father had made for her when she stood first in school. Nana kept it in the bank for safekeeping, along with her other jewelry. Master Sahib made me a pale pink outfit with tiny purple brocade, and matching pale pink skinny churidar pants and dupatta shawl. Cassim was dressed in a tiny, formal white silk shervani suit and a miniature white silk turban, matching the one on Uncle Salman's head. The wedding was held in a large multicolored tent in the backyard of Siddiqi House, and hundreds of people gathered to attend the ceremony. Guests entered the front driveway through a tunnel of well-wishers throwing rose petals. A crowd of children and families from the nearby slum collected in a ring around the crowd, jostling for a vantage point. The *hijras* were here, too, eunuchs dressed elaborately as women. Periodically they began to dance and sing, hinting at the full performance they would like to give. The *hijras* stared at me, and I tried in vain not to stare back. My uncle Waris handed out coins, thanking them for their blessings and asking them to disperse. Behind Siddiqi House the wedding feast was being prepared, as well as food to feed the crowd that had assembled to watch the festivities through the fence.

I waited for the arrival of the bride and groom with my cousin Sartaj and his new bride, Fatima. Sartaj was tall, with a trim goatee and short-cropped hair. He was only a few years younger than Uncle Salman and was starting to work as a banker in Karachi. Fatima held her dupatta halfway across her face while she smiled into the cloth, too shy to speak. I had heard my mother say that she was just nineteen and did not speak much English. I could see part of her face through the cloth; her large, dark eyes rimmed with kohl, and her shiny black hair pulled into a ponytail. Her face was so pale that she didn't look Pakistani to me; her skin wasn't brown like that of the rest of my relatives. I smiled at her, and she smiled back, tentatively.

"So, Sadia," he said, "are you going to be friends with my wife?"

It must have been an idle comment, but I took this question very seriously, turning it over in my mind.

"Yes," I said slowly. "I will."

"Good," said Sartaj amiably. "That's settled, then."

I looked at Fatima, her eyes lowered in modesty, and had the impression that she had a quieter temperament than Shehzadi.

The night was a burst of color—flashes of blinking lights, red silk, and fireworks. My eyes took everything in, assembling detailed notes that I carry with me still. Uncle Salman approached the house on a white polo pony, his turban dripping roses, his eyes showing amusement at and appreciation for the proceedings. In front of him, Cassim sat astride the horse, surveying the crowd, a tiny decoy to deflect the evil eye from Uncle Salman. Cassim took his role very seriously, sitting straight up in his saddle, tipping his tiny head at the crowd below, and waving. The horse was flanked by Uncle Salman's *baraat*, a group of male relatives who clapped and sang as he dismounted and walked through Siddiqi House to the backyard, where he sat on a dais and waited for Shehzadi's arrival. The walls, the platform, and the ceiling were covered in strings of fresh roses. We were enveloped in their scent. The sound of drums echoed throughout the space as Shehzadi entered the tent under the protective embrace of her female relatives holding an elaborate cloth above her head. She was dressed in a gorgeous hand-block-printed wedding outfit. Instead of the traditional red and gold, she had opted for an outfit chosen by my mother in shades of dark rose and deep purple. A long chain linked the large gold ring in her nostril to a set of small diamonds hanging in her hair above her ear, and her eyelids were shadowed with shiny metallic powders. I had never seen anyone so beautiful.

The wedding ceremony itself was shorter than I was expecting. A small mirror was placed underneath Shehzadi's veil. She looked into the mirror and saw Salman for the first time in several weeks. Cassim, ever vigilant, peeked into the mirror after him. There, in that very public moment of intimacy, rested the possibilities of the life unfolding before her feet. She was asked if she accepted this marriage, and she nodded. Two male witnesses from Shehzadi's family and two from our family signed the marriage document. The *maulvi* intoned his prayers in Arabic over a handheld microphone. Man and wife. They did not kiss, or even touch. When the ceremony was over, they continued to sit on the dais and people took their picture. Nana asked Cassim and me to sit at Uncle Salman's and Auntie Shehzadi's feet while relatives and friends approached the couple and congratulated them.

"Bee-yoot-iful bride, she is ve-ry fair. . . . *Mubarak, mubarak,*" the aunties said as they went by.

Even though she might have been happy, Mama told me that Shehzadi was supposed to look sad about leaving her parents' home, and she was supposed to look down as a sign of modesty. I imagined how frustrating it must be to have to look down while people are talking about you. I crossed my fingers and hoped that she was happy, even though she couldn't show it.

Nana had made sure to invite every person in the extended Siddiqi family, every last cousin and distant relation by marriage. She had tracked down all the servants who had ever worked for the family, their families, and the people my grandfather helped move from India to Pakistan. Uncle Salman was Ali Siddiqi's last son, and in this moment, the house rose to its full potential, brimming with all ten of its children, all three of its mistresses, prayers, song, long trays of food, and flashbulbs going off late into the night. My mother said the event would have made my grandfather proud. I had the unshakable impression that this grand performance was a taste of things to come, that the opulence of this night was merely a foreshadowing of the glamorous life Uncle Salman and Auntie Shehzadi were about to embark upon in America. It never occurred to me that this night might have been something else, a grand finale to Siddiqi House, to my grandfather's legacy, the highest fulfillment of my grandmother's promise to raise her husband's children as Muslims.

Cassim and I tried to stay clean and pressed throughout the night, but it was impossible. By the end of the evening, we were covered in the red stains of roses, our fingers tender from their thorns, our necks heavy with garlands, our fancy clothes crumpled and marked in too many places to count. When I look back at this night, I see it through strings of flowers, bruised and sweet. Since that evening, the idea of Pakistan, of Islam, has forever been linked in my mind with the perfumed excess of roses, their sweet stickiness. I would be reminded of this association when I visited Sufi shrines as an adult, carrying red petals in a wide, flat tray on my head, bowing over the saints' graves, my offering spilling out.

ON THE PLANE ride back to Boston, I tried to write my report for school in my blue notebook, drifting in and out of sleep. Half Pakistani, half American. Half Muslim, half Christian. Half-half.

"Have-have, sweetheart," Nana said, elbowing me awake, offering me her slice of plane-food cake.

"Thank you, Nana." I smiled, half awake.

I slipped my head onto her shoulder and inhaled the comfort of her scent: rose talc, rose soap, and rose water.

Reverse order: Karachi, Cairo, Frankfurt, New York, Boston. Home again.

9

SHANTARAM'S POND

PUNE, DECEMBER 2001

Shantaram."

A voice startles me, and Rekhev sits down next to me. He has an unsettling way of appearing seemingly out of nowhere, when I least expect it. Sometimes I am tempted to mention it, but something stops me, as if I might break a spell and then he will no longer appear.

I'm sitting on a crumbling stone step next to the empty cavity of an old man-made pond, a hole in the ground filled with vines and weeds. This is my favorite place at the Film Institute. If you look carefully, you can make out the borders of the original structure, the steps, and a crumbling statue of an elephant—a concrete relic from the Institute's days as a film studio, cracked in places, with green spilling out. Healed and solid in my mind, the place is easy to imagine as the setting for a Cecil B. DeMille movie, with bathing beauties sitting poolside in high heels. I wonder what its Indian equivalent might have been. I like to go there in the afternoons, to read and write, until the mosquitoes become too persistent.

"This pond is named for him," he says, looking straight ahead, as if I had asked him a question. "Shantaram was a film director who worked here in the days when the Institute was a film studio."

"Did he use this pond in his films?"

"See the ramp there? That must have been to wheel cameras in and out. You can see an alcove there. It must have been used as a small shrine, a kind of temple. . . ."

We sit looking at the pond in silence for a few moments.

"Place memory," he says. "The imprint of past action on an environment. We are surrounded by ghosts here."

"It feels that way," I say, nodding.

"Do you see those trees there?" he asks, gesturing across the pond toward a gathering of large, tall deciduous trees. They look like ficus trees, with large green leaves and knobby, wise-looking trunks. "Pipal trees," he says. "It is believed that the god Brahma resides in the roots, the god Vishnu in the trunk, and the god Shiva in the crown. People believe that the god Krishna breathed his last underneath a pipal, and that the tree is invested with a sacred thread. In the Konkan, where your Jews originally resided, I have read that people who are wishing for a particular outcome used to worship the tree, and walk around its base several times a day. There is also a belief there that the spirits of the dead are reborn in their descendants, especially if they have wishes that remain unfulfilled. Sometimes if a child resembles a relative who has died it is believed that the ancestor has returned to the family in the form of the child. You are seeking a ghost, aren't you? Perhaps that's why you like to come here."

I wonder for a moment if Rekhev talks this way to the other students, if they accept his long-winded theories as easily as I do.

THE NEXT TIME I see Rekhev, a week later, he is sitting on a campus bench, reading a book. He nods at me and goes back to his reading. I sit down and reach into my handbag, sifting through its contents, not sure what I am looking for.

"You're always looking in that red bag, as if it might have answers," he says, not looking up. "You look tense."

"It's my pictures," I say. They seem flat, hollow somehow. "They're no good."

"You should read for a year in India before you take out your camera," he says. We are silent for a few minutes. Then he gets up, shielding his eyes from the sun with one hand and not looking at me.

"Come," he says, and I find myself walking down the long campus path and Law College Road next to Rekhev. I'm not sure where we're going, but there's something compelling, urgent even, about his invitation. We reach an old stone bungalow set back from the road. The building is surrounded by leafy trees and flowering bushes. A curved signboard in an arc over the entrance reads "Bhandarkar Oriental Research Institute. Founded 1917."

We enter a large, dark room lined with glass-paneled bookshelves. On the right side is a long, low table holding academic books and journals published by the Bhandarkar Institute Press. I scan the titles: *Recent Trends in Indology, The Bhagavadgita as a Synthesis, The Vedic Sacrifice in Transition,* and *Ancient Indian Insights and Modern Science.*

"There's a *Mahabharata* department here where scholars have been working on a definitive edition of the *Mahabharata* since 1919. They finished the main text in the late sixties and are now working on the epilogue. Everything you could possibly want to know about India, to 'understand' it, lies here."

Rekhev moves slowly around the room, piling books of folklore in front of him. I sit down at one of the long desks and take in my surroundings. I feel as if I have been let in on a secret. Rekhev pulls out a large green volume, which he presents to me. The spine reads *Natya-Manjari Saurabha: Sanskrit Dramatic Theory.*

"It's fragile," he says. "Be careful."

Once Rekhev has assembled a large pile of books in front of himself, he begins to work through the stack systematically, taking notes in a large hardbound notebook with an old-fashioned fountain pen. I fight my impulse to read his notes over his shoulder and try to concentrate on the volume in front of me.

I open the book, curious why he has given it to me, and read about the five stages of dramatic plot construction in Sanskrit plays, trying to make sense of the unfamiliar words. The first stage, *prarambha,* is the beginning of action, where the dramatic hero's search for some great fruit, or goal, is identified. In the second stage, *prayatna,* or "effort," the hero recognizes that the achievement he is seeking will not be possible without using appropriate *upaya,* means. The hero investigates the means available to him and determines a course of action. The third stage, *praptisambhava,* "the possibility of attainment," occurs when a particular means becomes available. This is a stage of hope, expectation, and anxiety. The fourth, the *niyata phalaprapti,* "ordained attainment of the fruit," occurs when the hero's desired achievement is within grasp. He may visualize the achievement in his mind, or have a vision of his goal attained; the hero's objective will become a reality in the final stage, the *phalayoga,* "the accomplishment or attainment of the fruit."

As I am reading, I come across an illustration, folded into the body of the text. Captioned "Dramatic Plot-Construction: Relations and scope of Arthaprakrtis, Avasthās, Sandhis-Sandhyaṅgas," it shows some kind of manmade structure spanning a body of water. The construction has five arches held aloft by six pillars, and each arch is marked with a series of letters in Devanagari script. The building blocks of each arch are also marked with letters, as are the bricks above the arches, which form the top half of the bridge. It seems to be some kind of diagram.

Rekhev leans over my notes. "You found the drawing."

I nod.

"So—have you identified your goal?" he asks me.

"What?"

"Let's have tea," he says. "I have some ideas to tell you."

On our way to Lucky, Rekhev asks me if I have read *The Hero with a Thousand Faces* by Joseph Campbell. I tell him that I recall vaguely what I learned in college about Campbell's theory regarding the universality of myth.

"This idea is very exciting to me—the idea of a folktale as a structure. The ordinary world is established, and then comes the call for adventure. The hero denies that call. Again it comes, and the hero finds motivation to meet the call. He encounters threshold guardians, who express doubts. He

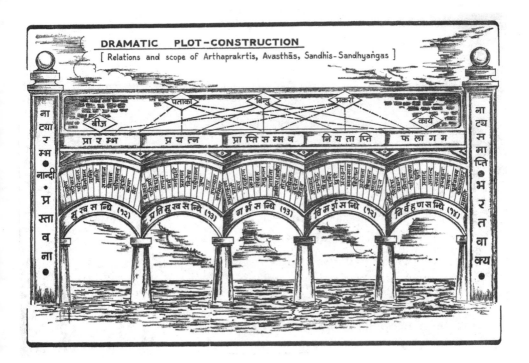

meets allies, tricksters, and shape-shifters. The hero meets a mentor, a fallen hero, someone who has already gone through a journey and knows routes, how to kill the villain. The mentor gives a sword to the hero, who is able to conquer the villain and return to the ordinary world with an elixir. In many ways, it closely mirrors Sanskrit dramatic theory. I always imagine my life like that, moving through time in a series of progressive stages."

We enter the café, and Rekhev chooses the table where we sat before, orders two cups of tea. He takes out a cigarette and lights it, offering me the pack. I shake my head no.

"The mentor is a kind of guru?" I ask.

"Perhaps, but a guru does not always come in the form of a wise old bearded man. A guru is not always someone who gives you something. He or she can also be someone you take something from, or someone who makes you realize something. The guru can even start a process without being aware of it."

"Do you think I am following this model? In India?" I ask.

"By being here, maybe you are writing your own story with each step you take, what do you think? Your grandmother gave you the call for adventure, the impetus. I could be a trickster in your path. I could also be an ally."

"So who is the villain? The mentor?"

Rekhev taps the burning tip of his cigarette on a small metal tin filled with the stubbed-out butts of previous patrons, and pauses for a moment.

"Perhaps you have not met them yet, perhaps you have. And perhaps you never will, not in predictable forms. Ultimately, the whole myth, every character, is you. You may find that mentor or that villain in the world, or you may find it within yourself. In Greek tragedy, the hero is the source of the tragedy. In the West, I find that your dramatic searches, whether in books or in films, are driven by a single emotion. Whereas in India the hero often finds the source of his information in one person."

"So I am walking across that bridge."

"We all are," Rekhev says, pausing again. "What was she like, your grandmother?"

I think for a moment, trying to figure out how to summarize her. For some reason, I find myself wanting to tell Rekhev details about Nana that I don't normally mention, tiny details that I never think of in succession. I want to create a portrait of her for him, an image that I can hand across the table.

"She had a bookshelf in her room where she kept small items she brought back from her trips abroad . . . odd things, a dog made of seashells, a teacup with the King of Sweden on it, a model of Big Ben. She didn't see kitsch. She didn't read it that way. She would knit baby clothes in strange colors, pastel greens and bright, bright yellows. My mother would say, 'Amma, why did you choose this yarn?' and Nana would say, 'Because this is such a beautiful color!' " I laugh, imagining her holding the balls of yarn and gesturing at my mother with them. "She had an entirely different aesthetic from her daughter, from anyone in my family."

Rekhev smiles slightly.

"She is familiar to me," he says. "You know, I can understand your Nana much better than I will ever be able to understand you."

We sit in silence, drinking our tea. I watch through the doorway of the café as a man tries to tie a large block of steaming ice to the back of his bicycle. He unfolds a woven tarp, which he wraps around the block; he winds a length of twine around the block and expends a good deal of effort to stop the block from slipping.

"Look," I say, gesturing outside. "That man is trying to carry ice."

Rekhev looks over his shoulder, unimpressed, and returns his attention to his teacup. I feel like a foreigner.

"What does your name mean?" I ask Rekhev, seeing it written on the cover of his notebook: *Rekhev Bharadwaj.*

"Bharadwaj is the name of my *gotra*. Do you know what a *gotra* is?"

I shake my head no. "My *gotra* is my clan, my lineage from the Brahmin sages, or *rishis*. We are Mohyals, Hussaini Brahmins who fought alongside the grandsons of the Prophet in the Battle of Karbala. Is your family Shia or Sunni?"

"Sunni."

"Too bad," he says, wryly. "We were allied with the Shiites. The Mohyals believe that an ancestor of ours named Rahab Sidh Datt became close with Imam Hussain while living near Baghdad—this would have been in the late seventh century. When Hussain was traveling from Medina to Karbala and was attacked by Yazid's army, Datt's family was part of the entourage. He and his sons fought alongside the Imam, and seven of Datt's sons died in the fighting. Those who survived settled across northern India, mostly in the Punjab. My ancestors were Hindus, but some of their traditions were quite influenced by Islam."

"Your family is not so different from mine, then," I say.

"I suppose you are correct," Rekhev says, looking doubtful. "This was centuries ago, of course. My family are fairly traditional northern Indian Brahmins now. But the history remains."

"Do people know about your community?"

"Not much—some. There are those who would like to erase this past, of course. But I had an old uncle who used to recite this saying: *'Wah Dutt Sultan, Hindu ka dharm, Musalman ka iman, adha Hindu adha Musalman.'* It means: 'Oh! Dutt, the king, who follows the religion of the Hindu, and the faith of the Muslim, half Hindu, half Muslim.' My uncle was an Urdu poet. He spoke better Urdu than many Pakistanis. You see, some threads continue."

"And what about your first name? Does it have a meaning?"

"All names have a meaning," Rekhev says, bristling. "In the Chandogya Upanishad there is a small reference to a *rishi* called Rekhev, just two lines. A king comes to him seeking *tatvagyan,* the knowledge of elements. He has his daughter with him, the princess. And Rekhev says that he will give the king knowledge only because his daughter is very beautiful. 'Why would he say that?' people wondered. There have been centuries of discussions among scholars about these two lines. Someone wrote a novel based on these two lines, called *Diary of Anonymous.* It's a shame you can't read it; it's in Hindi. Rekhev is the hero of *Diary of Anonymous.*"

"Is it the story of Rekhev's relationship with the king and the princess?"

"No, in fact it is the explanation of those two lines from the Chandogya Upanishad, of what came before that meeting."

"What was the story?"

"It's a long one. Shall we have another cup of tea?" Rekhev asks me, and I nod.

"Bhaiyya, do chai," he says to the waiter, who swiftly returns to the kitchen with our order.

"Rekhev had been looking for the princess for his entire life. In the beginning, Rekhev used to do meditation and *tapasya,* or penance, in the jungle, because he was a sage. He had never seen a woman in his entire life. On the day when this story takes place, it was raining hard. The princess was passing through this jungle and had an accident: her cart broke down. Because Rekhev had never seen a woman, he thought that the princess must be a man-god, a *dev-pursh.* Because she was wounded, Rekhev offered to carry her on his back. She said that this would not be proper, because she was a woman. 'What is a woman?' he asked her. She told him, and he understood, recognizing the idea as familiar, though it was outside of his experience. What is the English word for *manobhava,* for an idea of something . . . ?"

" 'Concept'?"

"Concept. She made him understand the difference between concept and something tangible, between concept and . . ."

"Matter."

"Exactly. Between concept and matter. He said, 'Because you have made me understand the difference between concept and matter, you are my guru.' "

"How did she leave the jungle?"

"I am not sure. The princess returned to safety somehow, and Rekhev sat down near the broken cart and started to meditate. He got a rash on his back because of the improper idea of carrying the princess on his back. He stayed in this position for a long while, for years even, scratching his back and meditating, trying to understand his guru. Then he went on a journey to find her. He found a very old woman who told him that he had information but he lacked knowledge, because he had not done *satsang.* Do you know the meaning of *satsang?*"

"*Satsang* is when people gather to sing devotional songs, right?"

"No, no. I suppose some people call that *satsang,* but the real meaning of *satsang* is 'noble friendship.' You see, Rekhev was all alone. He hadn't related to anyone."

"Did he go, then, in search of noble friendship?"

"He did. This is the preoccupation of most of the book. It might make an interesting film, actually. Now, this is my own idea, and you can make of it what you will, but I believe that when you take information from one sphere to another, only then does it transform. It changes from information to knowledge. I think this is why people travel."

"But you don't travel."

"I have not left Pune for some time," he says, lighting another cigarette. He suddenly looks very tired. "Shall we go back?"

"Yes, let's do that," I say.

As has quickly become our pattern, we walk back to the campus without speaking. Darkness has fallen, and the dinner hour is over. Once again I will have to make my meal out of wheat biscuits, potato chips, and bottled wa-ter, I think to myself. My head aches from the amount of information I have tried to absorb in one day. I wonder why Rekhev has chosen me to tell all these theories to. He seems to take it all so seriously.

"Good night," I say, extending my hand when we reach the entry to my compound.

"Good night," Rekhev says, shaking my hand quickly. "You may not see me for some time."

I try not to sound disappointed. "Why is that?"

"I have some work to attend to," he says, mysteriously. "But we will meet soon."

As he walks away, I call out, "Good luck, then."

"Luck?" he says, looking back at me over his shoulder.

"Good luck with your work, I mean."

"Luck is written in the Fates," he says, and weaves his way among the passing cars to the main campus gate.

His words make me smile. I turn around and walk back to my room, wondering if he was intending to be so cryptic.

10

RICHARD AND SAMINA

I first heard the story of my mother's fascination with America at a party my parents threw when I was eleven years old. It was a Saturday night in the beginning of December, and my mother and grandmother had spent the day preparing chicken *biryani,* filling the house with the smell of toasted cumin. The lights were turned down low, and my father had built a fire in the sunroom and put on one of his Pakistani folk records. The sunroom was in a far corner of the house, just off the more formal living room, and it was slightly sunken, one step below the rest of the ground floor, so that you had to make a small step down to enter it—a small but deliberate motion signaling that this was a different sort of room. This was where my mother and grandmother told stories. The walls were paneled in rosewood, and lined with large windows that opened like swinging doors, letting in sun in the daytime and letting out smoke from the fire at night. A pair of old Indian puppets hung above the fireplace, carefully placed by my father so that they faced each other with their arms raised and their mouths open, appearing to be in mid-conversation.

By eight o'clock, the house was crowded with my mother's friends from Pakistan and my parents' friends from Boston, drinking cocktails and laughing. Dinner was served on the thick metal *thali* plates with matching cups that we used for company. Guests praised the *biryani,* and several American women gathered around my grandmother, asking her how to make it. I heard her begin to explain, shyly, "Really, it's not hard. You just take ginger, garlic . . ."

After dinner, everyone gathered in the sunroom. Someone asked my mother to tell a story. Her friends referred to her anecdotes as "Samina stories," and that night, someone asked about her first trip to America. She laughed and said, "It all started at the movies. . . ." Cassim and I took seats on the floor of the sunroom, settling in next to Nana as the story began.

"When I was eight years old, my father took his three wives, eight sons, two daughters, four nephews, and five servants to the Paradise Cinema in downtown Karachi to see Cecil B. DeMille's *The Greatest Show on Earth,* and that day I decided I wanted to come to America. The movie was in Technicolor, and I had never seen anything so magnificent. There was a trapeze artist, an elephant trainer, a clown. . . . I remember thinking, 'Is this what America is like?'"

My father sat across the room from my mother, smiling. No matter how many times he might have heard these stories, he always looked as though he were hearing them for the first time.

My mother went on. "When I was fifteen, I began heavily campaigning to be allowed to apply to study in the United States. I convinced my first cousin Uzma to apply with me to the American Field Service exchange program. Uzma was fair, much fairer than me, with long shiny black hair and long eyelashes, and we were best friends. My brothers called us 'Beauty and the Beast.'"

The guests laughed. My mother liked to joke about not being pretty when she was younger, but I'd seen the pictures, and I knew she was exaggerating.

"Uzma had an aunt who worked at the Pakistani Consulate in Paris and periodically sent her French magazines and underwear, and Uzma was fascinated by Europe. She wanted to go to Paris, but I explained to her that America was a much better choice—it was the land of Elvis Presley, our favorite singer. I offered to help her with her essay and she relented. We completed our applications and hand-delivered them to the U.S. Consulate, and then we waited for a response. Every day after school, I would ask Majjid, the majordomo of our household, if any mail had come for me. And every day Majjid would say, 'No, *beti*, there was no letter,' shaking his head. 'Perhaps tomorrow.' It seemed like the letter would never come.

"One day, after more than three months, the telephone rang after dinner. It was Uzma. 'Did your letter come? Did it come?' she asked.

" 'I haven't had any letter. What does yours say?'

" 'Oh, Sam, it says I am going to Lockport in New York State! I am going to stay with a family called Parsons! And they have two boys in the family, and one girl, who is also fifteen! Oh, Sam, this is so exciting!' "

My mother shook her head sadly. "Truthfully, I was terribly unhappy. I thought to myself, How could Uzma have been accepted and not me? It seemed wildly unfair. Not only was I not going to America, I was also losing my best friend. Five days later, I shuffled home through the gate after school and Majjid was there waiting for me, looking jubilant.

" 'A letter for Her Majesty!' he announced.

" 'It's come?' I dropped my satchel and ran up the stairs to the kitchen storeroom—the only place where I could shut the door and open my letter in privacy. There it was. Thick, pale blue, and covered with American stamps. I was going to America! To Manhattan!

"There was so much to do. I had to pack my clothing for an entire year in two steamer trunks, and in these I had to fit gifts for my American family. And I had to do research. I went to the U.S. Consulate and asked to see photographs of Manhattan. The consul general's secretary got up on a stool and brought down the *Encyclopædia Britannica,* and showed me pictures of the Statue of Liberty, the Metropolitan Museum of Art, the Empire State Building. I studied these carefully, and imagined everything that I was going to do in America. I couldn't wait to get there."

My mother paused, smoothing the fabric of her salwar kameez.

"When it was finally time to go, Uzma and I were taken to the airport in a long caravan of cars, garlanded with strings of flowers, photographed, wept over—most of our relatives were convinced that a terrible fate awaited us.

"We took an Alitalia flight to Paris, where we planned to spend two days before meeting the steamship that would take us to New York. A cable had been sent to Uzma's auntie Seema. She was instructed to put us up and chaperone us in Paris. Our mothers stood close to one another on the airport tarmac, watching their fifteen-year-old daughters boarding a 747, looking very nervous.

"I remember that once we were inside the plane I was quite struck by the clean beige surfaces of the interior; I had never been on an airplane before. When the dinner service was distributed, I was quite amazed by the minuscule amounts of food placed into tiny compartments in the tray, and I began poking at it.

" 'Don't eat it. It might be pork,' Uzma whispered fiercely.

"Since it is forbidden in the Qur'an, we had been carefully instructed to avoid pork. Neither of us had any idea what it looked like.

" 'I'm eating it,' I announced.

"An hour later, the plane hit a patch of turbulence and we clutched each other's hands.

" 'It's because you ate pork!' said Uzma, frightened. 'This plane is going to crash because God is angry with you!'

"We prayed for God to forgive me, and asked for his blessings to safely land in Paris.

" 'Please, God,' I pleaded, 'I promise to be obedient if you will just let this plane get us to France.'

"Ten hours later, we landed at four a.m. local time. We sleepily emerged from the plane and entered the airport terminal to look for Auntie Seema. We found a bench and sat down, surrounded by our four trunks. After an hour, there was still no sign of her. The airport police approached us to see what the problem was. Uzma spoke a little French, and she managed to explain that Seema worked at the Pakistani Consulate in Paris. The police were clearly exasperated, unsure what to do with two lost girls, but eventually they rang up the consulate. This being August, Seema was on holiday in the French Riviera, and had not received the cable from Karachi. The consulate sent a car, and we were taken to Seema's apartment.

"We were very hungry. We looked around the apartment and found some spare change in a jar in the kitchen. We decided to venture out and see what we could buy with it, and found a small shop not too far from the apartment. We selected two bottles of milk and two croissants, which we placed on the counter. We laid all of our change on the counter and looked up at the cashier.

" 'Is it enough?' Uzma asked.

"The man waved us away dismissively with his hand, indicating that we should just take our breakfast as well as our change.

"We walked down the street, drinking our milk and eating the croissants. We couldn't believe our luck.

"The consulate sent a telegram to Seema's hotel, and she had to cut short her vacation and take a train back to Paris. In the interim, a car came twice a day to fetch us and take us to the consulate for our meals. In between, we wandered the streets of Paris, looking in shopwindows. Auntie Seema arrived just in time to put us on the ship that would take us to America.

"On board, there were games and dances, and we met students from all over Europe and the world. I spent a great deal of time talking to a friendly Danish boy named Steen, who was heading to Arizona and told me that he thought I was very pretty. No one in Pakistan had ever thought I was pretty—this was an exciting development. One morning, almost two weeks later, I woke up to hear shouts from the front of the boat; America was within sight. I ran to the front deck, watched, mesmerized, as the Statue of Liberty came into view. It was just like the picture in the *Encyclopædia Britannica*. We had arrived in Manhattan.

"The ship docked at New York Harbor and was met by a team of people from the exchange program, who all wore yellow shirts and went around with clipboards, passing out name tags and envelopes of information. Uzma and I stood next to each other and waited.

"A man with a loudspeaker announced Uzma's name. Next to the man was a pleasant-looking couple with two teenagers in tow, the Parsonses. Uzma's American family.

"I kissed Uzma goodbye and sat on one of my trunks, nervously waiting for my own host family to arrive. What could be taking them so long? After two hours, all of the students were gone and the dock was empty, littered with baggage tags. I sat with my chin in my hand, wondering what to do. The man with the loudspeaker approached me with a curious look.

" 'What's your final destination, young lady?' he asked, looking at his clipboard for my name.

" 'Manhattan,' I replied.

"The man looked carefully at my name tag and consulted his list.

" 'Oh no, young lady. You better put on your red shoes and call for Toto. You're not going to Manhattan, New York. You're going to Manhattan, Kansas!' "

The party guests erupted, looking at each other, and my mother, in wonder. Red shoes. Toto. Manhattan, Kansas.

"The man handed me an envelope that contained fourteen dollars and a bus ticket to Kansas, and fetched a taxi to take me to Port Authority Bus Terminal. I spent the next three days with my face pressed against the glass of a Greyhound bus, watching America unfurl before me. I had never seen anything so green, or so wide. People were very friendly to me on the bus, but I was careful not to speak to any strange men. A very nice woman from Missouri shared some of her sandwiches with me. She said: 'I have a daughter about your age at home, and you look awfully homesick sitting all by yourself.' I changed from a bus to a train in Kansas City; I couldn't believe how big America was. Finally, I reached Manhattan at four in the afternoon on August 18, 1961.

"There at the platform was the entire Manhattan High School Marching Band, playing 'For She's a Jolly Good Fellow' and waving a huge banner that read 'The Little Apple Welcomes Samina!'

"Manhattan was smaller than anywhere I had been previously, and I couldn't get over how clean it was, with rows of houses with no fences; I had only ever seen compound walls. And there was so much grass! I was from the desert, and I was amazed by all of the lawns and trees. There were no beggars, no poor people in sight, and everybody seemed to have a car. Everyone was smiling, and they all knew my name. There was a beautiful brown-haired girl in a matching yellow skirt and blouse who walked to the front of the crowd and extended her right hand.

" 'I'm Susie Beck, student body president of the senior class, and we're here to welcome you to Manhattan. We hope you'll be really happy here.' "

Mama pressed her hands together and looked around the room, her eyes shining.

"It was nothing like I'd expected America to look like. But there I was."

A couple of the guests turned to Nana. Wasn't she afraid to let Samina go?

"Yes," Nana cried, shaking her head at the thought. "She was such a headstrong girl, and it was such a long way!"

BY THE TIME I was old enough to wonder about it, my parents' life together made sense; it had a rhythm and an order. My mother had learned the Lord's Prayer and how to make a Thanksgiving turkey, my father knew the proper way to salute a Pakistani elder or, if need be, play a game of cricket. But what had compelled them to choose each other?

My parents met as graduate students at Yale—my father was studying to be an architect, and my mother was studying art and design, postponing her arranged match in Pakistan. My mother had mixed feelings about getting married, but had agreed to the engagement. Her fiancé, Hussain, was a medical student eight years her senior who had studied in the West, and my mother felt that marriage would give her stability and the freedom to pursue her goals in Karachi. In the late sixties, Pakistan was a new nation, and my mother was filled with plans. She hoped to work in public television and to create a magazine about Pakistan. She had no intention of settling permanently in the United States—but she thought she might experience romantic love just once before she got married. She wanted something to look back on as she grew old in Pakistan.

My mother first noticed my father's red bandana and cowboy boots while riding in the Art and Architecture Building's elevator. At six feet six inches tall, he towered over her, and she thought that he was the most handsome American she had ever seen, like a real-life Marlboro Man. My father says he'd admired my mother from afar, but was cautioned against becoming interested in her. "She's got a guy back home," the other students told him. "She's way out of your league."

My parents spoke to one another for the first time in a photography class. My father took carefully composed, carefully executed pictures of buildings and landscapes. My mother took all of her pictures on a single trip to Pakistan and returned with stacks of negatives, which she spent the next three months printing in the darkroom. Her prints were flawless, and my father asked her how she did it. What f-stop did she use? What kind of photo paper? Samina just shrugged. It came easily to her.

My father was mesmerized by my mother. He asked her if she would like to accompany him to Winter Carnival at Dartmouth College, from which he had graduated the previous year, not quite believing she would agree. Many men at Yale had asked her out—football players, law students, a doctoral candidate in philosophy who slipped ten-page love letters underneath her door every day for an entire semester. She went on dates to see what these men were like, but she was never interested. There seemed something different about Richard, something kind, thoughtful, worth knowing. She decided to choose one American man to have an affair with, and she picked my father.

The way my mother tells it, she suspected that my father was simply interested in her exotic looks; in those days, she wore her long black hair loose, down to her knees, and colorful, hand-block-printed Pakistani clothes. So, in preparation for the date, she made a visit to downtown New Haven and bought a weekend's worth of American clothes. When my father pulled his car up to International House, he found my mother in a pink turtleneck, a tweed skirt, and brown boots that reached her knees.

My father says that he decided just days into their relationship that he wanted to marry my mother; she was completely unlike anyone he'd ever met. She was focused, ambitious, confident. They were from drastically different places, but in that car ride from New Haven to Hanover, they found certain commonalities. They both had had difficult, charismatic fathers who died young; selfless, caring mothers who kept their emotions to themselves; and younger siblings that they worried about. They both cared a great deal about art, good books, and making their communities better. They both were in love with graduate school.

I was always intrigued by my father's ability to recognize in my mother someone that he wanted to spend his life with. How did he manage to convince her that he was destined to be more than a memory?

After her graduate work, my mother moved home to Karachi and did start a television show, in which she traveled through the countryside, introducing different regions of Pakistan to its people. After he graduated, my father worked in a small architectural firm in Denver and saved up money to bring my mother back to the U.S. One day, to his boss's surprise, he announced that he was quitting to go to Pakistan and get married. He sent a telegram to Karachi to let my mother know which day he was coming. He imagined that he would be garlanded at the airport and welcomed as a son. Instead, he found himself alone at five in the morning in an unfamiliar city, surrounded by beggars tugging on his sleeves and taxi drivers offering him rides to hotels. The call of the muezzin sounded, crackling over the loudspeaker, and most men vanished to pray. He was left in the terminal wondering what to do, faced with the sobering thought that perhaps marrying Samina would be more complicated than he'd thought.

He stumbled with his bags to the taxi stand and directed the driver to my mother's house, speaking the few words of Urdu he had learned: *"Bridge ke pas"*—"near the bridge." When they finally found it, he woke up the gate man and tried to explain that he was a friend of Samina's. My mother came down in her nightdress and a robe, with her long hair in a braid down her back. She put her hands through the bars of the gate. She told him, "I'm so sorry, my brothers wouldn't let me come and fetch you at the airport. We've been fighting about it for days. They said it wouldn't be appropriate."

That first night, my mother put my father up in a garage apartment adjacent to her home—where he would be out of sight from her gossiping relatives. The next day, she found him a flat nearby to stay in. To justify his presence in Karachi, my mother arranged for him to take music lessons, explaining that he was an American student who had come to learn from a sitar master. The neighbors said, "That Samina is up to something," and watched her closely. She hired a group of mural painters to come and paint a village scene on one of the walls of his new apartment. She surrounded him with a group of her friends, so that they traveled in a pack of young people, going to concerts, even to the disco. To see each other privately, they had to make elaborate arrangements, design complex alibis. My mother had said he was a talented musician, so her brothers wanted to hear Richard play. She had to keep finding new reasons why he couldn't give a concert.

It took my father a year to convince my mother to return to the States, and to convince Nana that he would be able to take care of her. He studied the Qur'an, he went to mosque with her brothers. Once my mother had agreed to marry him, he had to go to see Hussain, her fiancé, and convince him to let her break the engagement. Mostly, he says, it was thanks to Nana that he was able to do it all. Even then, the two of them had a special bond; she was on his side.

My father visited Nana in the afternoons. They would have tea together in the long parlor of Siddiqi House, their silences filled with the constant whirring of the ceiling fans. My father told Nana about his family in Denver, about how they had arrived in the United States in the 1600s from England and had moved from the East Coast to Colorado in the 1800s. About how close he was with his two sisters and one brother, and how he saw his future with my mother.

One day Nana asked him, "Are you sure, Richard? Are you sure you want my daughter? Because you are talking about taking her very far away, and she's a difficult child. You had better be sure that you want her."

When I ask him what he said to that, his answer is always the same:

"I told her the truth. I told her that I couldn't live without her."

No one talks about it much anymore, but when the time came, my mother's brothers objected to the idea of my parents' getting married in Siddiqi House. Once Nana had given her blessing to the marriage, there was little they could do to stop it, but they didn't want to be perceived as condoning the match by hosting the wedding. Though Nana pleaded with them, it was no use—they would not allow it. Instead, my parents were married a world away, on a hillside in my father's native Colorado, without the flashes of cameras and the glint of heavy sets of jewelry, without the decorated tents, the trays of food, the week of escalating celebration.

There is a film of the ceremony, in Super 8mm, that I've watched hundreds of times. They were married in 1973, standing with their friends in a circle, in a meadow down the hill from my great-grandparents' home in the Rocky Mountains. Nana came from Pakistan to the United States for the first time to attend the wedding. I remember her telling me that she had never seen a wedding so informal, "like a picnic," she said, with people standing outdoors in their sandals. My father wore a navy blue three-button suit, his hair almost down to his shoulders. He walked, with his siblings behind him, his mother and grandmother in pastel suits, down the hillside to meet my mother, who wore a white-and-gold sari. Her long hair was parted in the middle and wound in a thick coil at the nape of her neck, encircled in a garland of wildflowers. A friend of my parents' from the Yale Divinity School crafted a service using readings from the Bible and the Qur'an. To honor Nana's connection to Judaism, they broke a glass.

A YEAR AND a half later, I was born in Denver.

11

ANXIOUS-TYPE NATURE

PUNE, DECEMBER 2001

A knock on my door punctuates my hazy awareness of morning. It's late, too late to be sleeping, but I can't seem to muster the energy to wake up and get dressed, face the world. Lately I've been falling sick repeatedly. Illness takes hold in an entirely different way here from back home—it catches me quickly, without warning, and I feel caught in an endless cycle of headaches, fevers, and sore throats. I'm not sure what to report in my e-mails to friends. The Parliament of India in Delhi has just been attacked by terrorists, and there is speculation that India and Pakistan might go to war. I think about when I left New York three and a half months ago, kissing my friends goodbye as if I would see them in a matter of days, not months, with only the haziest impressions of what I was leaving them for. I thought that I could replace missing Nana with being here, as if I could fill up the hole created by her absence with stories. I'd thought that something grand was waiting for me here, something out of one of my mother's famous anecdotes. In New York, my plan made sense. Now I feel foolish.

I've been having trouble feeling accepted by the Jewish community in Pune. When I visit the synagogues, I feel like an interloper, a tourist. I've been making increasingly frequent trips to Bombay, where the community is more used to visitors and I have an easier time talking to people. There I can slip into the back of a synagogue and feel relatively unnoticed. I travel to Bombay on the night bus to avoid the traffic and heat and to fill up the hours of my insomnia, but the dust of the roads, the pollution created by the trucks and rickshaws, and the nights without enough sleep are wearing on me. Going to Bombay and back leaves me exhausted, but I feel mollified that at least I'm doing something to further my project.

The knock comes again, louder this time. I put on a robe and answer the door. It's Rekhev, scowling at me.

"You should read these," he says, handing me several heavy books. He looks at me sharply, noticing the contact sheets strewn all over my desk. "What's wrong with you?" he asks.

"I'm not feeling very well," I admit. "I'm not sure why." Every day now, I wake up with new, unfamiliar ailments: rashes, sore throats, eye infections. I have acquired what feels like asthma, something I have never experienced before. It's as if my entire body is allergic to India, as if my constitution was made for another climate. I feel trapped in a constant cycle of sickness and miniature, fleeting recoveries. Just as soon as I feel well again, I fall ill.

A few days later, Rekhev knocks on my door again. He is disappointed that I haven't read the books.

"What are you doing in here all day, then?" he asks.

I tell him that lately I don't have the energy to do much of anything.

"Come with me," he says, firmly.

"I can't, Rekhev, I really don't feel well," I say.

"I'm taking you to the Institute doctor; he lives not far from here."

We walk together through the leafy side streets to a residential bungalow. The doctor's house is one story, set back from the road with a small courtyard in front. Rekhev finds a bench in the yard and opens his book. I ring the doorbell.

An elderly lady in a pale pink sari opens the door. Her gray hair is pulled tight into a low bun, and her eyes are bright with curiosity. I assume she might be the doctor's wife. "Yes?" she asks.

"I am here to see the doctor," I stammer, feeling shy.

"Brother!" she calls, and then turns back to me. "Come, child," she says, putting her hand on my shoulder, and I feel instantly reassured.

I sit in their dark living room, waiting and looking at an odd collection of painted ceramic tiles hanging on the wall. The door opens, and I hear a man say: "Enter!"

I walk in and sit down on a small bench, taking note of my surroundings. The doctor is a kind-looking man who appears to be in his late sixties and is wearing a tan safari suit. His examination room is a kind of study, with books lining the walls and a large desk covered in papers. The only indications that he is a doctor are the stethoscope hanging limply around his neck and an ancient-looking medical chart hanging on the wall.

He examines me, shining a small light in each of my eyes and sticking a tongue depressor inside my open mouth so he can look at my tongue, searching for clues.

"Why are you here?" he asks me after a few minutes.

"Why am I here in India, or here in your office?" I ask him.

"Both," he says. "India first."

I tell him about my project, then about my health.

"Every week I find myself coming down with something. I've never been like this before. I have asthma attacks most mornings, and I can't seem to stay healthy for very long. In the daytime I feel like I need to sleep, but I can barely sleep at night."

"Where do you take your meals?"

"I eat in the hostel of the Film Institute."

"Ack, the worst. No nutrients there. Are you taking multivitamins?"

"No."

He gives me a disapproving look and draws blood from my arm.

"Are you traveling?"

I tell him I have been commuting to Bombay every week by bus.

"You are trying to live like a real Indian, eh? You have a viral infection, very common with the change of season," he says. "And allergies. Probably to dust and the like. You are not used to this environment and this level of pollution. This work you are doing in India, it's based in Pune or Bombay?"

"Both. But increasingly I think it's based in Bombay," I say.

"The back-and-forth is bad for your health," he says. "You should try and stay in one place. Also, I sense that your nature is an anxious one. You are worrying yourself sick."

He gives me a prescription for an antibiotic and a long list of vitamins.

He guides me back to the living room, where I find his sister waiting for me. "Drink juice!" he tells me. "Eat steamed vegetables!"

Through the open door, I see Rekhev in the garden, pacing around the small courtyard.

"May I show you something?" the doctor's sister asks me, motioning to her kitchen. "Come, come."

In one corner of the room she has created a small shrine, decorated with flowers, miniature pots, and plates that carry oil and water and flowers as offerings.

"Do you know about Sai Baba?" she asks.

"I don't," I admit, feeling sheepish and wondering where this is going. I know that Sai Baba is a revered Hindu saint, but not much more.

"How old do you think I am?" she asks, looking at me inquisitively.

She looks to be in her late sixties, but it seems hardly appropriate to tell an older woman how old she looks. I'm reluctant to do so.

"I don't know, how old?" I say.

"Guess!" she says, delighted at the game, her eyes sparkling with amusement.

"Sixty-five?" I say, tentatively.

"No, really, how old?" she replies, her smile deepening.

"Sixty . . . seven?"

"I am eighty-two. I'll be eighty-three in three months."

It really doesn't seem possible that this sprightly woman could be eighty-two. Nana was eighty-two when she died, her body knotted in pain.

"Oh, I used to be like a regular person," she adds quickly. "I had aches, I had suffering. But then I made pilgrimage to Shirdi. There is peace there, and that peace came into my life. You cannot imagine how wonderful he is. My life since that day has been very different. Three times a day I do *puja* here, to honor him."

"That is remarkable, Auntie."

She walks me to the door, pressing a short autobiography of Sai Baba into my hands. "Faith, child. It takes all forms." She smiles sweetly at me, and raises one hand in a wave as I walk into her courtyard to find Rekhev.

Rekhev glances up at me, looking worried.

"I ran into one of my teachers here," he says.

"What did he say?" I ask.

"He was concerned, he said: 'Are you sick?' I said, No, my *friend* is sick. 'I see,' he said, like he could tell you were a woman. You know, I've never taken anyone to the doctor in my whole life. My father's good at these things, finding train tickets, doctors. I've never done these things in my life."

As we walk home, I start to feel wobbly, conscious of trying to keep one foot in front of the other, and counting the minutes until I will be safely in my bed.

"It's very stressful, you know, being your friend," he tells me on the way home.

"What do you mean?" I ask.

"I normally distance myself from these attachments, from people. You want to know someone who understands how India works, and you think that's me. But I don't understand how India works any more than you do. You and I, we are both expatriates here. I am not a tour guide."

"I never asked you to be my tour guide," I snap.

"No, but that's what you want. Someone to write home about."

I feel suddenly exhausted.

"What's that in your hand?" he asks.

"It's a book about Sai Baba; the doctor's sister gave it to me."

"Are you acquiring another religion, then?" he asks.

I nod, too tired to argue.

We walk the rest of the way in silence. Rekhev drops me at my gate, and I head inside by myself, dreading the effort of opening the lock. Everything feels too heavy.

The next day, I purchase the medication and vitamins recommended by the doctor, and for the following three, I have bouts of fever and nausea; my asthma attacks are my early morning alarm clock. On the fourth morning, I manage to put on clothes and walk to the phone booth to call my parents. Their voices are bright and clear, and I try to make mine match theirs. It's so hard to describe my life here, what it feels like, how I am spending my time. I don't know how to account for my days. My mother can hear the frustration in my voice.

"How long have you been in India?" she says abruptly.

"Three and a half months."

"And you feel like that's a long time."

"It feels like forever."

"What are you frustrated about?"

"Well, I feel like I came here to do something, and I thought I understood what it was. But I don't know how to find what I came here for. I'm not sure if it's even here."

"Look, you're pretending you're in New York, setting up meetings, commuting to another city, making phone calls, trying to take pictures. It's too hot, for one, and you're making yourself miserable. Remember, a week there is equal to a day in New York."

"What do you mean?"

"Think about it. You're imposing your own sense of schedule on the place, but it's not meant for that. Everything moves on a different timetable there. Accept that, don't try and change it. Your primary responsibility right now is to make yourself well. Do that, and then you can do good work."

I begin to argue, and then I back down. I know that she's right, in that annoying way mothers often are.

It takes me almost two weeks to feel the outlines of myself re-emerging from the thick fog I feel surrounded by. I can barely lift my head; food seems like a capricious friend. I retrace my steps to the doctor's house; he tells me that my blood work shows a very low white-blood-cell count.

"Something about how you are living is making you unwell," he says thoughtfully. "You're wearing yourself down, not eating well, not sleeping well. That has to change."

"Do you think I'm allergic to India?" I ask him.

"Don't worry so much, my dear," he says reassuringly. "There's no such thing as being allergic to India."

ONE NIGHT, I dream of Nana.

In the dream, she looks healthy, perhaps sixty years old, the way she might have looked when I was a baby. She is cooling herself with a fan made of thin, fragrant sandalwood. Flap-flap, goes the sound as the fan hits her collarbone. We are sitting in an opulent living room that I don't recognize, surrounded by gilded Baroque-style furniture, drinking tea. There are one or two Pakistani women present, who are listening to Nana with rapt attention as she narrates one of her dreams. Nana is wearing a shiny green silk sari and emerald jewelry. Her lips are painted red with lipstick, something I never saw her wear. It's as if death has rendered my grandmother in brilliant, incongruous colors.

"I am trying to cross Lamington Road; all five of my children are around me, holding on to my sari; I am wearing a white sari. All the children are little, and I cannot keep track of them all at once. My husband has just died, and I am thinking to myself: How will I bear this life alone? How will I do it?" She pauses, making long swooping gestures with her fan. "And then he appears to me, he comes up beside me and places his strong hand underneath my elbow, like this." She demonstrates. "And he leads me across the street, just like that." She looks at me and smiles softly. "And then he is gone."

The dream fades, and I find myself awake, staring at the rotations of the ceiling fan. Woosh-woosh. The pigeons flutter outside my window, trying to land on the angled slats of opaque glass again and again. Flip-flap, go their wings. A soft, fluttering sound of regret. In the swamp of my sickness, I cannot remember if this is a story that Nana told me about one of her dreams, or if the dream is mine alone. Lamington Road. I have never heard of the place. It sounds like London.

The next morning, my fever breaks and I feel well enough to sweep the dust from my bedroom floor out into the yard. As I open the door and take in mouthfuls of new day, I feel drunk with the inhalation of fresh air. I put on the geyser to heat water for my bath and lay out clean clothes for the first time in a week.

I go to the library and look up Lamington Road. It's in Bombay. Nana always told me she would send me messages in my dreams. Now I am sure that she is telling me that it's time to move.

PART TWO

FIELDWORK

12

THE DIRT COLLECTORS

BOMBAY, JANUARY 2002

I feel anonymous living in Bombay. No one knows me here. I think to myself, I could stay inside all day and not speak to anyone. But I'm wrong. Bombay comes right to my door and knocks to be let inside.

My new home is a one-room studio apartment inside a three-story bungalow called Bilva Kunj, on a street in the Gamdevi neighborhood called Pandita Ramabai Road, which connects the busy intersection of Nana Chowk to Bombay's famous Chowpatty Beach. On my left side is Laburnum Road, named for the long-departed laburnum trees planted by the English. My landlady, the elegant Mrs. Murdeshwar, tells me that the laburnum trees used to shade the private residences of the neighborhood. Directly across from me sits a temple, whose keepers rise at dawn to light incense and lay flower garlands at the feet of their goddess. In the morning, the road is lined with the compact parcels of sleeping men, arranged in columns alongside the stone walls that border the street, cocooned neatly in white cloths, like caterpillars. A one-armed man lives in front of the house, where he props himself up on his intact elbow, his keen, watchful eyes surveying everyone who enters and exits my flat—a silent witness. Another man paces the block most afternoons; he's tall, with a gray beard and a brown-checked shirt. Each time I see him, I hear him speaking to himself in multiple languages, gesturing as if to an unseen audience.

It's January now, cool enough that I can walk around Bombay in relative comfort. People tell me that these temperate weeks will be fleeting, so I try to take advantage of them, getting to know the old Jewish quarter of the city on foot, taking portraits of the synagogues and their caretakers.

The day after I move to my new apartment, I hear the first knock. A man selling Hindi and English textbooks, brightly colored booklets with pictures of nouns—"A is for Apple, B is for Boy." The man thumbs through his collection, fanning them out over his slender extended arm.

"No, thank you. No, thank you," I say repeatedly. "No, thank you. No children here." I shake my head for emphasis and shut the door.

Another knock. Someone who has something to do with the television. He comes in and fiddles with my set, murmuring the entire time. The telephone man; the electrician; the air conditioner repairman, who takes apart the entire unit to very little effect. All sorts of people parade through my tiny room in the mornings, sent by my kind landlord. The bell starts ringing in the morning, and some days it doesn't stop until early afternoon. I have heard the tales of people in Bombay waiting months, years even, for a cylinder of cooking gas, and I understand more fully that the handsome rent I am paying is partly for the ability to move into a situation that is already set up.

One morning, I answer the door to find a boy of about thirteen or fourteen holding a typed, laminated letter and making wild hand gestures. He points to his closed mouth and makes a guttural sound, bugging out his eyes for emphasis. I cannot for the life of me figure out what's going on. He hands me the letter. It reads:

Dear Sir or Madam,

> *I am deaf and dumb. I cannot talk! Please give me a charitable donation that I will use to help myself out of my current miserable situ-*

ation and help others like me. Your donation goes to deaf and blind trust, which has been established by Gov't of Maharashtra, 1983 (Borivali, Mumbai).

Kindly see fit to donate generously.

As with the kids selling candy on the New York City subways who say they are subsidizing their high school sports teams, I sense something is amiss here. But I have to admit: the scheme has originality. As I try to decide if I should give him money, the boy places the tip of his tongue on the roof of his mouth, showing me the back side of it, pointing and hopping from one foot to the other. I see that he is attempting to convince me that he has no tongue.

"One minute, one minute," I say, closing the door while I look for some bills.

I rustle around and find some loose notes, which I give to him. Instantly businesslike, he calmly straightens up and hands me a sheet of paper, a roster of people's names and addresses. He hands me a pen, and I write: "Sadia, Gamdevi, Bombay, Rs. 100."

The next day, there's another knock. The same boy, the same routine.

"I gave you money yesterday!" I say, showing him my name on his petition. "See?"

He looks at my signature and nods, shrugs, gives me a look as if to say, I guess you have a point. He gathers up his laminated letter, clipboard, and pen, and walks calmly to his next destination.

The following day, I am woken up by a knock at 7 a.m. In no mood to haggle with the boy again, I open the door and am surprised to find a pleasant-looking woman in a floral salwar kameez. She appears to be in her late thirties, and has wavy light brown hair that she wears in a braid down her back.

"I am Julie," she says. "I work here. I come in?"

"You work here?" I say, a little confused, sleepy.

"I am your maid."

I stand aside and let her in, rubbing my eyes. She is carrying a small plastic bag, which she takes with her inside my bathroom; she closes the door. She emerges a moment later wearing a different, older salwar kameez and carrying a bucket of milky white water. The smell of ammonia rises from the bucket.

"Any mens are here?" she asks.

"Just me," I say.

She disappears inside the bathroom again and emerges a moment later, without her salwar pants on. She giggles.

"If girls only are here, I am cleaning without pant. If mens are here, I am putting on pant," she explains.

I watch as she squats and expertly swings a gray rag from right to left, swabbing the floor clean as she moves backward.

I'm not sure where to go. After I dress in the bathroom, I sit at the table while she goes about her work, lifting my feet when she reaches the area near the table. It seems rude to sit and make notes or read while she is cleaning my floor, but I don't want to get in her way, and it seems equally awkward to sit and watch her. I shuffle between the options and then try to make conversation.

"So how long have you worked here?" I ask.

"I am working here four, five years. One Germany girl was here, one English girl was here. French principal is upstairs. I work at French school. Main job. Thirteen years I am there."

I remember that my landlord mentioned that his daughter teaches at the Alliance Française; perhaps there is some connection.

"Are you friend of Lindsay's?" she asks me suddenly.

"No . . . I don't know Lindsay. Was that the girl who was here before?"

Julie seems relieved.

" 'Julie,' she said, 'you don't come every day, this is small room, you come three times a week.' Then, one day, she *go*. Monday she is here, Tuesday she *go*."

It occurs to me that perhaps this is why the apartment became available so quickly.

"She just disappeared? You don't know where she went?"

"I am not knowing anything. I am only maid. Mr. Murdeshwar is saying,

'Where is Lindsay? Where is Lindsay?' Xerox Wallah, across the street, he is saying, 'Where is Lindsay? She is owing me a hundred fifty rupees!' Dhobi Wallah saying, 'Where is your madam? I have her clean clothes!' Everyone asking for Lindsay. I say, 'She go!' I don't know where."

"What did Lindsay do while she was here in India?"

"She came for job. Then she left that job. She is staying home, she is asking Mr. Murdeshwar for cable TV. Then she does some yoga studies. She is going to ashram. She is mixed up with some no-good peoples, I think so. She takes up another job, then, one day, she go. *I* don't know where. . . ."

I'm fascinated by what became of my predecessor. I ask about her habits, trying to solve the mystery of her sudden disappearance.

"Lindsay is very fond of bread. All the time eating bread only. And sweets. Lindsay is getting fat in India, I think so." Julie giggles—a soft, warm, contagious sound. I'm not sure why, but I'm laughing, too. "Lindsay is very fond of my chicken. 'Please, Julie, make chicken. Make chicken,'" she says, imitating Lindsay. "Sometimes I am making."

Julie finishes the floor and cleans the bathroom. Watery sounds emerge—sloshing and rinsing, a rag hitting the floor, being hung up to dry. After she finishes, she changes into her other outfit and walks quickly through the room to the door.

"I come day after tomorrow. Okay-thanks-bye."

ONE MORNING, the phone rings. It's a man asking for Lindsay. I tell him that Lindsay has moved away, and he asks me if I'm a friend of hers.

"No, why do you ask?" I say, and he offers me a job as an extra in a Bollywood film. If I'd like, I can meet him and his partner at Churchgate Station the following morning, where a busload of young Westerners will supposedly be driven to Ahmedabad in a luxury coach to appear as background players in a scene meant to take place in Europe.

"You'll like it," he says, his tone ingratiating and slightly predatory. "Lindsay liked it."

I decline politely and hang up.

Each visit, Julie tells me more about Lindsay, or the peculiar habits of her other clients. She tells me, in bits and pieces, about her life. Her name is Julie Rocky D'Souza. "Julie" is short for "Genevieve," which she pronounces "Jen-vee." She is a Christian, originally from Mangalore. "Rocky" is her husband's name, and hence her middle name. Rocky is in the electricians' union, and has a good stable job that she hopes he will be able to pass on to their son when he retires. They have two children, a girl of thirteen and a boy who is eleven and a half.

Julie and Rocky's union was a love match, at least from his side.

"My husband saw me at festival time, with my mother, at Mount Mary Church, Bandra. He saw my hair. I had very long hair at that time, to here it is coming." Julie points to her waist. "I did not see him, but he remembered me. He was all the time asking for me. Finally, my mother agreed to the match."

"Did you get engaged?" I ask.

"I *was* engaged," she says, as if I had doubted the fact. "I am *going* Chowpatty, I am *going* Gateway, I am *going* Marine Drive, Juhu Beach. I am doing all these engaged things."

These are the sites of courtship in Bombay, where couples go to steal moments of relative solitude, to join the throng of sweethearts sitting side by side, hand in hand. All of these places command ocean views; in each of them, men and women sit looking at the water, a wide slate on which to imagine their futures together.

"Did you like your husband? Before you were married, I mean?"

"I am not liking mens. I am only liking girls—my sisters, my mother. My husband was mad for me, he was mad for my hair when we were married. 'Leave it open! Leave it open!' he would say. I am only thinking that he is little bit dark. But he's a good man," she says, genuinely. "He is a good father, good husband. He is never beating me, he is offering me money when he has it. But I have my own money. I have been working since I had nine years. Sometimes my husband is drinking. He is throwing money in the beer bar. Then he is saying, Julie, I need some money. I say, Where is

your money now? I will not give it. Now he is good. He is not drinking for
the last one year."

"Really? For a year?"

"He is a good man, Rocky," she concludes. "Okay-thanks-bye."

I BEGIN TO LOOK FORWARD to Julie's visits. She has a comforting presence, and I like to listen to her talk. While she works, we chat about her life,
and I ask her questions about how things work in Bombay. I ask her where
to buy a toaster, how to get my knives sharpened, where to get a sari blouse
stitched.

One day, when she notices that I have gone grocery shopping, she says:
"How much you pay for tomato? How much per kg?"

I tell her I'm not sure—maybe thirty rupees?

She shakes her head, admonishing me.

"Where did you buy?"

I tell her where I bought them: at the third stall from the left in the vegetable market.

"You are paying too much. You are paying foreigner rate. I take you."

On her next visit, Julie walks me to Bhaji Gali, quite literally Vegetable
Alley. It is a long, crowded, narrow passage of fruit and vegetable sellers that
links Grant Road Station and the next major thoroughfare, about a ten-
minute walk from my studio.

"This is my madam," she says to the man I bought the tomatoes from,
introducing me. I smile and nod. She points to the staples, and he weighs
them on scales: tomatoes, potatoes, onions. Then she says something to him
in Marathi that I don't understand; from the looks of it, she is giving him a
hard time for overcharging me. I feign innocence, feeling like a small, grateful child. After that, the vegetable man charges me Julie's rates.

Since we are next to the train station, and Julie will go home to Bandra
from here, I ask her why she doesn't do her shopping in Bhaji Gali.

"I have my own market. Price in my locality is cheaper than here,"
she says.

"Why is that?" I ask.

She gives me a patient look, as if she is speaking to her thirteen-year-old daughter.

"Because I am poor and you are rich, no?"

I DECIDE TO TRY TO find a Jewish school in Bombay where I might be able to volunteer. I think that perhaps if I have some way of interacting with people, some way of contributing, I will be less of a visitor here. It's for this reason that I go to ORT India in Worli, Bombay, a Jewish vocational school located coincidentally just a few hundred yards from Rahat Villa. It's only when I get there that I realize why the school sounds familiar: my uncle Moses, the one who thought my project was such a waste of time, had told me that his son Benny is ORT's director.

ORT is housed in a tall gray concrete tower, several stories high, and offers several different programs, from what I can tell from the sign. There's a beauty school, a travel-agency training program, a nursery school, and a bakery, as well as a Jewish library. I tell the receptionist that I'd like to see the director, and she asks me who I am.

"Tell him his cousin from America is here," I say. Her eyes widen.

After a few minutes, an attendant in a gray uniform comes to fetch me and takes me to Benny Isaacs's office, a large, sunny room with a wide desk, several phones, and bright color posters of Israel.

"What's this about you being my cousin?" Benny Isaacs says when I enter.

He is a tall, well-dressed man in his late fifties who looks unmistakably like one of my grandmother's brothers, my uncle Solomon. I haven't seen Uncle Sol in years, but I remember his face, and I find the resemblance remarkable—the same light brown skin, rounded nose, glasses, and gray mustache.

I introduce myself and explain who I am, that I am Rachel Jacobs's granddaughter. If I am not mistaken, his mother, Lily, was my grandmother's first cousin.

"Quite right!" he says, slapping his desk. "I remember your grandmother! She was an elegant lady."

The attendant places a cup of milky tea and a puffed pastry in front of me, and Benny points to the pastry with pride.

"Baked here on the premises!" he says. "In our kosher kitchen! So tell me," he says, leaning forward, "what can I do for you?"

I explain to Mr. Isaacs about my Fulbright and what I've come to do in India, and tell him that I am hoping to get involved with a school, to do some volunteer work, perhaps with a youth group, if there is such a thing. Mr. Isaacs tells me that he is sending a youth delegation of fourteen Bene Israel students to Israel in a few weeks. As chance would have it, he has been looking for a way for the group to explain their history to the various Israeli student groups they will be meeting while they are touring the country. He asks me if perhaps I could help them develop some kind of presentation.

"Like a play!" he says. "You know, funny, serious—to show about our history!"

"What do the students know about their history?" I ask him.

"Not much. And people will be asking them, 'How did your people come to India? What is the story?' All that. Do you know anything about dramatics?"

I tell him that I used to do some theater in high school and college.

"Excellent! Why don't you write a play, direct it, and we'll put it on in Israel?"

I learn that the Overseas Resource Training Institute of India provides young Bene Israel men and women with skills they hope to take with them when they immigrate to Israel. I begin to spend my afternoons here, and each time I walk through the building I marvel at the endless codes the students in the travel-agency department are learning how to punch in to find low fares, the strings of numbers and letters of C++ programming they are typing in the computer center, and the fierce concentration of young female students armed with scissors who pore over the rows of mannequin heads in the beauty school. The walls are decorated with bright murals painted by children, and fading color photographs of important religious sites in Israel.

My actors are a group of fourteen college students in their late teens and early twenties—nine confident, gangly young men and five very shy young women. I think of my earliest questions about the Bene Israel, about what they look like, as I notice that their dark hair and their light brown coloring are similar to the pictures that I've seen of Nana's family in Israel. My male students dress in white or gray dress shirts and dark slacks, the consistent uniform of urban India; the young women wear salwar kameezes in solid colors with matching dupattas. Unlike mine, which are cotton prints bought off the rack, the young women's suits are handmade, bordered with lace or appliquéd flowers.

I am assisted by two pleasant male teachers in their late twenties, Samson and Sharon, who have been tapped by Mr. Isaacs to supervise the project and act in the play. Samson is a sprightly, enthusiastic computer instructor with short, straight black hair, who laughs easily. Sharon's long, curly black beard, *kippah,* and round, scholarly-looking spectacles give him an air of seriousness that is quickly dispelled by the friendliness of his demeanor. His eyes are black and shiny behind his glasses, showing his amusement and interest in everything going on around him. He teaches Hebrew to a group of young men and acts as a *sofer* in the community, a certified Jewish ritual scribe. Both Samson and Sharon make an effort to make me feel welcome, throwing themselves wholeheartedly into the pantomime drills I introduce to try to get the actors warmed up. They encourage their students to follow suit, with mixed success.

Our meetings take place in a dark conference room decorated with curtains that feature miniature blue Stars of David. My play is a series of short vignettes chosen to represent the highlights of Bene Israel history. The group leaps awkwardly from an imaginary ship hitting the Konkan Coast to the circular motion of pressing seeds into oil, to picking up heavy, make-believe suitcases to show the arrival of the Bene Israel in Bombay in the 1850s, and lifting them again to show the community-wide migration to Israel beginning in 1948. Throughout the rehearsal, the actors are in constant movement, from sea to land, village to city, India to Israel.

When the students are speaking the lines that I have written, they stand stiffly, facing the audience, with their arms by their sides. The boys speak loudly, but the girls can barely be heard. When I ask them to intersperse Hebrew songs and prayers at appropriate moments in the narrative, however, they brighten, singing heartily and confidently. They tell me the names of their songs, and I write them down phonetically. Hebrew songs with Indian melodies, passed down 150 years ago by visiting cantors from the Jewish community in Cochin. I am struck by which fragments of their history these young people hold; many of them have not heard parts of the legend, yet they can tell me the Marathi names their ancestors used, even if these names have not been in use for over a hundred years. My knowledge of our common ancestors is gleaned primarily from ethnographies of the community written by Western women in the 1970s and 1980s. I find myself wondering how different the community was twenty years ago, when those scholars were working in Bombay.

At lunchtime, Samson, Sharon, and the students pile into the ORT cafeteria, reflexively touching the mezuzah with their right hands and kissing their fingers as they walk in the door. The ORT cook, Shoshanna Auntie, is an older lady with the protective demeanor of a den mother. She replenishes communal bowls of rice; dal; and cucumber, tomato, and coriander salad after the students spoon large helpings onto their own plates, joking among themselves. I listen to their conversations, trying to understand the unspoken allegiances between different members of the group. Toward the end of the meal, I ask the students if they are planning to settle in India or in Israel. A long silence settles on the room.

"Well?" Sharon says, looking around the room. "Why are you all so quiet? What do you think?"

After a long pause, the answers begin to spill out, like confessions.

"I will go when I finish my studies," one young man says confidently. "It is our homeland, and we should go."

"There, all are Jews, together," says another student. "You can find a job there where you are not required to work on Shabbat. It is more comfortable."

For some, the move is only a matter of time. For others, the decision is more difficult.

"What about you, Sharon?" I ask. "Will you go to Israel?"

"I have spent some time in Israel," he says. "I studied in the yeshiva for one year on a scholarship; that's when I became a *sofer*. Now I can make the parchment scrolls inside the mezuzah, the prayer that we place on our doorposts. I have returned to work here as a Jewish educator, but I'm hoping to settle in Israel. My wife and I have a daughter, and we would like to send her to a Jewish school. We are hoping to emigrate soon, perhaps in the next couple of years."

I ask the group, "Will you get married here or there?"

The girls titter, and I notice Judith, one of the young women, elbowing her best friend, Leah, who blushes deeply. Judith is a bright, pretty girl with wavy black hair, more socially confident than Leah, a tall, sturdy young woman with a quiet, unflappable nature. Leah wears her long brown hair pulled back in a perpetual ponytail, and salwar kameez suits in muted shades of brown and crimson. She strikes me as firm and directed when I speak to her one on one, but she is painfully shy in public. It is almost impossible to get her to speak her lines in the play so that an audience can hear them. Judith is her best friend from childhood, and they have an inseparable bond, so, to make them feel more comfortable, I have staged the play so that Leah and Judith are able to stand together for most of the time they are onstage.

The students tell me that many love marriages are occurring now, but some still favor the traditional arranged-marriage process, in which meetings between families are arranged by a community matchmaker or a family friend. They tell me that some will marry here and then go to Israel, but others will go to Israel for work and return home to Bombay to find spouses. Some will find a spouse among the Bene Israel community in Israel, which now numbers between sixty and eighty thousand people.

"Are any of you engaged?" I ask, and the students laugh.

"Leah! Leah!" they say, teasing her. "Speak up!"

The group tells me that Leah is engaged to Daniel, a Bene Israel man now settled in Israel. Leah and Daniel will be married next spring, and she will move to Israel immediately afterward.

"What does your fiancé do there?" I ask Leah.

"He's working in a job," she tells me, looking at her hands in her lap.

"What kind of job?"

"He's working."

I notice that most Bene Israel are not specific about what kinds of work their friends and relatives do in Israel. The important fact is that they are there. When I press them, I learn that many are working in stores, small businesses, and hotels.

"Is it different from what your relatives thought when they went there, or the same?"

The young people tell me about the initial racism that the Bene Israel faced in the 1960s, before the rabbinate decreed that the Bene Israel were "full Jews in every respect." I learn that some of the first Bene Israel to go to Israel returned a few years later. It wasn't what they expected. The work was too hard, the place too unfamiliar. But most have stayed, most are very happy.

"How do you get from here to there?" I ask. "How do you move from India to Israel and become an Israeli citizen?"

They tell me how community leaders help them to fill out the paperwork. There are a lot of forms to fill out, and then you have to raise money for the ticket, make sure that you are ready to go. When you arrive, you will be placed in an "absorption center," where you take Hebrew classes. Then you start to look for a job.

I ask them if they worry about the violence in Israel, and no one responds immediately.

"Even here there are bomb blasts," Samson says. "And in New York also. No one is safe anywhere. India is our motherland, but Israel is our fatherland."

The students nod vigorously.

"Are there things that you will miss if you move there?" I ask.

"You'll never get a social life like you get in India," says Samson, shaking his head.

"What do you mean?" I ask.

"Everyone here is joking, laughing, yelling. There people are quiet. I went to visit my brother. He moved into a new apartment complex. 'Who is your neighbor?' I said. 'He is a man, by himself, in his forties,' he said. The next day, I went to knock on his door. 'What are you doing?' my brother said. I said, 'I thought I would say hello to your neighbor, tell him that I am here for a month, maybe he would like to eat with us sometime.' 'No, no, no!' my brother said, vehemently, shaking his head very fast. 'We don't do that here!' 'But why?' I said. 'He's your neighbor. You mean you don't know him?' My brother said that's not how things are done in Israel. I couldn't believe it. How could you share a wall with someone and not know his face? Not eat with him? I found it very strange. Probably I would have to get used to that."

ON MY WAY home, I watch the chaos of city traffic as dusk becomes night. Every year, I think, more young Bene Israel migrate to Israel and make their lives there. More of their families join them, and fewer and fewer remain in India. I cannot help wondering if the ones who leave are making the right choice. But, then, I think, I did not grow up with the idea of Israel as my homeland, not the way my students did.

As I enter my driveway, I pass the one-armed man on my right, who watches me silently. The man in the checked shirt who speaks to himself in multiple languages crosses me on my left and addresses me as if we are in mid-conversation.

"It's only that the theorem doesn't prove anything, that's the trouble with it," he says calmly, matter-of-factly. He speaks English as though he were living in London. "That's the *trouble* with it."

On the walls of my room I have tacked maps of the city, and when I come home at night I rest my camera equipment inside the door and mark with a pencil where I have walked. There are deep grooves of pencil around the places my grandmother loved best. I live just a few hundred meters from Cama Hospital—where Nana studied nursing and became head matron—and three doors away from Mani Bhavan, Gandhi's house. Sometimes I think I see a glimpse of Nana just ahead of me in Bhaji Gali, a trick of the homesick mind. I can hear the sellers calling out their produce: "Tomatar, tomatar, tomatar . . . Alu, alu, alu . . ." It is a kind of song they have sung since childhood. I imagine Nana in the same alleyway, hearing these same sounds and keeping pace with their call.

"MADAM!" comes the call from Vivek, my vegetable man. He saves the "English" vegetables especially for me. I had never considered that broccoli could be exotic.

"Madam, you are looking tired," Vivek says to me this evening.

I nod, agreeing with him. "I am tired. I miss my grandmother, Vivek."

"She is in Eng-land?"

I nod, not wanting to get into specifics.

"She is also missing you. I know it," he says, solemnly, handing me four small parcels of vegetables. He adds a dozen tiny limes for free and winks at me.

I go home and play the audiocassette of Nana's voice I have brought with me. It is thirteen minutes long, a recording that I made as part of an interview assignment in graduate school. I am grateful for the likeness of her voice, the crackling immediacy of my faulty recording. There are so many questions I wish I had asked.

"Where was your mother from?" I hear my voice begin.

"She was from a village inside a fort."

"And where was your father from?"

"He was from Bombay, but his ancestors were from another village, near to my mother's village."

"What were their names?"

"My mother's name was Segulla-bai Chordekar. Chor-de-kar. My father's

Bene Israel name was Bhorupkar. Then later it was made to sound more English. Then our family name became Jacobs."

"What did you call your husband? Before you were married, I mean?"

"I used to just call him Mr. Siddiqi. . . ."

"Mr. Siddiqi . . ."

I REPEAT MY great-grandfather's and great-grandmother's original surnames over and over again in my head, memorizing them. Bhorupkar, Chordekar. Their ancestors must have been originally from the villages of Bhorupali and Chorde. I look for the names, circle their tiny dots on my village map. One of my books has a black-and-white photograph of a woman sitting on an old oil press, operated by a large ox. The picture was taken in 1992, and I wonder if the press is still there. I try to find other pictures of the Konkan villages, curious to see what they look like, if any Bene Israel families remain.

13

HINDI LESSONS

BOMBAY, JANUARY 2002

I am convinced that what separates me from India is more than the differences of where I grew up, more than my skin color, my height, my foreigner's taste for brightly colored salwar kameezes. ("These weird clothes," Rekhev said to me once in Pune. "I have never seen such funny clothes as you wear.") It's all of these things, but it's language, too. If I spoke Hindi, if I could turn my tongue around the particularities of accent and tone, if I knew, as the local saying goes, how to "ad-just," then I could make myself understood and, more important, I could understand what was going on around me.

On my way home from Grant Road Station every day for a month, I pass a small sign:

MR. V. SHUKLA, B.A., M.A. ENGLISH
Hindi Tuitions
Guaranteed Excellence in Learning
Many Foreign Clients of All Nations

I decide that I should investigate.

Hindi, a mixture of several Indian languages, is spoken all over northern India and shares great similarities with Urdu, the language of South Asian Muslims and the one my mother grew up speaking in Karachi. I grew up hearing the sounds of Urdu—my mother's lilting cadence and my grandmother's more halting staccato—the patterns of the language have left an imprint. So far in Bombay I've gotten by with my limited Hindi vocabulary and with hand gestures, but I am acutely aware of the nuances I'm missing. It's a kind of co-cooning, to not comprehend the idle conversation that envelops me like bird-song. Marathi, the language of Maharashtra State, was Nana's mother tongue; she learned Urdu only after her migration to Pakistan at the age of thirty. Like most Bene Israel, she spoke English at school, Hindi or Marathi in the streets of Bombay, and a mixture of Marathi and English at home. Now, like the rest of the Indian middle class, almost all Bene Israel speak English. The language of child rearing, of simple household transactions, is still Marathi. Those who are planning to immigrate to Israel take Hebrew classes at the local Jewish community center in Mahim. The sounds of Marathi scramble once they reach my ears; Hindi feels more accessible, and more necessary to learn.

One afternoon in January, I follow a series of small yellow signs from the alley to Mr. Shukla's door, on the second floor of an old apartment building, a dirty gray concrete structure decorated with what would once have been colorful painted wooden arches and balconies.

Above the door hangs a lime, skewered with a thread. The thread binds together four small green chilies and a piece of charcoal. I've been told that the sourness of the lime, combined with the spice of the chilies, will ward off the evil eye, which will in turn be absorbed by the charcoal. On the door is a sign: "Mr. V. Shukla, B.A., M.A." And another, smaller plaque below it, reads: "Educated Abroad." For a moment, I entertain the notion of making a similar sign for my own door.

I knock three times on the door with a brass knocker, and, hearing no answer, begin to walk back down the staircase. As soon as I do so, the door opens and a sleepy-looking woman who appears to be in her mid-sixties emerges, wearing a housecoat.

"Bolo?" she says, asking me to speak.

I tell her that I am looking for Mr. Shukla.

"Hindi tuition?" she asks, hopefully, and I nod, agreeing. "*Ek* minute," she says, and retreats inside the room for a moment. I hear her speaking to a man inside. Then she emerges, rips a man's shirt from the clothesline, and goes back in the room. A minute or two later, I am let inside to a room of about seven feet by nine feet, where an older gentleman is sitting at a miniature desk reading the newspaper, wearing the shirt from the clothesline. He appears to be in his mid-seventies, with thick spectacles and a small patch of white hair standing at attention toward the ceiling. The woman, who I now deduce is the man's wife, arranges herself on a mattress on my left, which is elevated on cabinets above the floor to make a couch in the daytime and, presumably, a bed at night. She places her dupatta over her head, and her hand over her face, to return to sleep. In one corner of the room is a hot plate, above a half-sized fridge and a freestanding plastic water tank. The right-hand wall of the room is covered entirely in books and manuals, stacked precariously on top of one another. *The Complete Works of William Shakespeare* mingles amiably with *Chicken Soup for the Soul.*

The man gestures toward a plastic chair opposite his desk and invites me to sit down.

"I hope I am not disturbing you?" I ask tentatively.

"Not at all. I am V. Shukla, Hindi tutor," he announces, somewhat grandly. "I am tutor to many foreign clients at all the embassies, I give workshops, I am holding lectures, I teach Hindi to be spoken within one month. And you are?"

I explain to Mr. Shukla that I am a student from America and am in India for one year.

"Hindi is an excellent language," Mr. Shukla offers. "Not difficult at all. Shall we begin? Please take out one sheet blank paper and one Pencil Number Two. Only Pencil Number Two is suitable for Hindi tuition."

I explain to Mr. Shukla that I did not come prepared to start learning today and do not have paper and pencil with me. He looks at me over his glasses, with his chin tipped down.

"Proper materials are necessary for Hindi language study," he says, shaking his head. "Never mind, I will provide. Jyoti!" he says, rousing his wife. "Paper and Pencil Number Two!" Jyoti scowls at her husband, rouses herself, and fetches his requests from a cabinet underneath the bed.

"First we place paper in front of us, like so." Mr. Shukla places one sheet of paper in front of himself, and the other in front of me. "Then we write 'Om' at the top of the page, like so."

Mr. Shukla writes "OM" in shaky capital letters at the top of his paper, and then at the top of mine.

"Then we pray to goddess Saraswati, Hindu goddess of learning. Shut your eyes."

I close my eyes, peeking occasionally to watch Mr. Shukla placing his hands together and reciting a short prayer.

"Then we begin," says Mr. Shukla. "At top of page we write *'Namaste.'* This is an Indian form of greeting, with respect." Mr. Shukla writes *"Namaste"* at the top of his page, then mine.

"Then we write, 'What is your name?' *'Aapka nam kya hai?'* Then we write, 'How do you do?' *'Aap kaise haim?'* Please note: *kaise* for males, *kaisi* for females. This is gender."

"Mr. Shukla, can you explain about how gender works in Hindi, and how the sentence is structured? For example, I have noticed that in Hindi the verb of the sentence often appears at the end, instead of . . ."

"That is an advanced lesson. We are conducting an introductory lesson."

"Oh, sorry—"

"Then we write, *'Aapko yahaan kaisa lag raha hai?'* 'Do you like it here?' *'Aap kis desh se hain?'* 'Which country you are from?'"

The lesson goes on in this fashion for well over an hour, until both sides of my sheet of paper are filled with phrasebook Hindi. When Mr. Shukla comes to *"Aapki yatra mangalmay ho,"* "Wish you a happy journey," he comes to the end of his first lesson.

"Now we pray to goddess Saraswati, Hindu goddess of learning, for what we have learned, and to ensure the successful completion of Hindi language studies."

We shut our eyes, as before, and Mr. Shukla recites another prayer.

"Now we have tea," Mr. Shukla announces, and, as if on cue, a grumbling Jyoti produces two cups of sweet tea. "What time will you come tomorrow?"

Hopeful that the lessons may improve when we move beyond the introductory material, I attempt to work out an arrangement that will accommodate both of us, suggesting perhaps sessions three times a week, at a time in the afternoon that might be convenient for Mr. Shukla.

"In Hindi language study, most beneficial learning time is seven a.m., after yoga," Mr. Shukla announces with certainty. "Do you do yoga?" he asks.

I shake my head no. He looks surprised.

"Foreigners are very fond of yoga. I myself do yoga practice all seven days, as does my wife. It is excellent for health! Never mind, you come at seven a.m. *ir*regardless."

I explain that 7 a.m. is a little early for me; would it be possible to come at 9 a.m.?

"Nine a.m. is not possible."

"Ten a.m.?"

"Not possible."

"Two p.m.?"

"Two p.m. is not preferable."

"Six p.m.?"

Mr. Shukla pauses, thinking this over with his eyes closed.

"Six p.m. Decided," he says, opening his eyes.

We decide upon a figure for his fees that is acceptable to both of us and make plans to meet the day after next.

"Memorize the paper, and come back with supplies. Remember, Pencil Number Two!"

I nod, thanking him for the lesson and Mrs. Shukla for the tea, and scramble down the staircase and down the lane to my house before Mr. Shukla decides to add to his lesson.

14

NATIVE PLACES

BOMBAY, FEBRUARY 2002

My brother, Cassim, graduated from college a year ago and won a fellowship to study the legacy of indenture and the racial politics of the recent coup in the Fiji Islands. He's been living there for five months—long enough to have walked the length of the main island, made friends in the local Irish bar, and been adopted by a local Indo-Fijian family. Suva, the capital city, where he lives, has a population of eighty thousand people. Because numbers are incomprehensible to me, it sounds big. Cassim chides me over the phone that I should know better: it's about the size of Newton, the suburb of Boston we grew up in. To illustrate his point, he tells me that the previous day he was frustrated with his research and walked to a movie theater in the center of the city. He thought to himself, "No one in the whole world knows that I'm doing this." When he ambled into the pub afterward, the bartender said, "How was the movie?" Cassim asked him how he knew he had been to the theater, and the bartender replied, "Fiji is not a very big place."

"Come visit me in Bombay," I tell him. "I need your help, and you'll be inundated with anonymity."

IT TAKES CASSIM THREE DAYS to travel from Fiji to India—retracing the steps that indentured Indian laborers took by boat in the 1860s, uprooted from home against their will, and forced by British authorities into long, unpaid contracts. Cassim crosses the black water in a series of planes: Suva to Auckland, Auckland to Sydney, Sydney to Delhi, and Delhi to Bombay. When he arrives at my apartment by taxi early one morning, we begin talking and don't stop until late afternoon. Fiji has given Cassim's skin a warm brown color. He seems instantly at home everywhere he is, in ways I wonder if I will ever be.

"You look thin," I say.

"Fijians aren't known for their cuisine," he says.

Julie arrives, and I proudly introduce Cassim to her. Julie, ever distrustful of "mens," gives his rumpled appearance a quick look and says, "He is needing clothes washing. I think so?"

It's true. Cassim and his Fijian friends thought that it would be an adventure to walk to the airport, which required a trek through a wet forest. Thanks to his waterlogged shoes, my brother smells like a tropical swamp.

He tells me about his work, and I tell him about mine. Cassim laughs at me and shakes his head affectionately at how rapidly I am speaking. He silently accepts my offers of tea, toast, lunch, and I feel as if we are at home, in our parents' house. It is so exciting to share my newfound knowledge and my frustrations with someone who knew Nana and who has the same associations. I lay out a map of Maharashtra on the floor, tracing the short distance south from Bombay to the Konkan Coast with my finger.

"Here is where the Bene Israel believe they were shipwrecked. . . . Here." I point to the village of Navgaon. "And this is the area they settled into, several Bene Israel families in each village, working as oil pressers." I point to a series of villages, mostly scattered along the coastline. "These are small synagogues, built in the mid-1800s, after the Bene Israel came into contact with British missionaries who recognized that they were Jewish."

"This is wild," Cassim says. "I had no idea."

I take out a hand-drawn map from a book about the Bene Israel.

"This is a map of Konkan villages in Raigad District where Bene Israel families lived. See, they took their surnames from the villages where they were based. *Kar* means 'from' in Marathi. So—see the village of Pen; those families would have been called Penkar."

"Nana's father—I remember he had the name of Bhorupkar."

"That's right. See, here's Bhorupali, right here," I say excitedly. "And Nana's mother was a Chordekar. I found that out from a taped interview I did with her. So her ancestors must have originally been from Chorde."

"I see Chorde. It's not too far from Bhorupali."

"If Nana's parents were typical of the time period, probably their grand-parents or their parents grew up in these villages, and they more than likely grew up in Bombay. But Nana did say that her mother was from a village in-side a fort."

"That sounds like a riddle," Cassim says.

"I know."

"Well, let's go check it out. I'm down for anything," Cassim says, poring over the map.

WHEN I CALL TO MAKE a reservation for a car to take us along the Konkan Coast, I ask Bimal, the owner of the rental company, if it's possible to hire a Marathi-speaking driver. Cassim studied Hindi in college. I figure that, between the driver's Marathi, Cassim's Hindi, and the maps, we should be able to fumble our way along.

"I myself will come," says Bimal.

"Do you speak Marathi?" I ask.

"Actually, I'm originally from Delhi. I speak Hindi only. But my friend will come. He speaks Marathi and is in need of a vacation."

The following morning, Bimal, his friend Vinod, Cassim, and I set off at six and drive south, toward the Konkan Coast. We leave the center of the city for its outskirts, passing through patches of green, then stretches of highway. I did not anticipate what a relief it would be to get out of Bombay, its thick air, the constant barrage of images crowding the brain. Within three hours, we are surrounded by a landscape of reassuring sameness: green and brown fields on both sides, a scattering of trees, local phone booths and cigarette shops, and the occasional bullock cart ambling by the side of the road.

Bimal seems unimpressed with the view, but his friend is enthusiastic. Vinod rolls the window down and breathes in the fresh air. "First class!" he exclaims, but then rolls it back up in favor of the air-conditioning that Bimal prefers.

As we get closer to our first stop, Bimal and Vinod inquire about my project.

"So you would like to meet some people who are from Israel?" Bimal asks me, creasing his forehead.

"Actually, they're from here. They speak Marathi and they live in this region, but, yes, they believe that they are originally from Israel. They believe they were shipwrecked in India two thousand years ago."

"But they are basically Israeli?"

"They're Jewish. They practice Judaism, but they have lived in India for many hundreds of years, so they are quite Indian."

"They look Indian itself?" Vinod asks.

"Some of them are quite fair, but, yes, on the whole they look Indian."

"I see," Vinod says, looking skeptical.

ALIBAG, OUR FIRST STOP, is a midsized town with beach resort aspirations. "Golden Sea Side Hotel Six Stars!" "Lilac Family Style Inn!" "Color TV!" proclaim the signs that adorn buildings in the town center. We approach a group of rickshaw drivers gathered around the central bus station, waiting for passengers, and we ask the men where we can find the synagogue; the request is met with stares.

"What is this place?" the drivers ask, gathering around. We explain that it is a Jewish temple, *yahudi ka mandir,* a place of worship.

"It's a kind of church?" one driver asks. I nod yes.

"Like a church," I reply, "or a temple. For Jewish people. Where they go to pray."

The rickshaw drivers shake their heads in dismay.

"No, there is no such place," one says to another. And then to me, in English, with gravity: "Madam, we are not finding this place."

I am using the word *yahudi* for "Jewish," a term with Semitic roots. It is clear that the drivers are unfamiliar with it.

"Have you heard of a community, a small community, that has been here many, many years, and they believe in one God, like the Muslims, but they don't work on Saturdays?"

Vinod asks me what caste they are. This might help to identify them.

"They used to be known as the oil-pressing caste," I say tentatively.

"Oh! You're looking for the Israeli *masjid!*" they respond instantly, in a kind of chorus. "Why didn't you say so earlier?"

Masjid means "mosque," and I am surprised to hear the word used to describe a Jewish house of prayer. There is a small scuffle over who will lead us to the "Israeli *masjid,*" and then it is decided among the drivers that the one who lives closest to it knows it the best and should be the one to guide the way. Despite the relative clarity of the conversation with the rickshaw drivers, we are taken in a cavalcade of rickshaws to a convent school, where the lead driver parks his vehicle in the driveway and walks inside the building. I wonder to myself if he has linked the Christians and the Jews together in his mind somehow, and wish that I could ask him.

The driver ambles back, looking nonchalant, and we make a U-turn, pointing ourselves in the direction we came from. We drive at alarming speed through shady lanes until Cassim sees something out of the corner of his eye.

"Sadia, isn't that a Star of David?"

I turn my head and see a star carved into a stone gate, with a series of Bene Israel names of people who donated money for the gate, and, in keeping with local tradition, the amount of money they gave. Behind the gate is a beautiful, crumbling old building that must be the synagogue. Bimal parks the car, and Cassim and I venture tentatively inside. The front of the structure is anchored with several pillars, which still hold a faint blue stain. The building has a kind of porch with inlaid tiles, and a large and impressive carved wooden door with an ivory mezuzah. A lone pair of sandals sits by the door frame, and we peek inside to see a very elderly gentleman dressed all in white performing his prayers on the raised platform in the center of the synagogue.

Cassim and I sit quietly on the bench. I fish out a yarmulke from my camera bag, borrowed from ORT India for this occasion, and hand it to Cassim to put on his head.

"I never thought I'd wear a yarmulke for one of your harebrained schemes. How does it look?" Cassim asks, chuckling.

"Perfect," I say.

WHEN HE COMPLETES HIS PRAYERS, the elderly gentleman walks slowly out of the synagogue and looks unsurprised to see us standing there. He gives us a vague, benevolent smile and waves as if he is in a parade, floating by us.

"Excuse me, are you the caretaker here?" I ask, a phrase I have been practicing with my teacher, Mr. Shukla.

He looks back at us, waves again, points to a building across the street, then back at the synagogue, and keeps walking. We watch him walk down the lane slowly, with the help of his cane. I'm not sure how to proceed.

Just then we hear a loud sound of metal pots and pans crashing into one another, coming from a house across the street, and another older gentleman, slightly younger and rather portlier than the first, bursts into the lane. He has blue eyes and a large white trapezoidal mustache, and is dressed in a stained shirt that looks as if it was at one point a uniform of some kind.

"Baba! Baba!" he calls to the older man, running after him. "Sorry, sorry," he says, and offers the man his arm, helping him reach a door several houses farther down the street. "I'm just coming!" he calls back to us, over his shoulder. "Wait right there! I am just helping Uncle here, then I will be there!"

Bimal and Vinod are parked on the opposite side of the street, listening to a cricket match on the radio.

"These are Jews itself?" Vinod asks, pointing to the men, and I nod.

When the man reappears, he does so with a flourish. He gives a small skip, then twirls his mustache as he approaches us.

"Please excuse me. My job is to help that uncle there, from his house to the synagogue and back. He is quite old now, and in not such good health. I was eating, and I quite forgot that prayers must be finishing."

"Are you the caretaker of the synagogue?"

"Yes, I am Mr. Ellis. I am the caretaker here. You are from which country, please?"

We explain that we are from the United States and that I am photographing the synagogues of the Konkan.

"Welcome, welcome. We have many foreigners who come here. From Israel, from U.S.A. Many people come here and see our synagogue. We are undergoing a renovation—this is why the building is in some disarray—but when we finish it, it will be more beautiful. You will have tea?"

He leads us to an open-air kitchen area in front of the house he originally emerged from, pointing to a *charpoy,* a kind of flat hammock bed, for us to sit on.

"Hello?" he calls, and an older woman comes out, looking sleepy and slightly cross. He speaks to her in Marathi.

"She's your wife?" I ask after she goes inside.

"No, no," he says hastily. "I am living alone here. This is a Hindu lady. She and her family are taking care of me, paying-guest type thing. They are giving me food on payment."

"Does she mind making tea?" I say, feeling awkward about giving the lady trouble.

"No, no, of course not. You are my Jewish guests! Shalom!"

"You said the community is restoring the synagogue?" Cassim asks.

"Yes, yes. We will have a car park! We will have A/C! It will be more beautiful."

"How many families are here? How many people come to the synagogue?" I ask.

"About fifty Jews are left here. And from the surrounding villages, people come to this synagogue as well. We don't always get ten men for a minyan, but we try. On the High Holy Days we have good attendance. And sometimes people come from Bombay, or from outside. Tell me, do you know St. Louis, Missouri?" he asks us excitedly. "Do you live close to there?"

Cassim and I shake our heads. "No, we come from outside of Boston and New York," Cassim says. "We are somewhat far from there."

"I have one cousin there, in St. Louis, Missouri. Reuben is his name. He is a very successful businessman. He's in middle management! I thought perhaps if you met him you could give him a message from me . . ." he says, looking disappointed. "Maybe you might see him one day," he says, brightening. "If you do, you tell him his cousin Ellis is waiting for him, I am now the caretaker of Alibag Synagogue and am waiting for him here. You will tell him?"

Cassim and I nod, unsure what else to do.

After tea, we take a tour around the synagogue, and I take some pictures of the renovation in progress. Mr. Ellis shows us a candle resting on a table toward the center of the room and tells us that one of his primary responsibilities is to keep the flame lit. Once a day, he changes the oil, which he demonstrates for us. As we are speaking, two white-haired ladies enter the synagogue. The decorative ends of their saris are draped over their heads.

"Shalom, Shalom!" Mr. Ellis says, greeting the ladies. In Marathi he explains who we are and our purpose here. They nod at us in greeting, and we nod back. The ladies say something to Mr. Ellis in Marathi, and he opens the Ark to reveal ornate silver scrolls with the Sefer Torah inside. The ladies approach the Ark and reach their hands out, palms facing the Torah. They close their eyes, and each says a short prayer. Then they kiss their fingertips in short, repeated motions, thank Mr. Ellis, and nod at us again to say goodbye.

"Do those ladies live in Alibag?" I ask.

"No, these ladies are from far-off villages, but perhaps they have some work in Alibag, so they come here. Before going home, they give respect to God in the synagogue. It's like that."

When we go outside, I ask Mr. Ellis if I can take his picture.

"Welcome!" he says. "Shall I sing a song?"

He begins to sing a favorite Bene Israel song. The words are Hebrew, he tells us, but the melody is from a Marathi film popular in the 1950s. It has a beautiful, mysterious sound, and I photograph Mr. Ellis singing on the porch while Cassim records the performance with my video camera. Cassim asks me to move out of his shot, and I walk into the yard. Mr. Ellis thinks I am losing interest.

"I have another song!" he insists, and breaks into a rousing rendition of "Havah Nagilah." He knows only the chorus, which he repeats, and then he breaks into a small jig, lifting his knees in the air and jumping around the veranda. Small children from the neighborhood peek inside the gate, watching Mr. Ellis. "The children, they love this one!" Mr. Ellis exclaims.

We make a small donation to the synagogue and bid our grateful goodbyes to Mr. Ellis. As we are driving down the lane, Cassim says, "Sadia, turn around."

Mr. Ellis is standing in the middle of the road, dancing to his a cappella rendition of "Havah Nagilah." He is surrounded by a group of children, who are clapping in time to the music.

"That's right, children!" we hear Mr. Ellis say. *"Ha-vah na-gi-lah. . . . Ha-vah na-gi-lah. . . . Ha-vah na-gi-lah. . . ."*

"I think this man is very happy to serve God," Vinod offers as we drive away.

WE SPEND THE NEXT THREE DAYS driving from village to village in similar pursuit. It seems that, the farther we get from Bombay, the more ob-

scure our mission appears to the people we meet along the way; but I am thrilled by the occasional moments when we ask for directions to synagogues and see a flicker of recognition cross people's faces. Every time we reach a new village, Vinod leans his head out the window and makes a smacking sound with his lips, calling the attention of the old men we find sipping tea.

"Why are you making that sound?" Bimal asks, annoyed.

"It's a Marathi greeting, *yaar*," Vinod says, looking ruffled. "These people understand it." He scowls at Bimal and does it again. "Uncle, Uncle," Vinod calls. "Israeli *masjid*, Israeli *masjid*?"

In Bombay, directions work on a system of landmarks; addresses are used only in the context of their reference points to hospitals, police stations, and cinemas. In the villages, the landmarks are temples, trees, and houses, which blur together in our unfamiliarity. We move through the small lanes in series after series of circuitous spins.

We take turns leaning out the window: "Israeli *masjid*, Israeli *masjid*?"

I try to make the smacking sound myself and fail miserably. Instead,

I begin to jot down people's responses to our questions, trying to feel useful.

Underneath a tree, by the side of the local PCO phone booth and *paan* shop, an elderly man sits on his heels, smoking a *beedi* cigarette.

"Israeli *masjid* . . ." one man says, thinking it over. "Oh, you mean the people who build the tent every harvest and dance in it?" he asks Vinod, who translates.

"Yes, yes!" I say excitedly when I understand. The man must be talking about the Sukkot holiday, when Jews around the world build an outdoor structure to remind themselves of their years in bondage in Egypt. At the end of the seven days of Sukkot is the festival of Simchat Torah, when they dance to commemorate the completion of one year's Torah readings and the beginning of the next. "That's them!"

"Where are they?" we ask in unison.

Often the reply is "Gone." We find empty houses and synagogues with their doors shut. I wonder about the lives their former inhabitants are living now. Whether they are in Bombay or Israel, and what they think about the life they left behind here.

In a village called Poinad, we find a small, well-kept synagogue on a residential street. It is painted bright blue, pink, and white and is reminiscent of a cake.

Cassim says, "I keep expecting these buildings to look similar to one another, but they're all different. I wonder what the significance of the color scheme is."

We ask neighbors who the caretaker of the Poinad Synagogue is; "Moses" is the repeated reply. We wander around Poinad looking for Moses, whom we find grooming a beautiful chocolate brown horse in a stable off the main road. Expecting an older man, we are surprised to find a boy of about eighteen. His family owns the horse, he explains, which they rent out for weddings and special occasions. He walks us to the Hesed-El Synagogue, which is not much larger than a small bedroom. A large oil lamp dominates the room, which Moses asks me to photograph. He points out the renovations that his family has undertaken, and tells us how much he regrets that they can't do more. He says his family is one of two Bene Israel families left in Poinad. His older brother has migrated to Israel, and now only he and his parents are left. I ask him if he plans to go to Israel in the future.

"I want to go," he says, "but I worry about it. Who will look after the synagogue after my father?"

Cassim asks him about the choices of colors. "Are they significant in any way? Are these traditional Bene Israel colors?"

"You like them?" Moses says, looking pleased. "I chose them myself."

We head farther south, to Murud-Janjira. This area was at one time a Muslim stronghold, followed by a period of Maratha Hindu rule, and it was one of the last areas to succumb to the British. Though it is known as a kind of seaside holiday spot, it seems to be resting on past glories. The main strip of the town is a dusty road populated by ice cream stands and a few restaurants with red plastic chairs. We opt for a small guesthouse, which seems clean and has rooms available: one for Bimal and Vinod, and one for Cassim and me.

The next day, the only remnant of a Jewish community we can find is an old cemetery in terrible disrepair—the graves are overgrown with weeds, and a housing development is encroaching on the property lines on one side. The detritus of the building, the garbage, the storage, and the laundry lines are already spilling out into the exterior fringe of the cemetery. It seems only a matter of time before the housing takes over and the graveyard succumbs to a new identity.

WE DRIVE ALONG THE COAST, then farther inland. Cassim and I are determined to find our twin ancestral villages: Bhorupali and Chorde. Whereas most of the villages we have visited still exist as footnotes in books, none of my archival searches have yielded any information on either of these two villages. As we get closer to the dot on my map marked Bhorupali, Vinod leans out the window to ask a crowd of young men. "Bhorupali *kidhar hai*? Bhorupali? Bhorupali?"

"Bhorupali?" the group repeats back to us, seemingly unfamiliar with the name. They either shrug or shake their heads no.

I keep staring at the dot on the map, trying to will the village into existence. Since my map has no modern roads, just a collection of hand-drawn lines, it's entirely possible that we have taken the wrong route.

"Can I take a look at that?" Cassim says, scrutinizing the map.

Bimal, Vinod, Cassim, and I take turns trying to figure out the right path: through a village, to the left of another one, over a small bridge. This area has sparse vegetation and wide, open-plowed fields. There are very few trees in sight. Occasionally we pass collections of small concrete houses clustered near a cold-drink stand. We get very excited when an old man acts as if he has heard of the place; maybe we are getting closer. He waves us in a new direction, and we are happy to follow. He tells us to look for a large tree and a bus stop. We keep our eyes peeled on both sides of the dusty road, trying to define for one another what constitutes a "large tree." Determining the definition of a "bus stop" is no easier. Does the bus come to a halt at this bench? This tea shop? Phone booth? Before I realize it, I have dozed off on Cassim's shoulder.

I wake up two hours later, when Bimal pulls the car to the side of the road. I sit upright, wondering where we are.

"This, I believe, is it," he says.

In front of us is an unmistakably large tree. We watch from the car as a large red bus pulls up underneath it and a woman and her young son get on board.

"Should we get out?" Cassim says.

Bhorupali, if this is Bhorupali, seems to be not a village at all, but in fact a literal bend in the road. Now that the woman and her son have left, there is not a house or a person in sight. We wander around in a small circle, wondering what to do next.

"I could take a picture," I say.

"Of what?" Cassim says.

A motorcycle whizzes by us, and Bimal flags him down, asking if this is Bhorupali. They have a short conversation and the man drives on.

"It may have been here a long time ago, but it's been gone for some time," Bimal informs us. "Basically, it doesn't exist."

"I see," I say, walking toward the car and trying not to sound disappointed.

In our search for Bhorupali, we have lost the better part of a morning and a good deal of momentum. We halt at the next cold-drink stand and sit in a row of plastic chairs underneath a tiny, barely functioning fan. The earth is cracked and dry here, and the air feels heavy. Vinod produces a small green mango from his pocket, and asks the owner of the stand if he can borrow a knife and some salt. He cuts the mango into pieces and sprinkles salt on them.

"This is very good for heat," he says sagely, offering each of us a piece.

Bimal shakes his head at him.

"You believe in all these old wives' tales," he says to his friend.

We sit for several more minutes, trying to cool off and regain some energy, gnawing on our slices of raw mango.

"This is totally weird," Cassim says.

"Shall we carry on?" asks Bimal.

"Well, let's look for Chorde," Cassim says, getting up and trying to sound cheerful.

"Yes," I say. "Let's find Chorde."

WE WIND OUR WAY BACK to a recognized road, and follow it, asking directions along the way. After our search for Bhorupali, finding Chorde seems relatively easy. I laugh with surprise when we see a small sign that says "CHORDE" in block letters in English and in Devanagari script. The road to Chorde is so small that we miss the turn twice and have to retrace our route to find it. We go down a long, wide path not accustomed to cars. At the end of the path we see a little cluster of small wood-and-mud structures, a few concrete buildings with tin roofs. The buildings seem to lie lightly upon the land, as if they might pick up and move on.

"This certainly doesn't look like a village inside a fort," Cassim says.

"No, you're right, it doesn't," I say.

We pass through passages so narrow that we are looking into the eyes of curious people not three feet away. Clearly our car and unfamiliar faces are an unusual sight. I roll down the window and say, "Chordekar?"

I have no idea if a single Bene Israel family still lives in Chorde, but I figure it's worth a try. I suppose that it's possible we might be led to a Hindu family, who will be no less bewildered by our arrival.

"Israeli? Israeli *log?*" he asks, asking for Jewish people. Bimal rolls the car forward at a snail's pace, scanning the row of onlookers for a glimmer of recognition.

A tailor, his lap full of shirts, looks up from his stitches. "Abraham Chordekar?" he asks.

Abraham Chordekar. He must be a Bene Israel. I nod vigorously.

We are instructed to take a right, then a left. The right turn reveals a large concrete structure that looks as if it might be the village school. The left yields another row of houses, each one a small square, faced by another row on the right. One of these houses, a blue freestanding building, is the Chordekar home. I notice a mezuzah on the doorframe and feel confident that we are in the right place.

Bimal, Vinod, Cassim, and I get out and approach the house cautiously.

"Hello?" I call out into the darkness of the open doorway.

A tall, lean woman in a pink sari comes to the door, and we try to explain our purpose to her.

"Vinod, can you explain that our great-grandmother was a Chordekar and we have come to see our ancestors' village?"

I see Vinod's hands moving quickly, covering the basic points of our journey, and the fact that we are from America.

"America?" she says, her eyes getting big.

"America," Cassim and I say, nodding and trying to look friendly.

She gestures to us to come inside and pulls out chairs for us to sit on.

When our eyes adjust to the light, we find ourselves in a room that seems to function as living area, kitchen, and storeroom. On the back wall of the room is a stack of canisters that smell as if they are filled with kerosene. To our right is a small color television, and above it, a hanging candelabra and a large bell-shaped oil lamp, the kind I have seen in Bene Israel synagogues. To our left is a ladder that goes up to a second floor. As we enter, two children scamper down the ladder, mystified by our sudden appearance.

Mrs. Chordekar says something to Vinod, who translates.

"It seems that her husband is not well. He is lying down, but he'll be here in a moment. He has some trouble with his eyes. If I understand her correctly, he is blind, or going blind. She has two children, a boy and a girl. I suppose that they are these children here." He points at the boy and the girl, who are staring at us with open curiosity. The boy looks to be about ten or eleven years old, the girl about thirteen.

Mrs. Chordekar smiles at us and urges us to sit.

I ask Vinod to ask her if she is from Chorde originally, or from another village. We learn that Mrs. Chordekar was born and brought up in the small Bene Israel community in Ahmedabad, in Gujarat. This was an arranged marriage, and she has lived in Chorde for fourteen years. She has a sister married into a family in a town about two hours away, and a younger brother working there as well. I wonder what it must have been like for her to make the transition from Ahmedabad, a city of over four million people, to the village of Chorde.

Mr. Chordekar enters the room with the help of his daughter, who leads him by the hand. He is a sturdily built man with white hair, very pale skin, and blue eyes clouded with cataracts, permanently facing an invisible point in the upper left-hand corner of his gaze. He says that he is sorry he can't see us better or speak to us in English, and we hastily apologize for arriving unannounced. We reiterate our purpose here, and he asks, through Vinod, for the name of our great-grandmother.

"Segulla-bai Chordekar," I say.

He shakes his head; the name is not familiar to him.

"Chordekar," he says, pointing to himself and nodding.

I say, "Yes, Chordekar."

We sit for a few moments, unsure what to do next. He asks us if we will have a biscuit, and I don't want to refuse his offer of hospitality. He gives five rupees to his son, who skips out the door and presumably to a nearby stand. When he returns two or three minutes later with a packet of biscuits, Mrs. Chordekar places them on a metal plate and passes it around the room.

Mr. Chordekar grew up in Chorde. There were at one time as many as ten Bene Israel families in Chorde, but those days have long passed; everyone has moved to Bombay or to Israel. Only he and his family are left. After the loss of his eyesight, he was not able to work. He is grateful to the American Jewish Joint Distribution Committee in Bombay, who gave him a grant to start a small business, which they run out of their home. People come with empty vessels to the door, and Mrs. Chordekar fills them with kerosene from their supply. She weighs the filled vessel on a scale and charges the appropriate amount. It is not much money, but in this way they are able to cover their expenses. They plan to migrate to Israel within the next year or so, hoping the prospects for their children will be greater there.

"Vinod, they are planning to move to Israel?" I ask, unable to keep the surprise out of my voice.

"It seems that is their plan, yes."

I try to imagine Mr. and Mrs. Chordekar living in Israel, learning Hebrew. Their children are clearly excited about the idea. The girl offers that she would like to go to a Jewish school, where she will meet other Jewish girls.

A young woman in a housedress comes to the door with an empty can, which Mrs. Chordekar fills, weighs, and hands back to the girl, receiving a few notes in exchange.

I ask Mr. Chordekar if I can take a portrait of his family to send to him later, and he seems to like the idea. I ask where they would like to be photographed and suggest perhaps in front of their house. Mr. Chordekar consults his wife, and they decide they would like to be photographed here, in their living area. The daughter suggests a backdrop that includes their color television, candelabra, and oil lamp. The son arranges four plastic chairs in a neat row. Mrs. Chordekar asks her children to change into other clothes; she suggests a pink salwar kameez for her daughter, who refuses it, telling her mother she wants to wear a Western-style dress and excusing herself to go upstairs and put it on.

When they are ready, the Chordekars assemble themselves for their picture solemnly, and hold themselves very still. None of the family members smile. All except Mr. Chordekar look directly into the camera.

After the picture, they show me their family photos, faded orange prints mounted behind cracked glass, in the hallway that separates the front door and the living area. They show us around their house. It includes a large room with four cots where they sleep, and an outdoor bench where they spend most of their evenings. Mr. Chordekar says his goodbyes and retreats to his room, and Mrs. Chordekar and her children sit on the bench. We are grateful for a small breeze, which signals the end of the sun's daily onslaught. They seem more relaxed now that they are out of the house and the rituals of formality are over. I

take more pictures of them, and they seem to enjoy it. Mrs. Chordekar smiles softly. She looks younger than her husband, and I wonder by how much.

She suggests that we might like to take pictures of the temple in town, and asks the children to take us there. We walk down a little path bordered by small huts. As we walk, we gather children, a few at a time, until we are surrounded by dozens of tiny bodies. Their voices create a kind of chorus, and more and more join our ranks.

"Sadia, look behind us," Cassim says.

I turn back and see what look like fifty children under the age of ten. A multitude of black eyelashes, shiny black eyes, and tiny brown limbs peeking out of grubby shorts and school-uniform skirts. The little girls wear their braids in two wide loops, one tied above each ear. When we laugh, they all laugh in unison; it is a giggling, swarming echo.

"Where are we going?"

"I have no idea," Cassim says.

"MY . . . NAME . . . IS . . . PETER!" comes the call of a bold little boy, and I turn around in surprise.

"Your name is Peter?" I say.

"MY . . . NAME . . . IS . . . PETER!" another one repeats, looking pleased with himself.

"You're both named Peter?" I ask.

"MY . . . NAME . . . IS . . . PETER!" yet another one says, and more little boys start to laugh louder. I realize it must be a line from an English lesson, or from a television advertisement.

"MY . . . NAME . . . IS . . . PETER!" a group of four or five boys shout from my left.

"My-name-is-Pe-ter," a little girl says softly, tugging on my sleeve and looking up at me.

The little Hindu temple is a tiny, dusty, empty structure. There's not much to see, but we don't want to disappoint our audience. Cassim suggests we take a group photo of the children in front of it and tries to huddle the group into his shot. Soon there's a mob. It looks like a hundred children are trying to clamber into the frame. They are shouting excitedly; their cheers and cries rise and ebb as one collective, gleeful sound. I have little experience with children. I worry that they might spontaneously erupt into a mound of tears.

"Quickly! Quickly!" I urge Cassim.

He tells them to count to three and say "Peter!" They do and collapse in a fit of uncontrollable laughter.

Cassim and I walk back toward the car, where we find Bimal and Vinod talking to some men from the village about the finer points of their car. Bimal and Vinod are clearly enjoying their role as Bombay celebrities. As we approach, Vinod greets us enthusiastically.

"So this is your native place itself!" he says, looking delighted.

We drive out of Chorde at a walking pace, surrounded on each side by a crowd of people who have gathered to see us off, resting their arms on the top and sides of our car. Small children press their hands and faces to our windows, knocking and waving, making Cassim and me laugh. As we reach the outskirts of Chorde, Bimal accelerates slightly, and a few of the young men in the group break into a run, keeping pace with the car. While the others give in to the inevitability of our departure, one boy keeps up, and we drive, in tandem with his sprint, for a few hundred meters. He is panting with exertion, his face contorted in the grimace of his effort. Finally, Bimal tires of the game and hits the gas again. We speed past the boy, and I look back to see him come to a halt, exhausted, in the middle of the road. He places his hands on his knees and watches us go. Behind him a group of small children wave at us, their small arms move in unison, until we are no longer visible.

By nightfall, we are back in Bombay.

"Take pictures of our challah bread!" Benny Isaacs says to me one morning at ORT India. "Only authentic challah in Bombay!" he says proudly. "Our baker is very good these days. A very nice young man, a Muslim. You might like to take his photograph."

Cassim and I ask directions and find ourselves in the cavernous industrial kitchen of the school, where a wiry, thoughtful-looking baker named Akhtar is kneading dough into ropes, which he glazes with egg and braids into loaves. He is pleased to pose for my camera, and dutifully shows us the process he goes through to make each loaf. When we tell him our names, his eyes gleam with recognition and surprise.

"Aap Musalman hain?" he asks Cassim, pointing to the small gold Qur'an he wears around his neck. Are you Muslim?

It's interesting to me how much more often Cassim is recognized as a Muslim than I am. I wonder for a moment if he looks more South Asian than I do, or if people approach him more comfortably because he's a man, or both.

"As-salaam alaikum!" Akhtar says with enthusiasm.

"Wa alaikum assalam!" Cassim and I respond reflexively.

While I continue to photograph the bakery, Akhtar takes Cassim aside.

"How many Muslims are there in America, brother?" he asks in Hindi.

"About seven million," Cassim says.

"Seven million?" Akhtar asks, shocked at the number. "I thought there were only Christians and Jews there."

"No, no, there are many Muslims in America."

Akhtar leans in conspiratorially to Cassim and speaks in a softer voice.

"Do you know how many Muslims there are in India, brother?"

"How many?" Cassim asks.

"We are forty percent of the population. The Indian government says that we are only ten percent, but we are very strong in number. There are many problems here between the Shiv Sena and our community. But we are forty percent, Cassim Brother. The Bombay government, they try and keep us down, but we are very strong."

Cassim looks serious as he listens to Akhtar. I know that he's aware that Akhtar's numbers are off; the Muslim population of India is closer to 15 percent of the population. But Akhtar is right about the Shiv Sena, the right-wing fundamentalist Hindu party currently in power. They believe strongly that Bombay's culture should remain predominantly Hindu, and have a violent history of oppressing Muslims.

"Today is Friday," he says. "You can come with me to prayers; I'm just going now to the mosque. Come, you must come," he says, tugging Cassim's sleeve.

"He wants me to pray with him. Do you mind if I go?" Cassim says over his shoulder as Akhtar leads him outside by the arm.

"No, go ahead," I call back.

As I walk upstairs to the fourth floor to photograph the ORT kiddush winemakers, the staff members I pass in the stairway ask me where Cassim has disappeared to.

"I think he is talking to Akhtar the baker," I say, unsure how to clarify that he has gone to the mosque without explaining our entire family history.

I watch from the fourth-floor balcony as Cassim and Akhtar re-enter the ORT driveway, and am impressed by how quickly they have formed an association. I can tell from the way Cassim leans in to hear Akhtar speak that he is fascinated by their conversation, and Akhtar is clearly in high spirits, clapping Cassim on the back repeatedly. I return downstairs to the bakery, and Cassim perches on a stool while Akhtar mixes ingredients to make a new batch of challah. Cassim asks him about his home in a rural area of central India, how he came alone to Bombay to find work, and how he sends money home every month to his village.

"You should come to my native place!" Akhtar says, stirring flour, water, and eggs with a large wooden spoon. "Then you can see Bihar for yourself!"

"Insh'allah . . ." Cassim says, smiling. God willing.

Akhtar removes his gloves and jots down my mobile number on a piece of paper so that he can communicate with Cassim, and for the next two weeks calls him from phone booths to say hello every couple of days. Cassim, who has a much better ear for languages than I do, tells me that Akhtar's Hindi is close to our mother's Urdu, and for this reason he finds him easier to understand than he does most people in Bombay. After Partition, many Muslims stayed behind in Bihar instead of joining Pakistan. It's an impoverished, mostly agricultural state that is considered somewhat backward by most of Bombay's middle class, and Akhtar is part of a large migration of young Bihari men who have come to Bombay in recent years to find work. He tells Cassim that he's never met a foreign Muslim before, or anyone who is partly from Pakistan; the idea of an educated, well-traveled Muslim is exotic and interesting to him. After one of their conversations, Cassim tells me that Akhtar has been offered a new job as an assistant pastry chef in the exclusive Athena nightclub in South Bombay. He begins his shift at midnight, and works until morning. He invites Cassim and me to visit him at work the following Saturday night, and asks us to come at 1 a.m.

The Athena nightclub is located on a quiet street in Colaba, not far from the Taj Mahal Hotel. A cigarette seller has erected a makeshift stall on the sidewalk near the entrance line, and is doing a brisk business with the patrons waiting to get inside. A family of small children peer out from a tent erected not far from the club entrance, watching as the young Bombay elite emerge out of their imported cars and enter the throng of people in tight jeans, iridescent shirts, and Italian shoes, pushing their bodies toward the door, trying to gain entry. Cassim approaches the bouncer and tells him our names, as Akhtar has instructed him to do, and we are handed two thick white cards,

entrance tickets worth fifteen hundred rupees, about thirty dollars each. Inside, the lights and music pulse feverishly. We are in a reality far removed
from the one just outside, not quite sure how we ended up here. An attendant in a black uniform bows at us and leads us past the lines of people waiting at the bar for their drinks and a group of people trying to make their way
onto the dance floor. He opens a series of doors, and we follow him into a
large, bright professional kitchen, where we find Akhtar surrounded by several other staff members, standing at attention, waiting for us. Akhtar is
wearing a chef's hat and a large white apron covered in flour and chocolate.
He is beaming.

"Cassim Brother!" he says enthusiastically, waving his gloved hands,
which are caked in dough.

"As-salaam alaikum, Akhtar Bhai!" Cassim says.

Akhtar nods respectfully in my direction and introduces us to the rest of
the Athena staff, who nod at us. It seems that, in addition to being a nightclub, Athena also serves as a restaurant. The seven staff members who work
the night shift are responsible for the restaurant's pastry and cakes. Akhtar is
an apprentice, and is learning his trade from a more experienced pastry chef,
an older, serious-looking man with a mustache.

I present Akhtar with the pictures of him baking bread at ORT, and he
is very pleased. He tells us that he will send these pictures to his mother, and
that she will be very happy. He has a big announcement to share with us.
His mother has found him a wife, and he will be leaving for his wedding in
three months.

"Cassim Brother, can you come to my native place for my marriage?" he
asks hopefully. "It will be a big marriage, with festivities for seven days. . . ."

Cassim looks genuinely torn and tells him that he will try. I know that it
would be almost impossible for Cassim to make the trip back from Fiji, but
I can tell that he's touched by the invitation.

"Now you must eat something," Akhtar says. "My friend will seat you."

Cassim and I are escorted by a smiling waiter in a tuxedo to a dark,
closed restaurant section and are served six different varieties of dessert: two
kinds of chocolate cream pie, various fruit tarts, and something approxi-

mating a cheesecake. From behind a glass partition, we watch the crowd of young people gyrate on the dance floor and hear the familiar bass lines of American hip-hop remixed with Bollywood vocal tracks. I watch as two young men push up against an attractive young woman with a sheet of shiny blow-dried black hair, one in front and one in back. The three move in unison, and I wonder what Akhtar thinks of the people who eat his desserts.

The cakes are delicious, but there are too many of them. We finish the first two slices quickly and then look at each other, daunted by the prospect of polishing off the rest. Akhtar peeks his head out from time to time from behind the door to the kitchen to check on our progress. I start to worry that he will get into trouble with his supervisor.

We return to the kitchen, where Akhtar is eager to show us all of the aspects of his new job: the professional mixers he uses to blend his ingredients, the large industrial ovens where he bakes his cakes, the frosting cones he makes miniature roses with. We admire each new appliance as we go, and Akhtar's ability to use each one. He proudly frosts a chocolate cake for our benefit, showing us his new skills, and we applaud.

"You have made me very happy tonight," Akhtar says, smiling. "You have honored me with this visit."

Cassim thanks Akhtar for his kindness, and tells him that we must go, that it's 2:30 a.m. and that I am very tired. Akhtar asks his manager if he can walk us outside to say goodbye.

We leave the kitchen and find ourselves in an alley adjacent to the club entrance, where throngs of people are still trying to push their way inside.

"Cassim Brother, try and come to my native place," he says. "You will love Bihar."

"I will try," Cassim says solemnly.

The two embrace, and I take a picture of them, arm in arm in the alleyway.

"We will meet again soon, *insh'allah*," Akhtar says as we walk down the lane in search of a taxi.

"*Insh'allah*," Cassim says, and salutes Akhtar goodbye.

15

SECOND-CLASS CAR

M ake sure you take the ladies' car on the local train," people tell me repeatedly. "Especially at rush time."

"When is the rush time?" I ask, and get various responses, most of which include most of the afternoon.

There are three kinds of compartments on the local trains: first class, where the businessmen ride; second class, where the majority of male passengers travel; and the ladies' car. First class is more expensive and slightly less crowded; second class fills up quickly with men who occupy every available inch of the train car. During rush hour, both classes of travel are packed to the brim, and I feel lucky that I am able to travel in the women's compartment, which is never as full. It's difficult to know where to stand while I'm waiting for the train in Grant Road Station, which spot will be an appropriate one to board the correct car. Most often, I stand near the nearest group of women traveling together and try to bundle into the train with them. Sometimes when the train arrives I get lost in the rush of people trying to board all at once, and I miss my chance. Other times, sensing my inexperience, other women grab me by the shoulder and push me in front of them, and I feel my body hoisted up by the momentum of the group. Once inside, we arrange ourselves throughout the compartment, and a young girl goes through the train passing around a flat, wide cardboard tray of hair ornaments, plastic jewelry, ladies' underwear, and coloring books for children. The women pick through the merchandise absentmindedly, holding earrings up to their ears and hair ornaments up to their braids, testing different items. The other passengers look at them and act as mirrors, giving signs of approval or disapproval in their choices.

One afternoon, I am on my way to Andheri, one of the northern suburbs, to visit a Bene Israel family and take their portrait. I find the station almost empty; I don't see any other women. When the train arrives, it is nearly deserted, and I find a seat easily in the second-class car. There doesn't seem to be any harm in riding in one of the mixed compartments in broad daylight, I think, and I keep my tripod between my legs and my camera bag on my lap for safekeeping.

As the train goes farther north, I watch the sun fading and realize that it is later in the day than I thought. I watch as the car fills up with more and more passengers, all of them men. They look at me with a little curiosity, but I stare straight ahead, determined to seem unfazed. I realize that the train is getting more crowded, so that I will have to stand up well before my station to make sure I'm able to exit. Reluctantly, I give up my seat and try to make my way toward the open train-compartment doors.

At each station, more and more men enter the car, each time more than I think is humanly possible. I have seen the clamor and rush of men boarding Bombay's trains before, but never from the inside of the train, only from the vantage of the platform. I watch as men on the ground reach up their arms to be pulled in, thousands of arms reaching to pull them up, up and inside. If they are light, their feet will not touch the floor; their upper body will fill the usable space just under the ceiling.

I feel a growing sense of panic that I am going to be trapped on this train. I see my station on the map, a chipped line of paint above the door of the compartment. Five more stations, then four. Men are packed on either side of me now closer than is comfortable. I am holding my tripod over one shoulder, and my camera bag above most of the men's heads, so that no one can reach inside and pull anything out. I begin to see how the men make their exits when it's time for their station, yelling that their turn has come and then being forcibly evicted from the throng as ten more men climb on board to replace them. I am getting frightened about how I will do the same, and try to make my way closer to the door. We are packed in so tightly now that my body is surrounded on all sides, pressed next to the men's bodies, my sweat mingling with theirs. Suddenly I feel a hand push between my legs from behind. My hands are caught, holding my bag in front of me, and I can't slap the man or push his hand away. Three more hands, four start reaching for my breasts, and there's nothing I can do—my hands are trapped above me, and I can't let go of my bag. I start shouting in English, barely audible over the din of the train and the mob of passengers.

"Get the FUCK OFF ME, YOU FUCKING ASSHOLES!" I yell, which only delights the crowd further. The men snigger at me. Some look away, embarrassed.

I struggle to turn around slightly and halfway face the man behind me. "DO YOU HAVE A SISTER?" I scream.

He withdraws his hand and tells the men in front of me to drop theirs. A man closer to the door looks back at me across the crowd, almost kindly.

"Come, come here," he says. "I'll help you."

I don't feel I have any other choice. I take his hand and let him pull me, firmly and with assurance, through the mound of people plastered to the door like bees in a honeycomb. "Go!" he says, when we get to the next station, and pushes me out the door. I hit the ground running, tripping over myself, gathering my bags, making sure that I have everything.

I stand on the platform of the unfamiliar station in the dark, looking up at the anonymous train car, filled with hundreds, what feels like perhaps a thousand men, and swear at the top of my lungs to anyone who will listen until well after the train has departed.

16

OMENS

BOMBAY, MARCH 2002

Every morning, I walk to the corner stall to buy copies of *The Times of India, The Asian Age,* and *The Hindu.* The news is filled with chilling stories of attacks being waged by right-wing Hindu fundamentalists against the Muslim population just across the border to the north, in Gujarat. Bombay experienced traumatic violence in the winter of 1992–93, which began with protests against the destruction of a mosque in the northern Indian town of Ayodhya built on what is believed to be the site of Hindu deity Ram's birthplace. The clashes swelled into an anti-Muslim pogrom that raged across the city, and in March 1993, this violent period in the city's history culminated in what was widely considered a "Muslim response"—the detonation of bombs at the Stock Exchange and several bus stations. There is concern that Hindu-Muslim violence could break out again, but so far Bombay is largely quiet, and I am grateful to be far from the storm.

On the afternoons when I'm not at ORT India or interviewing older members of the Bene Israel community, I go to the David Sassoon Library on Rampart Row. The library looks across the art district known as Kala Ghoda, or Black Horse, named after a statue of King Edward VII that once stood in its center. Inside the lobby of the building, an imposing marble statue of David Sassoon keeps watch over the entry desk, where a sleepy attendant checks out books with a large, loud stamp. I walk up the curving wooden staircase, tap my way across the parquet floor of the landing and through the reading room, where students sit hunched over their textbooks, and retired men sift lazily through the magazines and periodicals. I have lived in Bombay for almost three months, and it's nice to have routines, places that I frequent. The reading room has tall, open doors that face the veranda, a space filled with oversized wooden lounge chairs that look suitable for a country estate or the deck of a luxury ship. This is where I make my nest for the afternoon, books of Bene Israel and Bombay history in my lap. Several members have discovered that the chairs make excellent sites for naps, and are unabashedly resting, their books perched precariously on their stomachs.

The library faces a low, modern building which houses the Jehangir Art Gallery, where I go to look at paintings when I need a short dose of air-conditioned air, stopping for tea and *paratha*s in Café Samovar. One day, a familiar gesture catches my eye as I am walking inside. I look to my left and see Rekhev sitting on the steps of the building, holding a large green hardbound notebook in his left hand, pushing his hair out of his eyes with the flat of his right palm. It's been a few months since I've seen him, since I left Pune at the end of December. I realize, with a flash, that I've missed him, and the feeling pulls on me. For reasons I will wonder about later, it does not seem surprising to see him out here in Bombay. When I approach him, he looks up at me as if he was expecting me, and we speak as if we had been interrupted only minutes before.

"Are you speaking Hindi now?" he asks me casually.

"Hardly," I say, sitting down. "I've been taking lessons, but I'm not getting very far."

"What are you reading about in the library?" he asks.

"Bene Israel history, mostly material about the Christian missionaries who taught the Bene Israel Hebrew and tried to convert them to Christianity."

"It's a very punishing God, your God," Rekhev says slowly.

"What do you mean?" I ask.

"I have been reading the Bible. I have no training in Christianity; I can only appreciate it as a narrative. But this is how I read my own holy books, the Puranas. These, too, are stories. The Bible is full of stories."

"That's true."

"In our tradition, gods are often eating and drinking, visiting us on earth. Your god sends locusts. I find him quite violent."

I notice that Rekhev pronounces the "v" in "violent" like a "w."

"Why are you reading the Bible?" I ask.

"The Western canon—your entire education, for that matter—it's all based on the Bible. But I don't understand the references. I'll never make sense of you if I don't read the Bible."

I feel immensely flattered that Rekhev would want to "make sense of me." I look down at my sandals to hide how pleased it makes me feel.

"So, have you found your shipwrecked Jews?"

"Some," I say. "But there's a trip out of Bombay that I want to make soon, to a town on the coast. I've heard that there is one Bene Israel family left who still make oil out of local seeds in the traditional way—I want to meet them."

"Do you think they are still there?"

I open up one of my books and show him a black-and-white photograph of two women sitting on an old oil press inside what looks like a thatched hut, a bullock in the background.

"They were there when this picture was taken, nine years ago."

Rekhev pauses, looking at the photograph.

"Nine years is a long time. How will you go there?"

"By boat, rickshaw, car I suppose."

"You will go alone?"

"I guess so; I hadn't thought about it."

"This is not America," Rekhev says. "I will come with you." He looks serious, as if he has been debating this point with himself for some time.

"Really?" I say.

"When you have decided when you would like to go, call me at this number. I'm staying in Bombay for a little while to work on a film."

Rekhev tears off a corner of his notebook and writes a phone number on it.

"I would like that," I say. "Thanks, I could use the company."

"I know," he says, returning to his book.

I sit down on the step next to Rekhev and watch a man trying to sell handmade drums to tourists. He methodically moves a two-sided drum back and forth, hitting each side with a ball on the end of a long piece of twine, hurrying after a couple in matching khaki shorts.

"Very nice, very nice, very nice . . ." he says, trailing after them, as they wave him away.

"Bombay suits you," Rekhev says, turning a page.

"Thank you," I say.

"Perhaps we'll go next week."

"Next week."

I MAKE AN APPOINTMENT to visit the American Jewish Joint Distribution Committee and find out more about the family who makes oil. The AJJDC is a social welfare organization that has been active in Bombay since the early 1960s. Inside, the offices are decorated with posters of religious sites in Israel and poster boards pasted with snapshots from various youth-group camps and activities. Underneath each picture is a handwritten caption in Magic Marker cursive: "Dance Class," "Purim Play," "Getting to Know Israel."

I have an appointment with Nandini, a social worker who periodically visits the remaining three hundred Bene Israel Jews still living in the villages of the Konkan Coast. In Bombay, Nandini supervises the AJJDC's Cash

Assistance Program, which helps Bene Israel families who are below the poverty line meet their monthly expenses. On the day I visit, several elderly men and women are sitting patiently in the waiting area to receive free checkups from a volunteer doctor; each holds a folder marked with the village surname and containing medical records. As I wait to meet with Nandini, an elderly lady in a pale pink sari leans over to me and smiles.

"You are from Israel?" she says.

"I'm from the U.S.," I reply. "But my grandmother was from here. Bhorupkar was her Bene Israel surname before her father changed it to Jacobs."

"Bhorupkar!" she exclaims, looking delighted.

"Yes," I say. "Bhorupkar was my grandmother's father's side, and Chordekar was my grandmother's mother's side."

"Bhorupkar! Chordekar!" she says, turning to the women around me and putting her arm around me affectionately. The women express their surprise and gather around my chair, asking the first woman questions about me in Marathi.

"Your grandmother is in Bombay?" she asks me, translating.

"My grandmother is no more," I say, using the Indian-English term. "But she was from Bombay."

The lady squeezes my hand and looks at me with large, sympathetic eyes before she relays this information to the curious onlookers.

"You remind me of her, actually," I say, noticing a certain similarity in her coloring and her mannerisms.

A woman on my left speaks to me in Marathi, tugging on my sleeve. She has some problem that she seems to think I can help her with. When her predicament is roughly translated for me, I gather that she converted to Judaism at the time of her marriage but does not have the certificate of conversion she needs to begin the process of making aliyah to Israel.

The lady in the pink sari suggests that she go to the synagogue where she was married and ask for some documentation. "Don't bother this girl," she says protectively, from what I can understand. "She doesn't know anything about how to help you."

A young woman shows me to a desk, where I sit opposite Nandini—a

tall, strong-looking woman with wavy black hair and a string of white flowers hanging from her ponytail. I tell her I have read that there were several
families in the Konkan still practicing the trade of oil pressing as of the late
1980s and early 1990s, and ask her if there are any left.

"Very few Bene Israel are left," she says, shaking her head. "Most left for
Israel a long time back."

"Are there any families remaining? I heard there was one family who still
make oil in the traditional way."

"Perhaps one only."

"And where do they live?"

She opens her file and pores through a database of names and dates for
several minutes, shaking her head. Then she finds an entry of interest and
reads aloud.

"David Waskar, of village adjacent to Revdanda. Owner of private oil
press. Father of Benjamin Waskar, *chazan* and caretaker of Magen David
Synagogue, and Ellis Waskar, owner of private rickshaw. Last visit from social worker in December 1998. Described Mr. Waskar as 'difficult.' Social
worker thrown out of house. End report."

Nandini looks up at me from her file.

"Why not photograph the synagogues here in Bombay? Many people
from Israel have visited, taken photos."

I explain to Nandini that I would very much like to visit Revdanda.

She smiles kindly at me and closes the file.

"If you like, Miss Shepard."

REKHEV AND I set out for Revdanda at dawn, when the light is still hazy.
We speed down Marine Drive in a taxi, and I note the sharp contrast among
the different morning rituals that bring Bombay residents to her beaches.
Through the outstretched arms of a group of smartly dressed retirees doing
Tai Chi, I watch men returning from their morning ablutions. We buy our
ferry tickets at the foot of the Gateway of India, the majestic arch built for the
arrival of King George V and Queen Mary, which faces the back of the Taj

Mahal Hotel on one side and the sea on the other. For centuries, it was the Gateway that first greeted visitors to this city as they arrived by ship.

We travel one hour across the harbor to the port of Mandwa. It's a gorgeous journey; light plays off of the water and the morning is still cool. I feel grateful, calmed by the pull of a destination, and watch as the buildings of South Bombay fade and are replaced by a watery horizon. I'm slightly nervous to take this trip with Rekhev; we have never traveled together any farther than the center of Pune, and I have never seen him interact with anyone other than his fellow film students.

"Have you dreamt of crossing water?" Rekhev asks me suddenly. "Recently, I mean?"

"Yes. Why?" I ask.

"It's a good omen. I have been reading about omens in the Konkan," he says.

"What are some other good omens?" I ask, eager for more.

"To dream of a cow, a bullock, an elephant, a palace, a mountain, a woman dressed in white, swallowing the disk of the sun or the moon, a lamp, fruit, lifting a goblet of wine . . . so many things."

It strikes me as funny, the scholar's authority with which Rekhev recites this list.

"You memorized them?"

"No, I have them written here, in my notebook."

Rekhev opens his notebook and flips through pages and pages of notes and drawings. Careful letters, written with a fountain pen—some in Devanagari script, some in English. I wonder if Rekhev believes in any of this, or if he just likes the sounds of the words.

"Any bad omens?"

"Cotton, ashes, bones, singing, laughing, studying, a woman dressed in red, a red mark on the forehead, a cat, a prickly shrub, a contest between two planets—these are considered bad omens." Rekhev looks at the water for a moment, and then back at me. "Tell me something, Sadia. Do you ever dream of your Nana?"

"I have dreamt of her only three times since she died, but, yes, I dreamt of her my first night in Pune."

"Perhaps she was looking out for you."

"It's strange, I felt that way."

"It is not strange at all. In the Konkan, it is believed that ancestors who take interest in the welfare of their descendants appear in dreams. Sometimes they foretell future events, so that the dreaming person may take precautions. I'm quite taken with this idea."

FROM MANDWA, we board a bus that takes us through farms and small residential communities to Alibag, where Cassim and I began our journey. The bus leaves us at the depot in the center of town. From here, we are not certain how to get to Revdanda. We approach a rickshaw driver, who points in the direction of a tea stall across the street, where passengers bound in different directions are piling into six-seater rickshaws.

It takes about an hour to reach Revdanda from Alibag, as the heat of midmorning begins to rise, foreshadowing the coming discomfort of noon. The road takes a series of twists and becomes more densely populated with trees and vines; I am struck by how green everything is, greener than any place I have seen in India thus far. Periodically, a new bungalow can be seen through gaps in the foliage, sometimes a glimpse of an old farmhouse. The road is littered with the occasional coconut. Three young boys, their arms linked around each other's waists, walk toward a tiny, dusty temple. From time to time, I notice makeshift stalls set up by the side of the road: a tarp held up with tall sticks, shielding a table with a cash box and an attendant, two or three animal carcasses hanging from the roof.

As we move farther from Bombay, Rekhev and I settle into a comfortable silence. I watch as he calmly and quickly takes in his surroundings in each new place, occasionally jotting something down in his notebook. There is an effortlessness between us that I have not experienced with him before, and I feel fond of him, grateful for his presence. It would be difficult for me to make this journey on my own; I see that now. When his hair falls into his eyes, I fight the temptation to tuck it behind his ear.

The remainder of a large fortress wall marks the entrance to Revdanda, where the driver lets us off.

I notice a small flat stone embedded in the mossy ruin that reads: "On this site stood a monastery built by the Portuguese in AD 1510."

"Rekhev, this may have been a walled city once," I say excitedly, "a kind of fort. Look at the circular ring of rocks."

"We are close to the sea, to the port of Chaul," Rekhev says, examining the wall. "This must have been an important place at one time. . . ."

The Portuguese history of Revdanda is otherwise invisible. The main commercial area of the town is centered on a long main street, with a vegetable market at one end and small shops, each a small cubicle of space, occupying rows on either side. The vendors' shops have sets of double doors that open to the street, showing their wares. As we pass through, I peer into a tailor's shop; a grocer with bags of rice, tea, and cold drinks; a mechanic; and even a small restaurant. For reasons that are not clear to me, I feel instantly content here. Rekhev and I walk along the street and stop in a small stall to have tea. An old man in a cotton dhoti crouches in the entrance, frying onion *bhujias* in a wide, low black vat of oil. He looks at us and nods, and we sit at one of the two tables.

"There's something about this place," Rekhev says, watching the street.

"I agree—I can't put my finger on it."

"I have a good feeling," he says.

Rekhev smiles, which catches me off guard. I have become used to his scowls.

"Why are you smiling?" I ask.

"A donkey just passed the tea shop from the right and brayed—did you hear it?"

"I suppose. I wasn't paying attention."

"It's a very good omen for the start of a journey," he says, laughing. "Forgive me, I've been reading too many of these folktales."

I realize that I have never heard him laugh before; it's a convivial, warm sound that makes me feel like laughing, too.

After tea, we walk toward a group of rickshaw drivers who watch our approach with interest and curiosity. Rekhev asks them if they know David Waskar.

"Da-veed?" they say. "Da-veed Waskar?"

We nod in agreement. One of them volunteers to take us, explaining that the Waskars live in a nearby village. It will be twenty rupees to go there; are we willing to pay? We nod and get into his rickshaw.

The road to the Waskars' village is covered on both sides with thick green foliage: tall grasses, low brambles, and coconut trees. After several minutes along a narrow road, we come to what must be the center of the village, and Revdanda feels like a bustling metropolis in comparison. There is a tiny stall where a proprietor has just enough room to lean out over a waist-high partition to sell penny candy and homemade biscuits to children who have just finished school. Most people sit in open doors, facing the activity of the street, talking with those who walk along the road on their way home. The occasional bicycle passes down the lane, ringing a bell to alert those in its path. A bored-looking woman fetches water from her well, dropping a bucket down and waiting for the noise of wood hitting water before she lifts it up again.

We stop in front of a house where a woman is sitting on her heels, her arms resting on either knee. I practice my elementary Hindi, trying to sound natural.

"David Waskar khidar hai?" Where is David Waskar?

"Here, naturally," she says. "Where else would he be?" She waves us ahead.

After driving a few more hundred meters, we pass two men on a scooter. Rekhev leans out and asks them if they know David Waskar.

"Know him?" the driver of the scooter says. "Everyone knows him. Go to the end of the lane." His friend makes a forward motion with his arm. "It's a big house, you'll see it."

The lane narrows, and at a turn toward its end we see a blue house set in a compound, with two adjacent buildings. At the top of each building is a Star of David, carefully carved and painted. There can be no mistake.

"This is it, Rekhev," I say.

We get out of the rickshaw and walk gingerly into the yard. There is a strange sound, a kind of seesawing song, coming from behind the building on our right. An old man wearing a dark blue cloth cap, a sleeveless shirt, and shorts emerges. He appears to be in his early seventies, but walks with a sprightly step. His eyes are unmistakably bright, as if he is perpetually amused. He looks at us and stops singing. I feel an eerie sense of the familiar.

"*Shalom!*" I call out. "*Aap David Waskar hain?* Are you David Waskar?"

His face breaks into a deep, wide smile.

"*Haan,*" he says, laying a hand on his heart. "I am David Waskar. *Shalom.*"

I introduce Rekhev, and he explains the purpose of our visit, that we have come to find out if there are any Bene Israel who still make and sell oil in this area. I'm surprised, and a little pleased, to see how adept Rekhev is at making an instant connection with the man. I see how he speaks deferentially, even affectionately, to the older man, and how the man responds.

"You've come all the way from Bombay to find *us*?" he says, laughing, and we tell him yes.

"Come, come," he says, putting his hand on Rekhev's back. "You are my guests, come and sit. The electricity is shut off now for the afternoon, but it will come on after some time. Rest awhile and drink something."

He places two plastic chairs underneath a large tree for us to sit on and squats on the ground nearby, where he takes a machete and slices open a coconut. He fetches two glasses from the inside of his house and pours the coconut milk into the glasses. We thank him for his kindness and drink the sweet liquid, surveying the compound. There are three buildings and a wooden shed surrounding a large yard, where a deep trough of brown seeds are laid out to dry. Behind us, two bulls stand in their pen, placidly chewing tall grasses. Several chickens wander by our feet, picking at scraps and occasionally letting out a squawk. Two carpenters sit on the ground of the woodshed, planing logs. In the center of the compound is a large, hand-made wooden swing held up with iron fasteners bolted into an old, knobby tree. It's a peaceful place; the only passing traffic is two girls in school uniforms riding by on matching bicycles.

"I love this house," Rekhev says to me.

A strong-looking young man with a mustache emerges from one of the buildings and sits on the swing, looking at us with friendly curiosity.

"My son," David says. "Benja. Benjamin."

We say hello and shake hands, apologizing for arriving unannounced.

"It's nothing," Benjamin says, smiling. "You're most welcome."

Three small children, two tiny dark-headed boys who look about five years old and a girl of about seven, run out of the house to stare at us.

"Tell them your names!" David says, and the little boys smile and hide behind the older girl. "Who are you?" he asks them. The children twist their little bodies in shyness, afraid to speak up.

Finally, one of the little boys raises his head and chants a high, singsong recitation of his name, village, and district, as he has clearly been taught to do in school.

"My name is Siyon Ellis Waskar, staying in Revdanda, Bazaar Pada, Ustancha Ustan, Alibag, Jillah Raigad."

"Very good!" David Waskar says. "That was good! And you two?"

"My name is Eleizabeth Benjamin Waskar, staying in Revdanda, Bazaar Pada, Ustancha Ustan, Alibag, Jillah Raigad," says the little girl. She has a husky voice, as if her age belies her true personality.

"Elan?" he says, trying to catch the attention of the smaller boy. "Elan?"

But Elan won't speak. He runs from behind his sister to behind a nearby tree to avoid the task, and we laugh.

"Foolishness!" David says, then turns his attention to us. "My grandchildren. Siyon, Eleiza, Elan." A little boy, perhaps just over a year old, stumbles out of the house and across the courtyard toward his grandfather. He has clearly just learned how to walk, and seems surprised that he has the ability to move himself from one location to another.

"Ah!" David says, amused. "Israel!" He scoops up the child in his lap, and the baby adroitly straddles David's knee, his tiny fat legs hanging down on either side, watching us.

"His name is Israel?" I ask.

"His name is Israel," David says. "We have named him Israel."

"How many of you are there in your family?" I ask, and Rekhev translates.

"I had two wives, but one is no more," David says. "Two sons are here, Benjamin and Ellis, and their wives and children. I have two sons here, two in Israel. And me. David Waskar. Hindus call me Da-veed, Muslims call me Da-wood. Da-veed, Da-wood." David Waskar smiles at the thought. "What to do, I am an Israel Jew. Anyway, I have no problems here. I am friends with everyone. People respect me a lot. They should, we have been here a long time."

David speaks Hindi tinged with Marathi, the local language of this province, and he speaks it very fast. Rekhev doesn't speak Marathi and tells me under his breath that he finds David's accent difficult to understand. "He's

fascinating, though, don't you think?" he asks me quietly, and I can tell that
he's intrigued by their conversation.

"How long have the Jews been here in your village?" I ask.

"Oh, that's an old story. Many, many years. There was a ship. It came
from Israel; it took a month to get here. Now it takes only five, six hours on
a jet airplane. My wife can tell you—she has just come back from there on
a visit. But back then it took a month. Over a month. And then there was a
shipwreck. We landed here, we began to make oil, we sold it in carts from
village to village. People called us *teli,* oil presser. They thought we were low-
caste; they didn't know we were Jews. Still, we got along with everyone. The
problems of the Hindus and Muslims are not our problems."

"Do you still make oil?"

"We make the oil all year, and then my wife and I go and sell it. It is difficult now, now people buy oil in a shop, and they are not as used to buying
our oil, but I still do it. I go to very small villages where they need it. I enjoy
it—traveling on the bullock cart, seeing the different places. I enjoy the
travel a lot. But then I enjoy coming home a lot, too. God has blessed me. I
have a good family, a hardworking family. Whatever we grow, or we sell, we
eat. Nothing more. God has given me enough, and I am grateful."

"I want to show you something," I say, taking out a book of Bene Israel
history from my bag. "Do you know these people?" I show him the picture
of two women sitting on an old oil press, with two bullocks in the background.

"*Mustt!*" David says—"Wow!"—shaking his head in astonishment. "She
is our cousin! She has gone to Israel. This one, too, she has gone to Israel.
We have not seen them in so long, and now they are in a book? *Mustt.*
Where did the book come from, from Bombay?"

"No, from America," I say.

"*Amreeka se?*" he says, surprised. "*Mustt.*"

David calls his wife to come and see the photograph, and she walks
slowly out of one of the buildings, scratching her head and looking annoyed. Her hair is slightly unkempt, as if she must have been taking an afternoon nap. David quickly explains who we are and that we have brought

a book about the Bene Israel all the way from America, a book that has their cousin in it. Mrs. Waskar looks at the photograph, then at us, in astonishment. She turns the book over and looks at the spine, marveling at it and talking rapidly, her voice rising. The younger women of the house, the wives of the two Waskar sons, come into the courtyard to see what all the fuss is about. The two women appear to be about the same age, in their midtwenties, and are dressed in floral-print housedresses. One woman is lean, with a handsome, kind face. The other is shorter, with rounder, softer features and a quick smile.

"What's happening?" says the shorter one, tucking Baby Israel under one arm.

Mrs. Waskar passes them the book, and each looks at the picture, pointing to the page and presumably talking about the two women in the photograph. Ellis, David's other son, ambles up the path to find the group gathered around the book. He is stockier than his brother Benjamin, and slightly less interested in the book, but he dutifully looks at the picture and at us and nods his greeting.

"Do you still press oil in this way?" Rekhev asks.

"This part is the same," David says, pointing to the base of the press, a round drum. "But we no longer use the bulls to turn the press."

"How do you turn it now?"

David raises his eyebrows and wiggles his head from side to side.

"*Yeh* mechanic *hain*," he says proudly. "It's mechanic."

David leads us inside one of the buildings. It is a small, dark space with a packed mud floor and a thatched roof. The oil press sits in one corner of the room, flanked by an antique-looking rocking chair and bales of hay. The press is a large, mysterious-looking object that consists of a deep tray filled with seeds and a log protruding from the center of the tray, which is rotated by a motor to mash the seeds.

"How does it work?" I ask, and just then a bare bulb above our heads turns on, seemingly of its own volition.

"The electricity has started again!" David exclaims suddenly. "Come, I'll show you how we make oil."

David turns a switch on the wall, and the press lurches into motion. The log begins to turn in circles, pressing seeds against the walls of the container and making a brown mash. David squats and jams a stick repeatedly in a hole at the base of the press to free the passage of debris and make way for the oil. Once the passage is clear, a thick, opaque beige liquid is expressed and collected in a tin receptacle. Later, he tells us, this liquid will be strained and refined before being sold.

I take some pictures of the oil press and shoot some video of David making oil.

"How long have you been making this oil?" I ask him.

"My father, and his father, and his father before him. Jews have made this oil as long as we have been in India. *Teli* means 'oil presser.' Shaniwar means 'Saturday.' The local people used to call us "Saturday Oil Pressers," the oil pressers who did not work on Saturday. This is an old story," he says, shaking his head. "I have become an old man listening to old men tell this story. . . . Now we're the only ones left who know how to make oil in this way. After my sons, I don't think anyone else will do it. My sons don't want to teach their children to make it."

"Why is that?" Rekhev asks.

"College!" David says in a booming voice. "They want college for their children, to go to Israel when they are grown." He wags his head back and forth to emphasize his point, and returns his attention to the press, gathering fistfuls of the mashed-up seeds in his hand and throwing them into the center of the well to be crushed again.

"How many books have I read?" David asks me, as if I am being quizzed. "Two books," David says, smiling. "I'm not literate; I didn't have money to study." David puts his hand on his head to mime wearing a hat. "Wear a cap, then go to study. Where was the money for the cap?" He laughs. "Even still, look what a life I have had. I have worked here, I have worked in Bombay. What times I have seen! I have good children. They work hard; whatever we make, we eat. We take care of the *masjid,* and Benjamin has learned some Hebrew. God has been kind to me. Come! Let's have tea. I'll tell you more."

David nimbly gets up and walks outside to sit on a *charpoy,* a wooden-framed, string-laced bed heaped with old clothes, swooping down to place Baby Israel on his lap. He asks his wife to make tea.

"How long were you in Bombay?" Rekhev asks as we pull up two plastic chairs.

"I worked there nine years. I was a young man then. I made seven rupees a month, then fifteen rupees a month, and I would send it to my parents. They used to show it to everyone in the village, show them that their son had sent fifteen rupees. These are the kind of days I have gone through. . . ."

"Those days were good, or these days are good?" Rekhev asks.

"These days are good!" David says vehemently. "I earned little by little. Then I got married to my first wife. We didn't have any children, so I married a second wife. Then both wives got children. What to do? I was already married to both." David laughs at the thought. "Then we all lived together. Two sons have gone to Israel, two have stayed; my daughter is in Bombay. Most of the Jews have gone to Israel, only four or five of us are left in the area. There are five Jews in my village. In Chaul there is one man, and eight kilometers after that there is one man. We meet at Eid."

"Rekhev, he said Eid?" I ask, surprised that he would use the Muslim name for the holiday that marks the end of Ramadan, the month of fasting. Rekhev asks him what he means and clarifies that David is using the term as a catchall for the High Holidays. Then he bursts into a long monologue about Muslims that I don't understand.

"Now that so few Jews are left, will you stay here, or move to Israel?" Rekhev asks.

"Somehow, I have this feeling that we should stay here," David says, looking at his compound. "If we go, who will take care of the *masjid,* of the graveyard? My first wife's grave is there. I don't want to leave her behind. Israel is my fatherland, but India is my motherland."

"What about your grandchildren?" I ask, looking at Israel. "Will Israel stay in India, or will Israel move to Israel someday?"

David looks at Israel, who is staring up at him.

"If he wants to go he can go," David says softly. "If he wants to stay he can stay."

Israel grunts in response, and David laughs, bouncing him on his knee.

"Right? Let the people who want to go, go! You can stay here! With me!"

Mrs. Waskar brings us tea in three piping-hot chipped cups and hands David a plate with several tablets on it, which she instructs him to take.

He gives her a begrudging look and winks at us.

"My wife is trying to kill me with medicine!" he says, teasing her. "She complains about me, but she would be sad if I went before her, isn't it!"

Mrs. Waskar shoots back a shrill retort in Marathi before returning to the kitchen. David winks at us conspiratorially.

"I ENJOYED THIS TRIP," Rekhev says to me in the six-seater rickshaw back to Alibag at the end of the day. "It's so different here from where I grew up; it's as foreign for me as it is for you. You've been invited back, by the way. In September. For some kind of festival. David was going on about some kind of hut they make, with lots of dancing and smashing of fruit."

"Sukkot and Simchat Torah!" I say. "It must be. It's the harvest time. Jews construct a sukkah, a temporary structure outside of their homes and synagogues, to commemorate the forty years the Jewish people spent wandering, and they spend time in it for seven days. Then, on Simchat Torah, there's rejoicing in the synagogue, they celebrate the completion of the annual cycle of Torah readings. . . ." Suddenly it seems necessary that Rekhev come with me when I return to Revdanda; I can't imagine coming back without him. "Will you come with me?"

Rekhev looks straight ahead, as if he is thinking over what I have suggested.

"I don't think so," he says. I feel a twinge of something, of disappointment.

"So what did he say about the Muslims?" I ask, trying to change the subject.

"Oh, it's very interesting. It had nothing to do with the Israeli-Palestinian conflict—perhaps you thought it did."

"I was wondering."

"He seemed mostly unaware of it, in fact. No, his trouble with Muslims was some theory of his about how they marry their brothers' children. According to him, it's proper for a Bene Israel man to marry his father's sister's children, but not his father's brother's children. He got very upset about it. I've read some anthropology—kinship patterns and that sort of thing. It reminds me of that."

"But that's the reason he doesn't like Muslims?" I ask. "It seems like there must be more to it."

"Of course there is," Rekhev says. "Sadia, the relationships between different communities in India, they're not as simple as your family has made it seem to you growing up. I like your story, growing up with three religions, learning about these different paths. It's a very American idea. But, frankly, I am closer to understanding David Waskar, who is from a region and a religion that is foreign to me. . . ." Rekhev gestures at the landscape outside the rickshaw. "I know nothing about Revdanda. But these prejudices, growing up with a fear of the man next to you, I understand that. I may have had Muslim friends as a child, I may have grown up with people of all castes and all communities, but when I used to come home from school at night my mother would get angry if she found out that I had eaten dinner in a classmate's home."

"Why is that?"

"Because we are Brahmins. And that's the way we were raised, to keep apart. Even now, that old bias stays with me. I don't believe in it, but it's ingrained in me somewhere. I have a very difficult time eating in friends' homes. You and I, I'm not sure that we will ever be able to be friends, not in the way you want."

"Why not?"

"You have an idea about India, you want to find something here that is going to make you more complete. Somehow, you've decided that I am a part of that plan, that I can teach you things. You have an idealized concept of friendship. I have no such illusions. The whole notion of your work here is predicated on the idea of a search. I don't actually believe that you are searching."

"Of course I am. . . ."

"I think that when you were growing up you were not actually very confused about who you were. But confusion is a natural impetus for a journey, and so you have entered a state of confusion. What you are seeking, in fact, is not greater clarity but greater disorder."

I look out the window at the tall grasses whipping by our rickshaw, trying to figure out how to respond.

"Don't you think that if I am compelled to take this journey—seeking disorder, as you say—then experiencing confusion is a necessary stage? If I am not here seeking something, some greater understanding, then why do you think I'm here?"

"It's a surface understanding, what you want, and you'll get it. You will work hard, and you will get these people to accept you, and you will photograph them and tell their story, and you will return to the world you came from and feel proud of yourself."

"How can you say that?" I ask, feeling a sharp rise of anger. "You don't know anything about me or the world I come from."

"Perhaps not. But I know something. You will spend months and years unraveling the questions that you've muddled into here. Some of these questions you haven't even formed yet; you cannot imagine them. There will come a time when you'll want to do simpler work. You will feel this acutely, many times."

"You're telling me not to give up."

"I'm telling you that something about your story, about your grandmother, affects me, and that is why, against my better judgment, I'm helping you. You are ambitious and you want to do good work. I like that."

"So will you come back with me, to the harvest festival?" I ask, feeling bold.

Rekhev shuts his eyes for a moment.

"This is why I don't make friends," Rekhev says.

"Why?" I ask.

"People always leave. Books are much more reliable."

17

JEWS AND INDIANS

BOMBAY, APRIL 2002

Magen David Synagogue of Byculla stands like a relic, a great, faded yellow old lady by the side of Sir J.J. Road. Built by the Baghdadi Jewish community leader David Sassoon in 1861, it was enlarged and renovated to accommodate the then thriving Jewish community of Baghdad, many of whom relocated to Bombay in the mid-nineteenth century. I have read about the difficult relationship between the Baghdadi community and the Bene Israel. In their early years in India, the Baghdadis, lighter in skin tone and more European in their manners, felt more culturally aligned with the British and distanced themselves from the Bene Israel. But in recent decades, as numbers in both communities have decreased, the gulf between them has diminished, and the two groups now share synagogues and celebrations.

I walk in the gate and look up at the Gothic structure, four frontal pillars holding up the edifice, supporting a long, tall spindle. It's imposing and impressive. The interior of the synagogue is dark; the pews are covered in protective cloths, and the lights are off. I wonder if anyone is here.

"Who is it?" comes a woman's voice from a side chamber of the synagogue, on my left.

I pass through a door and find an older woman fanning herself with a newspaper, her cheeks slick with sweat. She has pale pink skin and is wearing a flowered housedress that billows around her frame like a curtain, her remaining strands of white hair tied into a tight bun. She is surrounded by the sedentary layers of many years: stacks of books, folding chairs, old papers. Her cot is visible in the background, and I realize that this room might be her home. Perhaps I am intruding.

"Are you the caretaker here?"

"I am, by the grace of God," she says. "Flora. Sit down, I can't see you."

I pull up a folding chair and bring it close to hers. She looks at me closely.

"You've come to see the synagogue?"

"I'd like to take some pictures, if I could."

"You come from Israel? America?"

"America," I tell her. "But my grandmother was a Bene Israel, from Bombay."

"Ah, so you've come back. What was your grandmother's name?"

"Rachel Jacobs. She was raised in Thane, Pune, then eventually here."

"This was when, child?"

"This would have been in the thirties, the forties—before Partition."

"I knew a Flossie Jacobs. Was she related to Flossie?"

"I'm not sure. She had a sister named Lizzie. . . ."

"I knew Flossie. Flossie was a very pretty girl, got married, moved to Israel. I haven't seen her in thirty years. But, then, I haven't seen my own children in almost ten. What's your name, then?"

"My name is Sadia."

"Muslim name."

"My grandmother married a Muslim."

She pauses for a moment, considering her response.

"I'm a Baghdadi Jew; you know, we came from Iraq two hundred years ago. Baghdadis built Bombay, you know: Gateway of India, Flora Fountain, these were built by Baghdadis. The British were very good to us; things worked properly then. Now there are very few of my community left. . . ."

"Your family is here with you?"

"Here? No. My children are in Israel. The people here are good to me, give me a place to stay; people come to visit the synagogue, they give me fifty rupees so I can buy sugar for my tea. Muhammad and I are otherwise alone here. You want the lights turned on so you can take pictures? Muhammad, are you there?"

A man in a rumpled tan uniform appears, his Nehru-style cap resting precariously on his head like a deflated balloon. Over his shirt pocket is an embroidered "M." He looks at the floor and removes his hat quickly.

"Show the girl the synagogue, turn the lights on for her, all that," Flora says.

I walk into the hall and marvel at the size of the place. This synagogue must have been built to house quite a large congregation at one time. I take some pictures of the empty space, but I am much more interested in Flora and Muhammad. After a few minutes, I slip back into the side hall, where Flora is fanning herself with an old calendar.

"Blasted heat," Flora says, as I sit down across from her.

Muhammad appears a few minutes later with three small hot glasses of tea. He places a little side table by Flora and sets down a scrap of old newspaper on it. He fishes out four biscuits from a tea tin and places them on the newspaper, motioning for me to take one. Flora looks pleased and accepts her tea glass quickly. She blows into the tiny chamber, then tips the glass back and sucks the liquid between her teeth slowly.

Muhammad drinks his tea standing at the room's edge, looking out at the courtyard, both inside the room and outside of it. I wonder how many times a day they repeat this ritual, and for how many years they have been living like this; invisible people, side by side.

"How many Baghdadis are there left in Bombay, Auntie? Do you have services here in the synagogue anymore?"

"Most everyone has left. To make a minyan the directors call on the Bene

Israel men. Some of my congregation wouldn't have heard of such a thing back then. But people all get along now, there are not too many Jews left."

"What about your relationship with the Muslim community? The synagogue is surrounded by a Muslim neighborhood—do you feel safe here where there is violence in Israel?"

The Israeli Defense Force's Operation Defensive Shield has been escalating in recent days, and the news is filled with reports of casualties on both sides; I wonder to what extent the local Muslim population feels a connection with the Palestinians.

"The problems in Israel are not our problems here. We Jews in India have had good relations with the Muslims, and they with us. During the Six-Day War, do you know there was rioting in the streets here in Byculla? We were very afraid of looters. The Muslims from the neighborhood wanted to make sure that no one would harm our synagogue. They joined hands and made a wall of their bodies across the gate of the synagogue, so that no one could get in. 'This is a house of God,' they said. I will never forget the kindness of the Muslims that day."

"How many synagogues do you think have Muslim caretakers?" I ask. "In the world, I mean. It must be very rare."

"India is the only place it's possible. Here Jews and Muslims are both minorities. We're both settled in India, isn't it? Jews have experienced no anti-Semitism here. Not by the Hindus, not by the Muslims, not by the British. No, the British were very good to us."

I WALK UP the long staircase of ORT and greet teachers and students as I go. The school feels familiar now, like a home base of sorts. My students have returned from Israel with high, excited voices—enthusiastic streams of stories about where they went, what they saw.

"Did you perform the play?"

"It was a huge success, Miss Sadia! First-class!"

They tell me about how they practiced their lines on the bus that took them between religious sites and the college campuses they were staying in, how they would call out the lines to one another, chiding those who forgot their parts. They tell me how two lines of the play became a kind of cheer for their trip, repeated over and over again: "Who are we?" someone from the front of the bus would call, and one group would respond, "We are both Indians and Jews!" And another, "Jews and Indians!"

I poke my head into Benny Isaacs's office on the second floor to see if he has time to meet with me. I have with me a copy of my grandmother's family tree, two mimeographed sheets taped together.

"Ah yes . . ." he says, poring over the paper eagerly and offering me a seat. "The Jacobs boys, your grandmother's brothers. They were my mother's first cousins, and she was very fond of them. They were a spirited lot, you know. She used to tell me stories about them, how they used to dress up and play tricks on one another. . . . We used to visit Rahat Villa sometimes; I remember playing on the veranda as a very small boy."

"What about this branch of the family tree?" I ask. "Is there anyone else familiar on it?"

Benny Isaacs takes another look, and I see his eyes light up with curiosity.

"So!" he says. "Look at that—seems you're related to Mhedeker!"

"Who is Mhedeker?" I ask.

"Oh, he's a very big man in the community, very big indeed. He's the president of Magen Hassidim Synagogue, the biggest Bene Israel synagogue in Bombay. His family came down here from Karachi after Partition. Quite a story, in fact—rags to riches. Now he's a very successful businessman, has given a lot to the community. You should meet him."

On the fifth floor I find Sharon, one of the ORT Jewish educators who helped me with the play, sitting with a ten-year-old boy. He is instructing him in Hebrew, and I listen in on their conversation. The boy sits across from Sharon with an open notebook, trying to form Hebrew letters and sound them out.

"Good, that's good. Now try it again. . . ." he says.

The boy starts again, and Sharon turns to me.

"You want to sit in on my class, Sadia?" he asks, smiling.

"Sure," I say, and sit down to watch them work.

People have told me that Sharon used to be quite liberal, secular even. He was a student of chemistry and not particularly religious. Then, in his early twenties, he began to study Judaism and became more observant. He's now one of the more fastidious younger members of the Bene Israel community. He wears a long black beard and a perennial *kippah* on his head, and he works to promote Jewish knowledge in the community, much of which he learned in yeshiva in Jerusalem. Yet something about Sharon's easy manner helps me not feel judged or uncomfortable, the way that I sometimes feel around pious people. His faith seems to be a personal matter that he's happy to share with others, if they're interested.

When the boy returns to his notebook, Sharon turns to me.

"Sadia, when are you coming to my home for Shabbat dinner? My wife, Sharona, and I supervise the ORT boys' hostel, in Byculla. We have a large place, and we often have people come for Shabbat, for holidays. Perhaps you might have some questions, or just want to talk. Please feel welcome in our home."

"Thank you, Sharon," I say gratefully. "I've been wanting to learn more about Shabbat. Sharon, your wife's name is Sharona?" I ask.

"Yes," he says, smiling.

"And you're both Jewish educators?"

"Yes."

"What a nice match you found!"

"I'm very lucky," he says, nodding. "You know, we have found over time that Shabbat is not a hindrance for us, it is a kind of gift. Often during the week we don't have time for more than five minutes to spend together. On Shabbat we can spend time together, talking, playing with our daughter. We enjoy it. Shabbat can be fun, a chance to be together. To pray, yes, but also to discuss, to enjoy each other's company."

"I look forward to it," I say, and find that I mean it.

THE FOLLOWING WEEK, I am back in Bombay traffic on my way to Magen Hassidim Synagogue, to meet Mr. Mhedeker. When I reach the densely populated neighborhood of Agripada, I glimpse families living in crowded, cubicle-sized rooms above rows of shops. Unlike the subdued residential area where I live, here the street littered is with paper, the air is filled with the smell of roasting meat. Street carts wend their way between the cars, offering cups of crushed ice, colored bright green and red with syrup. Each lane features a different specialty. In one, a row of paper vendors sell stacks of discarded newspaper bundled with twine. In another, a shiny row of gold merchants weigh their wares on scales. Boys of twelve and thirteen play cricket in the street, their balls rolling underneath the parked cars. Women, some in colorful saris, others in black burqas, walk through the streets with white plastic bags of vegetables hanging from their elbows. Men watch them as they pass, smoking cigarettes or chewing *paan,* which they spit out in bright streams into the thin, full gutter—a red rivulet winding its way through the neighborhood.

When I walk through the synagogue gate, it is surprising to enter the spacious, walled courtyard and be instantly surrounded by quiet. Magen Hassidim is a large structure and quite beautiful, with separate sections for the women to sit upstairs and the men downstairs. People have told me that this synagogue is the most desirable location for a Bene Israel wedding to take place, and that on High Holidays the large hall is packed to capacity, with standing room only in the back. I am greeted and ushered inside the main door by a man who won't shake my hand; he must be Orthodox, I realize. Inside the office I find a very tall, imposing-looking gentleman who is presumably Mr. Mhedeker, sitting behind a large desk. He has salt-and-pepper hair cropped closely to his head and a trim pencil mustache, and he nods at me when I enter, indicating that I should sit down next to his desk.

A boy produces biscuits, tea, and a bottle of mango nectar, which he places in front of me. Mr. Mhedeker offers me a biscuit from the plate, and I bite into one eagerly, wanting to show my gratitude for his hospitality.

He lifts one up and closes his eyes, praying before he takes a bite.

"I'm sorry," I say quickly. "I should have waited for you to pray."

He shakes his head to reassure me that he doesn't mind.

"So. Benny Isaacs tells me you're doing research?" he asks.

I place my family tree in front of him and point to the section that Benny had noticed.

"I understand that you are related to the former jailer of Karachi? Who was a Bene Israel? See here, he was my great-grandfather's brother. . . ."

"Is that so? The jailer was my grandfather! He served the British; our family was in Karachi for generations. We were quite well established there."

"And you grew up there?" I ask. "Before you decided to come to Bombay, I mean?"

"I did not make the decision!" he says forcefully, and then calms himself. "I will tell you."

Mr. Mhedeker leans his body back in his chair comfortably and begins to talk. I take out my notebook and pen.

"I was raised in Karachi," he starts, "when it was a part of India. This was before Partition. In Sindh we had a very big farm—eighty-five to ninety mango trees, apples, limes—it was a big business. We used to have a camel cart, and we would sell to the wholesale market. We had our own building in Karachi. We were very happy there. Then Partition happened. I was thirteen years old. In 1947, everything changed."

"Were you asked to leave Pakistan?"

"There was no asking. Two hundred people came to my house. They had come from India. They said to my mother: We have lost everything, we have left everything behind. You go on now. Go to India. Whatever is on your body is yours. This is our house now."

"They were refugees?"

"They were people who had lost their homes. My mother said, 'How can I go? This is my house, I have small children here. . . .'" Mr. Mhedeker shakes his head at the memory. "They said, 'We have lost everything, now this is ours.' My mother reached for her cupboard, where she kept her cash, and a man stopped her. He said, 'Madam, please close the door. We have told you; whatever is on your body is yours. We will not harm you, but you go now. If you reach for the cupboard again, what is on your body will also become our property. You go now.' "

"And so you left. . . ."

"Within ten minutes we had become beggars. My mother gathered us children up, and somehow we got to a boat—I don't know how she did it. We came to Bombay by ship. We went to my auntie's house, and we stayed here with the Jewish community. At that time there were full buildings of Jews here—this whole area was filled with Bene Israel."

"What did you do when you arrived in Bombay?"

"Our position was very bad. We had no money. In those days, I used to take my shirt and pant to be darned. The darning man would say: How can I darn these clothes? They have been patched too many times. I left school at sixteen years old and worked in a toothbrush factory. I made two rupees, eight annas per day. I was thinking as I made the toothbrushes that I have to become a big man; I had this in my mind. I wanted to become a business-man. I was not so religious at that time. I thought to myself, 'What has God given us? We had our lives in Karachi, and he took all of that away. Why?' Then my brother's wife told me to come to the synagogue for New Year's prayers. I said to her, 'Why? God has forgotten us.' She said, No, you must go. I said, 'How can I go? I have nothing but these old clothes to wear, one shirt and one pant.' My brother's wife was a wonderful lady. She provided new clothes for me to go to the synagogue, new clothes for the new year, and I began to go for prayers. I was twenty-two or twenty-three at the time. Day by day, God has helped me. Everything in my life began to change when I started coming to the synagogue."

"How did you go from that time to being a successful businessman?"

"I began to sell chocolate, handkerchiefs, from a basket on the road. I sold them for eight annas, twelve annas. Then, with one hundred borrowed rupees, I began to sell toothbrushes. After some time I thought to myself, 'I must have my own factory.' This was in 1964. I took on a small place, where I made a toothbrush machine. I had an idea of how to do it from working in the factory. In two years' time, I had it. It was the first toothbrush machine made in India. Before that, toothbrushes were all imported—from London, Germany. I began to export toothbrushes also. To Russia, to Israel, to Dubai. Two hundred people worked for me. There were different units in the factory—the toothbrush unit, plastic molding, sealing and cutting, bristling machine, trimming machine, packing. My company was called Menorah Industries. I sold these toothbrushes like hotcakes, I tell you."

"Will you go to Israel?" I ask. "Do you plan to migrate there?"

"I have one son in Toronto, three daughters in Israel. I have thought about going, but my life is here. I became president of Magen Hassidim twenty-eight years ago. As president, my duty is to look after the synagogue, property, marriages—so many decisions. Maximum weddings take place here—I would say fifty weddings take place in Magen Hassidim per year. We have one coming up in a few weeks."

"I think I know the bride, Leah—she was one of my students at ORT. Who is she marrying?"

"Young man who is settled in Israel. They will go there after the marriage. You'll see." Mr. Mhedeker pauses for a moment, as if he is thinking over a final point. "In India we are happy. But there are very few Jewish businesses now, so there are fewer job opportunities for our youths. Now, by the grace of God, call centers have come up. So our young people are working there. El Al Airlines is there, they are working there also. But mostly they are migrating to Israel. Young Bene Israel are saying, 'In Foreign, we get more salary.' Every week, a family is migrating to Israel."

"What will Magen Hassidim be like in twenty, thirty years?"

"It will be like an antique. Like a museum. Like in Cochin, in Kerala. Like the synagogue there. The government will protect it."

"Do you still think about Karachi? Do you remember the synagogue there?"

"Ah, the synagogue was very beautiful. I remember it was bigger than this; so many people used to come for holidays. After Partition, the leader of Pakistan, General Zia, said, 'I will destroy this building.' He was anti-Israel. The Jewish people, the few who were left, said, 'Let's make a library, so that the building will remain.' 'No,' he said. He would not listen. He crushed it.

And within three months his plane crashed. General Zia was in pieces, just like he crushed the synagogue. You ask anyone—this is true."

Mr. Mhedeker shakes his head with regret.

"I will stay in India," he says suddenly, as if he is in the middle of a thought. "My people need me here. They will not let me go."

18

WHICH CASTE

BOMBAY, MAY 2002

As usual, I have not allowed enough time to cross town in rush-hour traffic. My taxi struggles across Nana Chowk, past Bhatia Hospital, through Tardeo, up toward Byculla. We are moving slowly through gridlock traffic, and I look nervously at my watch. It's ten past six. I am on my way to Sharon and Sharona's house for Shabbat dinner, and sundown is at six-thirty. I'm annoyed at myself for not leaving earlier. I should have known better. Outside my window, a man struggles to navigate his vegetable cart, a wide plank perched atop two large wooden wheels, between the tightly wedged cars, trying not to let too many of his tomatoes roll into oncoming traffic.

I watch the neighborhoods change. Just a few months ago, they would have looked equally foreign to me, would have read as one Bombay. Now some of the differences register. As we go, I notice how we move through affluent to less affluent areas, from predominantly Hindu areas to predominantly Muslim ones, and how as we go the shops and styles of dress change. The tinkle of temple bells is replaced with the crackling loudspeaker of the *azaan,* a sound I always associate with my childhood trips to Pakistan. Several days earlier, three Pakistani nationals dressed in Indian army uniforms carried out an attack on a cantonment near Jammu, where Rekhev is from originally. As a result, India has placed its military forces on high alert, and tension has increased between the two countries. Near J.J. Hospital, we pass Magen David, the old Baghdadi synagogue on our left, and I think of Flora and Muhammed inside.

I find the landmarks Sharon's wife told me on the phone to locate their apartment—the bridge, the petrol pump, the second petrol pump. Even though it is the end of the day, it is hot, and I am sweating. I wipe my upper lip with my dupatta. It's now just past six-thirty. I hate being late. I point to the building where I'd like the taxi driver to drop me, a large multistory building with shops on the ground floor. It's difficult to find the entrance. When I do find it, it looks more like a gap between buildings than the way inside. I ask a few young men lingering on the sidewalk, and they nod, indicating that this is the entrance. I check my watch again. I know that Sharon and Sharona have probably already lit their Shabbat candles and are wondering where I am.

As I pay the fare, the taxi driver asks me if I wouldn't rather go back to my hotel. I am sure he is more accustomed to dropping foreigners at the same handful of spots: the Taj Mahal Hotel, the Ambassador, the Oberoi shopping complex.

"I *live* in Bombay," I say in Hindi, by way of explanation, surprising myself.

"These are your relatives?" he asks, pointing at the building and looking doubtful.

"Yes," I say, to make things simpler.

I get out and try to affect a nonchalant look as young men standing in the street watch me. Their look is one of curiosity, laced with a kind of sneer. I can guess, but I'll never know, the exact source of their resentment. It's not an entirely comfortable feeling, but it no longer seems unusual.

I am dressed, as has become my custom, in a loose-fitting cotton salwar kameez and sandals. I have given up the idea of blending in. Instead, my clothes are an attempt to make it clear that I have made an effort, and that I am not leaving anytime soon. Many young Indian women in Bombay wear Western clothes, but in a pair of pants and a shirt I feel like a visitor. I want to make it clear that I am something else.

I walk up a long flight of wooden steps, passing a thin bench where a very old man is sleeping on a matted layer of blankets. Water pools in worn sections of the floor, and on one landing, incense emanates from a low burner, emitting a smoky odor. I wonder again if I am in the right place.

Several flights up, I reach a large door painted a deep blue and a dusty white. This has to be it. The ORT boys' hostel that Sharon and Sharona oversee is a large apartment reserved for young men who grew up outside of Bombay and are completing one of ORT's vocational programs. Now that more and more Bene Israel have left India for Israel, the hostel serves a grow-ing number of young men from the Bnei Menashe community, a small group from Manipur and Mizoram, in eastern India, who have been in the news recently for their claim that they, too, descended from one of the lost tribes of Israel.

I ring the doorbell but it doesn't seem to make a sound. I bang on the door, hoping that someone will be able to hear me. It seems that the main living area is somewhat removed from the front door, and it is well past six-thirty now; I fear that they are in the midst of their prayer. I recall that one of the forbidden actions is to "complete a circuit," and that doorbells are one of the things turned off after sundown. But what about answering the call of someone else ringing a doorbell? Is that forbidden also?

I rest my head on the milky glass panel embedded in the door, feeling suddenly exhausted, and wonder what I should do next.

Two little boys in Muslim-style prayer caps bound down the staircase, followed by a pretty young woman who must be their mother. She is wear-ing a long silk kaftan with pants and a matching dupatta over her head, a costume vaguely Arabic in style and one I recognize instantly as Muslim.

"Why don't you ring the doorbell?" she asks me kindly, in English.

"I've tried, but they don't seem to answer," I say, shrugging. "I've come

a long way, and I'm late. Do you know my friends Sharon and Sharona?"
I ask.

"I know who they are," she says, nodding. "There has been some work
going on in the building, so I have seen them when they come to collect
water from upstairs, or when repairs are going on. Upstairs is my granny's
flat. I live there with my boys." She points to the children.

"Your sons?" I ask.

"One is four and one is two," she says, with a hint of pride in her voice.
"The older one studies with a Qur'an teacher downstairs. What's your name?"
she asks.

"Sadia."

The young woman looks at me with recognition. "Muslim," she says,
smiling.

"Yes," I say. "What's your name?"

"Hajira."

"That's an auspicious name you have," I say, and she looks pleased. "Hajira" is the Islamic name for Hagar, Abraham's second wife and the mother
of Ishmael.

"Where are you from?" she asks.

"I'm from the States," I say, "but I have family in Pakistan also."

For some reason, I want to cement my status as a Muslim, so this young
woman will like me.

"Are you married?"

"No," I say. "I've got my family in Pakistan worried. . . ." I cup my hands
in a gesture of prayer, imitating one of my anxious aunties, and she smiles
with amusement.

"It will happen when the time is right. Maybe you should bang on the
door, louder, so they can hear you. Come, I will help you," she says, walking
to the door and banging loudly on the wood.

"They have their prayers on Friday night," I say. "I wonder if maybe they
can't hear me."

"We pray on Fridays, too," she says. "Come, let's bang louder."

We bang on the door in unison, beginning to laugh at our exertion. I watch Hajira's face, just a few inches from my own, and feel a flash of curiosity. I wonder what her life is like, when she got married, how often she leaves this building.

I see a female figure on the other side of the glass, and a woman opens the door.

"You are Sadia?" the woman asks. She must be Sharona, Sharon's wife.

"I'm sorry I'm late." I turn back toward Hajira. "Thank you, Hajira. *Khuda hafiz.*" May God protect you.

"Allah hafiz." She gives me a small wave and leads her sons down the stairs.

I enter and feel as if I am entering a different world. As in ORT, the walls are decorated with photographs and drawings of life in Israel. Sharona is a handsome woman with a headscarf wrapped around her head. There is an authoritative feeling about her manner; she is someone I would not want to disagree with.

"We were worried about what had happened to you!" Sharona says as she leads me down the hall toward her living room.

"I'm so sorry I'm late," I say. "There was traffic, and then I wasn't sure if you could answer the door on Shabbat. . . ."

"Who was that you were talking to?" she asks, turning around.

"A young woman from upstairs. I told her you have prayers on Friday; she said that they also have prayers on Friday."

"She's a Muslim," she says.

"Right. We had a nice conversation."

"She spoke English?" Sharona asks, looking doubtful.

"Perfectly."

"Did she wonder about why you didn't ring the doorbell?"

"I . . . did ring the doorbell. I wasn't sure if I was supposed to. Is it forbidden on Shabbat?"

"We don't use the doorbell on Shabbat. But for you . . . well, it's up to you, really. Do you observe Shabbat in America?"

"I'm just learning about Shabbat."

"You're Jewish?" she asks.

"It's a long story," I say.

"I love long stories," she says. "You can tell us over dinner. Come, my father-in-law is just starting prayers."

At one end of a long wooden table, Sharon's father, an older man in a dark blue cloth cap, recites the Hebrew prayers. Sharon blesses and drinks from a large goblet of kiddush wine, a handmade beverage from fermented raisins, and passes small glasses around the table. His small daughter sits on his lap. Sharona holds the cups to the little girl's lips, making sure that the juice does not stain her Shabbat dress, laughing at how eager she is to drink the sweet purple liquid.

Sharon leads the little girl in reciting a blessing over a plate of dates and bananas.

"Barukh ata Adonai . . . " Sharon says, pausing for his daughter to repeat after him.

"Barukh ata Adonai . . . " she repeats.

"Eloheinu melekh ha'olam . . . "

"Eloheinu melekh ha'olam!" she says excitedly.

Two loaves of challah bread rest underneath a white sateen cloth embroidered with Hebrew letters. Sharon, noticing that I don't know the words to the Shabbat songs, hands me a guide to the prayers, mercifully in English, and I am able to sing more confidently.

"I could sing all night," Sharona says when we have completed the first portion of prayers and begin to pass around dishes of food. "I just love Shabbat songs. In Israel, we used to sing until quite late."

"You used to live in Israel?" I ask.

"I studied there for a year. Sharon did, too. And we hope to go back to Israel to raise our family." She smiles at Sharon, and he squeezes her arm affectionately. "We want our daughter to go to Jewish schools, with other Jewish children."

"When are you planning to move?" I ask.

"It's an interesting question," Sharon says with a laugh. "Every year, for eight years, we have said 'Next year.' Every year we have meant it, but we have not been able to go. One thing keeping us here is our community. I am a Jewish educator, and I feel like I should help. In India I have job security; I know the language; I know the people. Still, I do not feel at home. In Israel, I feel at home. I have much less security there—I don't really know the language, I don't know as many people. But there I can practice my religion."

Sharon thinks for a moment.

"Look around you. Up until now, we haven't really settled in our lives, not in our careers, not in our house. We have not bought real furniture for our house, because we think, what is the point of buying furniture if we are going to leave it?"

The time comes for the blessing of children, and after Sharon's father blesses Sharon and Sharona, he lays his hand on my head. "What's her name?" he asks.

"Sadia," Sharon says.

"What's your father's name?" he asks me.

"Richard," I say.

"And his surname?"

"It's Shepard."

"Rich-ard Shep-ard," he repeats, trying out the unfamiliar syllables. He inserts my father's name when he comes to the correct portion of the prayer, and asks God to make me like the matriarchs of the Jewish people: Sarah, Rebecca, Rachel, and Leah.

"Amen," he says at the end.

"Amen," I repeat.

After dinner, Sharona passes around a bowl of watermelon, and we take turns stabbing the large red squares with a fork. Sharon's father lies down on the nearby *charpoy* and falls asleep quickly. His granddaughter uses his body as a cushion, resting against him comfortably as she plays with the pieces of a large plastic puzzle.

"So," Sharona says, "what's your long story?"

"Oh . . ." I say, feeling shy, "it's about why I'm here, in India."

"Are you a student? We have a lot of students who come through here."

"I am a student," I say, "though I am not really in school. I came to India because my grandmother was a Bene Israel from Bombay. Sharon has heard this story before."

"No, no, it's interesting. Go on," he says.

"And she left the Bene Israel community to marry my grandfather, who was a Muslim."

"She married a *Muslim*?" Sharona says, looking surprised.

"She married a Muslim with two other wives, and she moved to Pakistan, where she raised her children as Muslims."

"I can't imagine any Bene Israel girl from Bombay marrying a man with two other wives," Sharona says.

"Well, it was a different time then, I suppose, and he was a close friend of her father's, and was quite wealthy . . . and also she was in love with him."

"She really moved to Pakistan?" Sharon asks. "I didn't realize that part of the story."

"She did."

"Your mother is Jewish or Muslim?" Sharona asks. "Of course, according to Jewish law, she's Jewish."

"Well, my mother was raised a Muslim, and she's a practicing Muslim now. She's curious about Judaism, but she feels comfortable with her faith."

"And your father?"

"My father is Christian."

"And you?"

"I'm here to learn more about my grandmother's community, about what she left behind."

"You know, Sadia," Sharon begins, looking thoughtful, "your situation is much more complicated than I realized. You have a choice to make, isn't it."

"You think she has to choose, Sharon?" Sharona asks, picking up her daughter and bouncing her on her knee.

"I think she absolutely has to choose."

"Do *you* think you have to choose?" Sharona asks me.

"I didn't think so before I came to India, no. In America people sometimes grow up with more than one religion. Not often three religions, but there it's more common to acknowledge more than one tradition. Here I have begun to question that. I wonder if I should choose."

"Sadia, may I speak frankly, as your friend?" Sharon asks, and I tell him I would be glad if he did.

"I think, Sadia, that if you are not going to go into depth, then you can be quite comfortable with all three religions in your life. There are certainly a great number of things that Judaism and Christianity have in common, and a great number of things that you will find similar in Islam and Judaism. But if you look at all three in depth, I think you will see that there are also a great number of contradictions. So that, if you believe fully in one, you cannot believe in the others."

"Sharon, give her an example, so she understands," Sharona says.

"Oh, I'm not smart enough to do that," Sharon says modestly.

"Of course you are!" Sharona and I say in unison, asking him to continue.

"Well, okay, it's like this. In Christianity you have the Holy Trinity. If you believe in the Holy Trinity, then you believe that the divine can take forms that are holy besides God. This concept comes into conflict with the concept of monotheism, in my opinion. In Islam, from what I have read, the Muslims believe that Prophet Muhammad was the last prophet, and there will be no prophets after him. And they believe in Moses, that he was a prophet, and they believe in the Book of Moses. But if you follow the Book of Moses, then you believe that God has said that he has laid down these rules and they should not be changed. In Halal, in the concept of Halal, it says that you can eat the blood of an animal, but in the Book of Moses it says expressly that you cannot eat the blood of an animal. So this is a case of revision. There is a Muslim gentleman downstairs, and he gives lessons in the Qur'an. We meet quite often, and he gives me books about Islam—he is often trying to convince me to turn to Islam. And we have good discussions. Basically, he tells me stories from the Qur'an, and I listen, and privately I break apart those stories and put them into contexts that I understand, placing the different pieces of information in different places in my mind, like shelves. If you speak to anyone of any of these three religions, they are always going to feel preferential to their holy book. I am a Jew, so of course I think the Torah is correct. But I think the thing that you should do is to get yourself a copy of the scriptures and read for yourself. And teachers—get yourself good teachers. You might find a very good Christian teacher and a bad Jewish teacher and you will end up a Christian, or vice versa—it is important to find good teachers and then decide for yourself. You have a lot of work to do, Sadia."

"I think you're right," I say.

"What kind of person will you marry?" Sharona asks. "Will you marry a Jew or a Christian or a Muslim?"

"Oh, I'm not sure," I say. "I suppose I will find someone and then we will have to decide how we'll raise our children."

"I am not sure that you should wait until you marry to start this," Sharon says seriously.

"You should know who you are *before* you marry," Sharona says, matter-of-factly.

"You should learn about religion, and then choose a person from within the faith that you feel most tied to," Sharon says.

"Sharon and I, we are raising our children in a Jewish home. You would not want to marry someone and then study religion and realize that you do not respect the religion of the person you married. . . ."

"Oh, I see," I say, smiling. "I see what you mean."

"You have a lot of work to do," Sharon repeats. "I don't want to seem like a spokesman for Judaism, but for me, the Torah makes a lot of sense."

LATE THAT NIGHT, later than Sharon and Sharona would prefer that I travel on my own, I hail a cab and am filled with the usual apprehension that I feel entering Bombay taxis after dark. "Remember to write the cab number down!" older people often say, and I am amused at the thought of finding myself in a tricky situation, fearing robbery or worse, with the number of the vehicle carefully printed in my notebook. Most often the fear dissipates quickly after the ride begins, and I feel silly for being worried.

"Which country, ma'am?" the taxi driver asks soon after I get in, and I expect that our conversation will follow well-worn patterns: where I am from, how I like India, and what his impression is of the United States.

"U.S.," I say, watching the crowded streets of Byculla pass by my window.

I look for the sights that have become familiar and favorite: the window into an old man's apartment lined with a gigantic collection of commemorative plates, the makeshift wooden stall no larger than four feet wide that sells pet fish out of a large stagnant-looking aquarium, behind a sign that reads "Fish Paradise."

I know that Sharon and Sharona would have preferred that I stay the night. The truth is that I have a lot to think about. Our conversation has left me with many unanswered questions, and I want to make sense of things in my head, on my own.

"What is your caste?" the cab driver asks.

Of course, I think. How fitting that he would ask me this tonight.

I am not sure how to answer the question. For one thing, his query might imply that he assumes that I am Indian, or part Indian, and I feel flattered, accepted even by the assumption. But it could also be that his English limits his ability to phrase his real question, and that he's just curious about why a young woman is traveling alone late at night. Either way, it is not a typical start to a conversation. To ask someone's caste is a loaded question, and, in most circles, plainly rude.

I decide to answer him with the truth.

"My mother is Muslim, my father is Christian. My grandmother was Bene Israel; they are a small Jewish caste in Maharashtra."

"Haan," he says, nodding, as if he knows whom I am referring to. I wonder if he does.

"And you? What are you?" he asks.

"I am studying religion."

"It is good to study," he replics. "I am Brahmin. We are study caste."

"Yes," I say, not sure what else to say.

"Hindus are very good people. No drinking, no bad words, no fighting, no . . . bad words . . . no drinking. . . ."

I have heard these arguments before. "Don't leave out vegetarian," I add, looking out the window as streetlights streak past my view.

"*Haan!* No meat!"

"Right."

"Muslims are bad people," he says, taking on a more serious tone. "They are all terrorists. What do they want? I don't know what they want. Can you tell me what Muslims want?"

"It's a complicated question," I say. "I don't know how to answer that."

"They attacked your country. They attacked my country also."

"It's more complicated than that."

"You are married?"

"Not yet."

"*Not* married?" he asks, turning in his seat to look at me, as if he can't believe my answer.

"No, not yet."

"What is your age?" he asks.

I hesitate, reluctant to tell him.

"Twenty-eight," I say finally.

"Oh-ho-ho-ho-ho . . ." he says regretfully, shaking his head and knocking his temple with his left hand, as if his head is a block of wood. "Oh-ho-ho-ho-ho . . ."

I think of Tony, whether if I had never come to India we would be engaged by now. The driver pulls his composure back together in order to deliver some statistics.

"In India, in village, people marry at eighteen. In city, people marry at twenty-four, twenty-five. When do people marry in States?"

"It depends. Sometimes twenty-five, sometimes thirty, sometimes later. It depends."

"What caste will you marry?"

"I don't know yet," I say. "I will wait and see."

"Your mother is Indian?"

"She was born here."

We pull up next to my house, and I instruct him to drop me at the gate.

"This is your mother's house?"

"Yes," I lie. "She's inside."

"She must be wanting you to find hus-band," he says, raising his eyebrows. "No?"

"Good night," I say, counting several small bills to give to him.

"You should find hus-band from the same caste, it is better."

"Good night," I say, annoyed, slamming the door on the way out.

I unlock the black iron gate of Bilva Kunj and drag my feet the ten steps up the driveway to the door of my apartment. Once inside, I drop my bags, shed my shoes, and sit on my bed, turning on the television. It's late morning in New York. A thirty-eight-day standoff between Palestinian militants and Israeli forces at the Church of the Nativity in Bethlehem has come to a close; thirteen of the militants inside the church have agreed to be deported to various countries. I fall asleep, and dream that I am walking in Manhattan, trying to cross Canal Street on a Saturday afternoon. As I walk, I hear the cries of the hawkers around me interspersed with my sandals hitting the pavement, and a constant refrain, like a heartbeat: "Which caste? Which caste? Which caste?"

SOMETIMES, AFTER I HAVE finished my vegetable shopping, I stop in at B. Merwan, an old Irani café behind Grant Road Station, whose décor does not seem to have changed much since it opened in 1914. B. Merwan's tabletops are made of marble, and its wooden chairs are dark and well worn by a steady stream of ancient-looking customers, almost all of them men, who come faithfully each day. It's dark inside, and a few patrons seem permanently in place—I wonder if they ever go home. The menu features a steady diet of milky tea, coffee, eggs, and bread for under twenty rupees each, a fraction of what it might cost elsewhere. I come to B. Merwan for its famous milk cake, and to read. Because I know that the look of the place has not changed since it opened, I know that this café existed, in much the same way it does now, when Nana lived here.

One day, I notice an elegant elderly woman in a sari drinking tea by herself at a table adjacent to mine. Her white hair is pulled back in a bun.

"Excuse me, but where did you get your bracelet?" she asks, pointing to the black elastic hair band I wear on my wrist, and I take it off and show her.

"Actually, it's a hair elastic," I say. "I keep it on my wrist so I don't lose it."

"Oh, I see," she says. "I asked because we have a shop at home, and the black people are always asking for rubber bracelets to wear on their wrists, but I cannot find them. They believe they will not get electric shocks if they wear them. It's not true, of course, but they believe it."

"Where is your shop?"

"Back home, in South Africa."

"Are you from South Africa?"

"I've lived there all my life."

"But you have family here that you visit?"

"My family is lost."

It takes me a moment to register what she's said.

"Lost?" I ask.

The lady pauses for a moment, with a strange smile on her face. I recognize the look, one of an older person who has decided to let someone younger in on a secret.

"My grandparents were brought from Assam to South Africa during the time of indenture. This was in the 1860s. They thought they were going on a month-long holiday. The British rounded up so many people and told them this story. My grandparents took all six of their children, and they went. They didn't know they were going to work in the sugarcane fields. They were fooled; they signed a contract—they couldn't read, they didn't know what they were signing. The British were very cunning, also very cruel. For years, my grandparents and my parents kept up with the family back home, they wrote to my uncles and aunts in Assam. They knew all the family news. Then we didn't hear from my uncles for some time. When I was going to India for the first time, I said to my father, 'Why don't you give me the address? I'll see what's happened to them.' We came by ship, in 1963. When we arrived in Bombay, I showed my family's address to the Tourist Office here. They said, 'How long has it been since you have heard from them?' I told them that it had been several years. 'But don't you know?' they said. 'This whole area has been flooded.' So that's how my family was lost. The rest of my family was in South Africa. Quite a lot of us."

I scoot my chair closer to hers and rest my elbows on her table.

"And when it came time for you to marry, you found other people from the same community?"

"Oh yes, we wanted to stay to our own kind. Actually, my mother was from Amritsar. My father's family was from Assam. My grandmother, my grandfather, they all had Chinese eyes. As children we were confused; we used to say, If you are Indian, why do you have Chinese eyes?"

"You have beautiful eyes. How do you think you got your gray eyes?"

"I have diabetic eyes! My eyes have turned a different color with time. If you see in my passport, or photographs from my wedding, I had black eyes."

"Really? I have never heard of that."

The waiter puts a dish of milk cake in front of her.

"Oh, perhaps you don't want that—there's so much sugar," I say, conscious of her diabetes.

"Why not?" she says, with a girlish shrug of her shoulders. "You know, you only live once . . . and you only die once."

"Quite right," I say. "Plus, you're on holiday."

"Indeed. When I came to India for the first time, it was on holiday. I had never been here before, but somehow I liked it. It all felt very familiar. I didn't feel out of place. I came with my three sisters, my cousins, my sister-in-law. We thought, We may never come again, let's make the most of it. We stayed three months. We went to Kashmir, to Simla, all over. Now I try to come here once a year. I go to Bombay, to Delhi, other places."

"What do you do when you are here?"

"Oh, I visit places. I go shopping, of course. After all, I am a lady!"

"You wear saris always?"

"Oh yes. All we wear back home is saris. My grandmother, she brought India with her, you see. She never left her food, her ways, her *Gita.* She taught us everything. After the contract was finished, my grandmother saved money her whole life to come back to Assam. She used to tell us stories of the rains, of the floods. In those days, Assam was always having floods. She was crying of home until her dying day. But she never saw India again. My grandfather died, and it was too difficult to travel. . . ." She gets a faraway look, then interrupts herself to focus back on me. "What brings you to India, young lady?"

"Well, I'm looking for my lost family, actually, in a way. My grandmother was from here, from Bombay. She was from a small community here that practices Judaism. I am here to learn about them, and to learn more about my grandmother."

"We're not so very far removed from that in my family. My granddaughter has married a Jewish person, someone she met here in Bombay, and they have moved to Israel."

"Did she marry an Indian Jew?"

"No, no, an Israeli Jew. He was working here in Bombay. My granddaughter is in the law, and she met him in her company. Oh, we were not very happy about it all. We were all against it, especially my husband. The Jewish religion is so different from ours! But my granddaughter said, 'No, Ma.' All my grandchildren call me 'Ma.' She said, 'Jews are just like Hindus—they are very family-oriented.' Now my granddaughter and her husband live in Israel, and they are quite happy, they have two children. If they like each other, who are we to say different?"

"I'm sorry," I say, extending my hand, "I didn't introduce myself. My name is Sadia."

"I am Mynavathi."

"That's a beautiful name. Myna, like the mynah bird."

"I used to chatter like a bird when I was small," she says, getting up and giving me a twinkling smile.

Somehow, I can imagine it.

"I hope you find what you are looking for, Sadia."

"Thank you," I say. "You, too."

PART THREE

DEPARTURES

19

PEOPLE OF THE BOOK

KARACHI, JUNE 2002

I have never traveled to Pakistan without my mother and grandmother, and never as an adult. This trip will also be the first time I have traveled to Pakistan from India, a replication of the journey Nana made after Partition with her two children, my mother and her younger brother Sibtain. The flight between Bombay and Karachi is a mere hour and fifteen minutes, a span of time almost too short to comprehend the gulf that separates the two. Both are cities by the sea, both are bustling metropolises, and when I have been asked about Karachi while living in Bombay I have been tempted to bridge the gap. "It's like here," I've heard myself say. "Karachi is the financial center of the country; the television industry is there. It's fast-paced; people come from other cities to work there, to reinvent themselves." But I know that the two cities, though linked, are wholly different. They are like distant cousins who share familial traits but were raised apart.

In Bombay, I line up for the security check with the ubiquitous Australian and Israeli dreadlocked backpackers, outfitted in tank tops, short skirts, and the occasional Indian scarf. My own arms and legs are covered in a long, loose salwar kameez. My bags are filled with embroidered Indian purses for my female cousins, sweets for my aunts and uncles. I wonder what they will think of my gifts—what I can bring them from Bombay that they don't already have in Pakistan.

From the moment I board the plane, I am aware that I have entered a culture different from the one of the airport. There are fewer people in Western dress; I hear Urdu spoken all around me. Two young women in matching makeup and headscarves say *salaam* to me as I take my seat next to them. As the flight takes off, they bow their heads and I hear them murmur the Traveler's Prayer. Islam shifts from a faraway idea, a hidden aspect of my life among the Bene Israel in India, into the center, the forefront of my mind. I close my eyes and instinctively repeat the First Kalimah, the prayer my mother taught me to say as our childhood flights to and from Pakistan took off.

I look out the window and imagine my grandmother on a flight like this one, her arms wrapped protectively around her two children as she watched her birthplace—grand colonial structures, dense slums, the sweeping arch of the Queen's Necklace hugging the bay—recede and become incomprehensibly tiny.

Nana told me how she learned that she was leaving India for Pakistan— she was instructed by her husband to gather a few clothes and belongings together for a two-week trip. "Things are not safe in Bombay," he said. "I think we should visit my sisters in Karachi, leave town for a little while, until the violence calms down."

Nana had an ominous feeling; there was too much uncertainty in the air. She went to the bank and withdrew twenty thousand rupees, more than she had ever carried on her person at one time. She hastily filled a trunk with the family silver: goblets, table settings, picture frames, a ceremonial sword given to Ali by the Jam Sahib of Jamnagar, her grandfather's walking stick, and a set of ornate water pitchers, shaped like a family of penguins. Under her sari she wore every piece of gold jewelry her husband had ever given her, necklaces heavy around her neck, a pouch of rings and earrings strapped around her waist.

"You haven't brought any valuables, have you?" her husband asked when she reached the Bombay airport. "It's not safe. What have you packed in the trunk?"

"Just some clothes for the children," she lied, rushing ahead to speak to one of her husband's nephews, Aijaz. She pressed a wad of bills into his hand quietly.

"I need you to get that trunk on the plane," she told him. "Bribe anyone you have to."

Nana met the other two Mrs. Siddiqis and their children on board. In India they had lived separate lives, with separate, independent households. Now they were traveling as one family, with three wives, one husband, and several children.

"It's temporary," Nana reassured herself. "This will pass, and we will all return to life as before, in India."

Once they were in Karachi, the newspapers and radio broadcasts were filled with news of communal unrest back home. The Siddiqis tried to acclimate to life as houseguests in this new, unsettled reality. A few weeks after they arrived in Karachi, my grandfather received the news that the properties he had placed in the care of his Hindu business partner had been confiscated, declared Evacuee Property. Overnight, their financial situation had changed. Ali sat at his sister's dining room table, his head in his hands. He would have to start all over again.

"I have the silver," Nana said quietly.

"What do you mean?" her husband asked.

"Look," she said, opening the trunk. "It's all here."

"How the hell did you manage it?"

THIS STORY, Nana's account of Partition, was the only time I ever heard her use the word "hell," and she always laughed after she said it, as if she were still marveling, all these years later, at her feat. *How the hell did you manage it?* It's this phrase of my grandfather's, repeated by my grandmother, that I think of when I think about Partition. The silver was only a remnant, a sentimental reminder of their life before, but these objects, over a period of years, began to accrue a significance that far exceeded their monetary value.

As my plane nears Karachi, I wonder how much it has changed since 1948. I see the blurred, dusty edges of the city, a wide expanse of low concrete buildings. Almost everything is the color of sand, but for the occasional daub of blue of a hotel swimming pool. From here, Karachi looks like dice shaken and scattered on the desert.

I AM FLYING TO KARACHI to attend the wedding of two cousins. My mother has also asked me to look in on Nana's flat in Siddiqi House, to make sure it is in order. My aunt Zaitoon, one of the last Siddiqis still living in the family home, has been collecting rent for the flat from long-standing tenants for the last fifteen years, and the money has been accruing in Nana's account at the Habib Bank. But there are other reasons, reasons that I keep to myself. After nine months of living in India and learning about Indian Jewish life, I want to find out what it feels like to spend time with my Muslim family in Pakistan. I want to see the place that Nana came to when she left Bombay, to imagine what it might have been like for her to leave home, now that I've made a home in her city.

Two of my second cousins, Saira and Asad, are getting married. Though the two met as teenagers and this was technically a love match, the general assumption is that the marriage was arranged.

"Did they choose it, or did their parents?" I ask one of my aunts on the phone.

"It's an arranged-cum-love marriage," she says.

As I walk through the Karachi international terminal, I am acutely aware that I am the only non-Pakistani, the only foreigner, and the only woman traveling alone that I can see. When I was a child in the 1980s, every major airline flew to Karachi. Now there are far fewer; the main flights in and out of the airport are operated by PIA, Emirates, and SriLankan Airlines. The airport has been refurbished in bright, gleaming marble, and I am surprised, again, by the sight of a McDonald's outside. A line of men wait behind a metal fence, holding signs with names written in English and Urdu. Many men wear long beards, prayer caps, and white kurta pajamas, traditional South Asian Muslim garb that I rarely see outside of Muslim neighborhoods in Bombay. I notice a dark stain, like a shadow, on some of their foreheads, a callus of piety formed as their heads touch the ground five times a day. I am aware of a multitude of eyes on me, a flash of curiosity about why I'm here. I scan the crowd for a familiar face; I am not sure who is picking me up.

"*As-salaam aleikum,* Sadia Apa!" comes a friendly young voice. It's Aliyah, the daughter of my first cousin Farah. Aliyah is seventeen now, and looks more grown-up than I remember her; I can tell that she is going to be a beautiful woman. I'm taken aback by how much more assured she looks, with her confident way of throwing her dupatta over her shoulders and the direct, steady look of her eyes, but she has the same wide-open, curious face that I remember from previous visits, the same excited, breathy way of speaking quickly, the same quick laugh. When she was thirteen, she pulled me inside her room, sat me down on her bed, and showed me the copies of teen magazines that she kept underneath her bed for safekeeping. It was only a few years ago, but it seems like a long time now.

Loping behind Aliyah are her two younger brothers, Saleem and Naeem, good-looking, lanky kids with spiky hair and a mischievous air, as if they might crack a joke at any moment. They are close in age, and I'm embarrassed that I can barely tell the two apart.

"*Walaikum asalaam!*" I stammer, and smile.

On this trip I will see my Pakistani American cousins, who are in town for the wedding like me, as well as my Pakistani cousins, who were born and raised in Karachi. It used to be that they aspired to come to the United States to study and work. Now stories of the prejudice Muslims are facing in the U.S. after the World Trade Center attacks have made them want to pursue their education at home or in the United Kingdom. In the car ride back to their house, Aliyah, Naeem, and Saleem fill me in on who is in which school, pursuing which degree; who is married or engaged; and who has decided to wear the hijab since my last visit.

As I settle into the backseat and watch Karachi speed by the car window, I remark on the number of trees, more than I remember.

"Enjoy them," Saleem says. "This is the last green that you'll see in Karachi."

Familiar landmarks, neon signs. Fewer words in English, more in Urdu script. I chose my outfit carefully this morning, a white salwar kameez with a blue border and a matching blue dupatta, but already I realize that I am hopelessly out of fashion, and anticipate that I will be taken hastily by my female cousins to boutiques and tailors to supplement my awkward wardrobe. Even the feeling of being different here is an old, childhood feeling, like re-entering a memory.

Aliyah, Saleem, and Naeem are the grandchildren of my mother's half brother Waris, the elder son of Bari Amma. Until several years ago, Waris and his wife, Mehreen, still lived in Siddiqi House, but they have since moved to a newer part of the city, into two handsome modern bungalows, side by side: Uncle Waris and Auntie Mehreen in one, their daughter Farah and her family in the other. Their son lives in the United States with his family, while their other daughter lives in another part of Karachi. For the first time, my first stop here will not be the ritual multitiered visit to the various flats of Siddiqi House, the complex negotiation of different entrances and exits, navigating in which order to visit the elders of the family. Instead, we pull into Uncle Waris's driveway so that I can say my *salaams* to him and to Auntie Mehreen before putting my bags down in my cousin Farah's house, where I will be staying for the next week. The *chowkidar* opens the house gate and nods to us. I try not to stare at the large gun strapped casually across his chest.

Uncle Waris and Auntie Mehreen's house is long and white, with a large, well-kept lawn in front and a wide veranda. As I come through the screen door to their parlor, I recognize the angular early sixties furniture in protective plastic that they kept in Siddiqi House, as well as the pictures they had on the wall—the same formal wedding portraits hung just a few feet below the ceiling. On a side table, there is a single black-and-white portrait of my grandfather, imposing and elegant, the same picture that used to sit on our library bookshelf in Chestnut Hill, common to all of his children's homes.

It has been several years since I have seen my uncle Waris—not since he attended a family wedding in the U.S. He is now the eldest male member of the Siddiqi family, and he wears his stature well; he is as tall as I remember and dressed entirely in bright white, from his hair and beard to his kurta salwar.

"Beti!" he says, offering me a seat. "Welcome, child."

He tells me that I should call my mother to let her know that I have arrived safely; a car bomb exploded in front of the U.S. Consulate in Karachi, and she will be anxious.

My cousin Sartaj, his wife, Fatima, and their three daughters are visiting from Georgia, where they own and operate a small grocery store, and enter the room from the kitchen when they hear me saying hello. Sartaj and Fatima have become increasingly involved in the Muslim community in their neighborhood in recent years, and they wear their new roles with authority; my mother has told me that they regularly speak about Islam at schools and community centers. Fatima is a small, fair-skinned woman with a direct gaze and a strong presence. I remember how shy she was when I first met her at Uncle Salman's wedding. Fatima has worn a headscarf for the last several years, one of the first women in my mother's family to do so, and she can clearly articulate the reasons for her choice, citing passages from the Qur'an.

I remind myself not to hug my older male relatives, several of whom have become more conservative in recent years and do not generally touch people of the opposite sex. I sit on the floor opposite Sartaj and wave an enthusiastic greeting, putting my arms around Fatima when she comes forward to embrace me. It has been two years since we have seen each other, since Nana died, and I am happy to see them again.

"Your mother tells me you are in Bombay," Sartaj says. "How do you find it?"

My instincts tell me that I should tread carefully when talking about India, aware as I speak of the strained relationship between the two countries.

"I love it," I say. "It's a very exciting city—very diverse, with people from all over Asia, all over India, and a great number of foreigners."

"Really?" Fatima says, looking curious.

"You're on a scholarship?" Sartaj asks.

"I'm studying at the National Film and Television Institute of India, on a Fulbright Scholarship," I say. I don't tell them about my project. I don't say that I am studying Jews. I want to get to know them better, and I don't want to say anything that will alienate them—not yet.

"Do you like it better here or there?" Sartaj asks, and I'm not sure what to say.

"I have not spent time here in a long while. I'm looking forward to getting to know Karachi a bit more."

"But you like Bombay," Sartaj says.

"Nana was from there, and she missed it all of her life. It means a great deal to me to be in her city. I feel connected to her by being there."

"Ah, you miss your grandmother," Fatima says, looking at me kindly. I remember how Fatima guided me after Nana's death and showed me how to perform the Muslim prayer with the rest of my mother's female relatives, and I nod, suddenly worried that I might cry. In India, when I talk about Nana with the Bene Israel, I do so to explain why I am in India. Nana is an abstraction, an idea. Here she is a person, a departed matriarch.

What I have forgotten is how time passes with my mother's family, how one conversation melds into the next, people drifting in and out of rooms, offering, making, and serving tea. Off the main living room is Uncle Waris and Auntie Mehreen's bedroom, crowded with dark wood furniture. I go in search of my aunt and find her lying down on her large bed with the curtains drawn. Mehreen married my uncle Waris and joined the Siddiqi family when she was just eighteen, and my mother has told me repeatedly what a lovely bride she was. She has always been famous in our family for her fair skin and long dark hair, those regional hallmarks of feminine beauty, and my mother, then nine years old, insisted on following her around from the moment she joined the household. The wedding albums attest to this fact, a tiny Samina hovering in the edges of the white-bordered black-and-white images.

"Mehreen Auntie!" I say, finding her in the dark and kissing her soft, round cheeks. "It's Sadia—I have come to see you. . . ."

"Oh, *beti*!" she says. "For you I have put new sheets and cleaned my room!" She sighs deeply and lays her hand on her forehead. "I have been working all day, and now I am very tired."

"I'm honored, Mehreen Auntie. These are very nice sheets," I say, touching them and tracing the floral print with my index finger.

"Roses!" Mehreen Auntie exclaims. "My favorite . . . always roses! Like Mysore . . . All the time I am choosing roses, my favorite flower."

I give Mehreen Auntie some *mithai* that I brought with me for her.

"All the way from Bombay!" she exclaims. "Special Bombay sweets!" she says, fingering the silver box. "My, my!"

"You were from Bombay, right, Mehreen Auntie?" I ask. "I've been wanting to ask you about Partition."

"No, no, I was from the south of India," she says. "From Mysore. Back then, it was a city of gardens—so many gardens were there! All green around all the time. We were there until '47."

"Then you moved to Karachi?"

"I'll tell you—there were so many problems in India at that time; people were after my brothers. I had older brothers, and people said that a mob was going to come for them, crowds were attacking Muslim houses. Our Hindu friends told us to get out, in fact. My parents did not want to go, but they said, Let's just make the trip, we need to be safe. My father said, I will put the boys in school in Karachi, and the rest of us will come back to Hyderabad. We packed a few things and we went. We couldn't even take our old dog. Such a sweet dog he was! He always stood watch over our *haveli*; he would bark and bark if he didn't like the look of someone. We left him with our old cook, Mukhtar Bhai, and we came to Karachi. I was so sad to leave the dog, and our garden. It took so many days to get here at that time, and such a difficult journey. I was nine years old. As soon as we arrived, my father said that he wanted to go back, but my mother said: Are you mad? We have just arrived, and the news is filled with stories of Muslims being killed. You must stay here with us."

"What was Karachi like at that time, Mehreen Auntie?"

"Oh, it was a such dusty place then! I thought, I have come from gardens to *this*? To what desert have we come?" Mehreen Auntie laughs, a soft, rolling sound, and shakes her head from side to side for emphasis. "Such a confused family we are!" She laughs again. "We don't know who we are and where we come from!"

Mehreen Auntie takes hold of my hand and squeezes it affectionately.

"Why have you come, *beti*?" she asks me.

"I am living in India, Mehreen Auntie, in Bombay. I am studying there. And I'm so close by, I wanted to come on my own, to see you and the family. And I miss Nana. I want to learn more about her life."

"I can tell you," she says. "I was there. I joined the Siddiqi family when I was quite young. People used to ask me: What is it like to have three mothers-in-law? Do they all get along? I just smiled when they said that. What is the family's business is the family's business. What is the use of discussing it? Your grandmother was a good, kind woman."

I nod, knowing that she must be alluding to the complicated relationships of Siddiqi House. Even with me all these years later, she won't go into specifics.

"Tell me, *beti*, when will we hear good news from you?"

"Good news?" I ask her, looking blank.

"About your marriage! Have you decided on someone?"

I laugh, not sure how to explain, and look at my watch. "I was timing this, Mehreen Auntie—you waited a whole half-hour before you asked me. I'm impressed!"

In Karachi, my female cousins typically marry young men who are suggested to them by mutual friends. After an exchange of pictures, the two families meet. Sometimes the young man and the young woman will spend a few minutes alone, talking about their likes, dislikes, and career ambitions. If the match is agreeable to both the young woman and the young man, the families will agree to an engagement, and preparations will begin for the wedding. From the moment the two meet, the relationship goes in only one direction, a linear path toward marriage and children. How can I explain to Mehreen Auntie that in the system I'm a part of we meet many different people, and that the process of choosing and marrying a compatible partner can take years?

"I have not decided, Mehreen Auntie." This is all I can muster. "I will marry when I find the right person."

"You must be serious about looking, *beti*!" Mehreen Auntie says, appearing concerned. "I have told this to your mother, but I have not had the chance to tell you. Time is running away, and then it will be more difficult! You must be serious about finding someone now. Do not be too choosy!"

It amuses me to think of my love life this way, that I am "too choosy." Suddenly Mehreen Auntie looks at me, remembering something.

"And do you know? Do you know what happened to our dog in Hyderabad?"

"What happened, Mehreen Auntie?"

"The dog refused food after we left. He would not eat a thing. He was waiting for us! For a whole month he did not eat. And that dog died. He died of *mohabbat*, of love. . . ."

JUST OFF THE MASTER BEDROOM is the library, bordered on one side by a large picture window facing the garden. In the center of the room is a large color television perpetually tuned to Pakistan Television, the other walls dominated by built-in bookshelves filled with English books. I'm intrigued to find a series of handsome older volumes with tooled leather spines, and open up a copy of *The Count of Monte Cristo*. On the flyleaf, I find a stamp with my grandfather's address in Rajkot, in Gujarat—the household he kept with his first wife, Bari Amma, and her two sons. My grandfather must have taken these books with him from India. When I hear the call to prayer broadcast from a distant loudspeaker, I put my dupatta over my head instinctively and put the book aside. My family members are offering their prayers privately, in their bedrooms, and a quiet stillness has slipped over the late afternoon. It is hot, too hot to feel the impulse to walk outside, even if there were somewhere I wanted to go.

I don't remember the order of standing, kneeling, and prostrating well enough to do it on my own. Instead, I listen to the Arabic and mutter the English translation under my breath. I think about why I am here. I am struck by how deeply familiar the sound of the prayer is, and think of a fragment of prayer my mother taught me: "O Allah bestow your favor upon Muhammad and the family of Muhammad as You have bestowed your favor on Abraham and the family of Abraham." The people of Abraham. The people of Muhammad. Through a series of historical accidents, I find myself tied to both, the same way I am tied to Christianity.

I feel a welling up of resentment at the idea of choosing one faith, one affiliation, over the others. There's an element of subterfuge in the way that I live, chameleonlike, presenting different sides of my religious background to different people. But it also allows me to keep asking questions, to hear what is really said behind closed doors. I'm not sure that I'm willing to give it up, not yet.

"COME, *BETI*. TEA."

Uncle Waris shuffles slowly through the library and to the adjacent dining room. Unlike many South Asian men, he is over six feet tall, and as he moves, his glasses swing like a pendulum from a string around his neck. I follow him, and we sit at the large dining table, covered in a thick plastic table-cover. A servant brings the tea tray and sets it down in front of us, pouring the hot liquid from a piping-hot teapot into our cups. We stir in teaspoons of white sugar; Uncle Waris opens a jar and pulls out a few biscuits, which he dips in his tea, and offers me one.

"Your mother said on the phone you want to know about the family."

"Yes, that's true," I say, taking out a notebook from my bag.

"What's that for?" He points to it.

"Just so I remember." I am uncapping a pen.

"What do you want to know?"

"I want to know about the Siddiqis, how they came to India and where they settled, and how my grandmother met your father. Nana told me that they met in Bombay; is that true?"

"Not at all. They knew each other much before that."

"Really? But I always thought . . ."

"My grandfather's father was originally from Arabistan—Saudi Arabia—and came to India to fight in the Mysore War, in Tipu Sultan's army against the British. Later, my grandfather became a sergeant major of the Indian Army, and after he retired, he joined the rest of the family in Ajmer. In Ajmer, our family had a neighbor who was also Indian Army retired. That man was your Nana's grandfather. So Nana's grandfather Jacobs and my grandfather were friends. The two families used to meet, have dinners together."

"What year would this have been?"

"Oh, my father was born in the early 1900s, so this would have been in the late 1800s."

"It's remarkable to me that a Muslim and a Jewish family would have been close friends in the late 1800s In India. . . ."

"Why is it remarkable? We had no problems with Jews, and they had no problems with us. Now there is this problem, this is because of Israel. If you look at the Qur'an, you will find conflict only if you take things out of context. Islam respects Judaism and Christianity—my father used to say: 'And dispute ye not with the People of the Book . . . unless it be with those of them who inflict wrong (and injury); but say, "We believe in the Revelation which has come down to us and in that which came down to you; our

God and your God is One; and it is to Him we bow (in Islam)" '[Qur'an, 29:46]. Your grandmother's people were always good to us. *Ahl al-kitab,* we used to call them, People of the Book. We had no problems with the Jews."

"Uncle Waris, were people aware in the family, growing up in Siddiqi House, that Nana was different, that she was born in a different religion?"

"Why bother about this now, sweetheart?" he asks, looking up at me over his teacup. "This time is long gone."

"I know, Uncle Waris, but I want to know. Did people think of her as Jewish?"

"The only time it ever came up, as I recall, was if someone was upset— 'She's a *yahudi,*' they might say, but this rarely happened. She was part of our family. We children did not discriminate among my father's wives. 'I have three mothers,' I used to say, and I treated them equally."

"Did my grandmother practice Islam?"

"In Islam, if a woman is one of the People of the Book, it is not required that she change her religion when she marries one of us. But, yes, I believe she lived her life as a Muslim. Who can say?"

"Did she say her prayers?"

"She was perhaps not as punctual a Musalman as I am," Uncle Waris says, opening his palm, "but, yes, she did say her prayers."

"When did my grandmother and your father get married? Do you know the story of their marriage?"

"My father," he begins, "had an eye for young, beautiful women. That is all I will say on the matter."

I nod, wondering at the continuing mystery of my grandparents' relationship.

Uncle Waris looks thoughtful for a moment.

"I have met missionaries at my doorstep, *beti.* And I have given them tea, and I have said to them, Thank you, I will take this Bible and read it." Uncle Waris pantomimes accepting a book and placing it in his lap. "I believe in all three books of God."

. . .

"OH, HERE YOU ARE, Sadia Apa! We were wondering where you were!" my cousin Aliyah says, bursting into the living room, where I am looking at old photo albums.

"Are you coming for dinner?" she asks. "I have to offer my prayers, and then we will start preparing the food."

"Where will you pray?" I ask her.

"Where, Sadia Apa? Well, my room, I suppose. Why?"

"I was wondering if I could pray with you."

I surprise myself. I hadn't planned to ask her this.

"I don't remember how to do it on my own. If you don't mind, I mean," I add.

"Mind! Sadia Apa, of course I don't mind. It would be a blessing for me, too, to pray with you, Sadia Apa. *Allah mian* would be very happy with me for showing you how. Do you want to go now?"

I nod and follow Aliyah the thirty steps to her house next door. We walk up a central staircase to her brightly colored bedroom, on the second floor of her parents' large, well-appointed house. On each of my trips to Pakistan, Aliyah's interests—music, styles of dress, favorite subjects—eclipse the ones she had the last time I saw her, and I have to relearn the rules of her quickly shifting universe. In her room, I notice framed snapshots of Aliyah and her school friends, and cassette tapes of contemporary Islamic singers singing devotional songs. This visit, I notice that she seems more religiously observant. She peppers her conversation with *"al-hamdulillah"* ("thanks be to God") and *"insh'allah"* ("if it is God's will") and tells me that she is thinking of adopting the hijab soon, perhaps after her next round of exams.

"It's a big decision," she explains as we sit on her bed. "You have to be ready, and it's a sacrifice. It really is." Aliyah pauses for a moment and then looks wistful for a moment. "I really love earrings." She sighs deeply, and then brightens noticeably. "But, *al-hamdulillah,* I am kind of a role model in my school, Sadia Apa, so I am thinking about it. I really am."

I nod, thinking about Aliyah's choice. I have read the passages in the

Qu'ran that pertain to women and how they should cover themselves. In my mother's interpretation, Islam asks its women followers to dress modestly but does not require that women wear a veil. Mama is in agreement with her relatives that to wear it is a highly personal decision, but the debate continues between them on its merits. My mother feels that the hijab draws unnecessary attention, but some of her family members argue that it provides protection, promotes discussion, and is an integral part of being a pious Muslim woman.

According to custom, my mother does cover her head when she prays, and I miss her acutely as Aliyah shows me how to tie my dupatta around my head so that no hair shows, making one side longer than the other and wrapping it around my skull, tucking it into the cloth across my forehead as I go.

"Like this, Sadia Apa!" she says, but I keep doing it incorrectly. "No, like this!" She's patient with me, guiding my hands in place.

"There," she says proudly. "You look like a real Muslim now."

We place two prayer mats on the floor and face in the direction of Mecca, our two angled rugs lying side by side.

Aliyah recites the Arabic of her prayers beautifully.

"Allah hu Akbar," she says, lifting up her palms on either side of her body. *"Allah hu Akbar."*

I follow her motions, bending, kneeling, and bowing my head as she does, Nana's key on the chain around my neck hitting my forehead as I prostrate myself on the floor. It is a deeply comforting rhythm, and I am taken aback at my attraction to the ritual. But would I do this five times a day, as this branch of my mother's family does, rising at five-thirty every morning to offer their prayers to God? I wonder if it would give my life a direction, as I've read converts to Islam argue it does. I wonder if I have to choose one religion above all others. I wonder what my Pakistani family would think if they knew that the real purpose of my work in India is to forge a connection with the Jewish community.

At the conclusion of the prayer, we carefully roll the prayer mats up, and I thank Aliyah for guiding me.

"Sadia Apa?" she asks. "What's that around your neck?" She lifts up Nana's key and turns it over in her hand, looking at it.

"It's something that belonged to my grandmother," I say. "I wear it as a kind of reminder of her."

Aliyah nods, looking serious. "I was wondering if I could ask you something. Is it true that she embraced Islam before her death?"

The question catches me off guard. I wasn't prepared to speak of Nana with Aliyah, and I didn't realize that the younger generation of my family thought of Nana as anything different from the rest of the Siddiqis.

"She was Muslim from the time of her marriage," I say, almost defensively. "She converted when she married my grandfather."

"Really?" Aliyah says, looking surprised. "Well, that's wonderful. I really didn't know that. I thought she was . . . was she . . . Jewish?"

"She was, originally, yes," I say. "Until she married."

I pause on my way to the kitchen, halfway down the stairs, with my hand on the railing, thinking about what Uncle Waris said about conversion. I have always believed that Nana converted to Islam, but I suppose that it's entirely possible that she might not have done so formally, much as I have always suspected that her marriage ceremony to my grandfather was never made official. There is no way of knowing which religion Nana considered herself. But if her greatest desire was for me to study the Bene Israel, surely she must have ultimately considered herself Jewish?

I brush these private thoughts into a corner of my mind and join the family in the kitchen, where Aliyah is helping her mother to prepare dinner.

THE NEXT DAY, all of my cousins, those who are from Karachi as well as a contingent of Pakistani American cousins from Michigan, Los Angeles, and Staten Island, gather at an uncle's home for a joint *mehndi* or henna ceremony, to bless the bride and groom. Though both bride and groom grew up in New York, they have opted to have their wedding in Karachi, and are using their two-week vacations—the bride's from law school and the groom's from his job as a financial analyst—to get married in Karachi. The *mehndi* has been organized by the bride's and groom's mothers, who in this case are sisters and presiding over the function like jeweled birds, equal in pride and glimmer. Family friends have lent their front yard for the occasion; it is decorated with strings of marigolds and roses. Folding chairs have been set up to face a decorated, gilded love seat where the couple will sit to receive blessings from their friends and family. The guests sit in the chairs, sipping Sprite and Fanta and a bright green soda called Pakola, chatting among themselves about what the other guests are wearing, comparing the starched and embroidered outfits decked with heavy gold thread.

Traditionally, families held separate *mehndi* ceremonies for the bride and the groom. In recent years, wedding functions have become more streamlined and slightly more Westernized, and it has become fashionable to have joint *mehndi* ceremonies, for both the bride and the groom. In a marriage like this one, where the two sides are related, a joint ceremony makes sense, but Aliyah tells me that her branch of our family still prefers single-sex *mehndi* celebrations, because her mother and father believe that men and women who are not related should not socialize with one another, that to do so is *haram,* forbidden. I try to not look shocked when she tells me this. Gone, too, are the choreographed dances, usually performed at the *mehndi* by the bride's sisters, friends, and female relatives.

"I used to love to plan them," Aliyah explains as we settle on our folding chairs, sipping our sodas. "But then my mother pointed out that it was not perhaps such a good idea."

"Why not?" I ask, feeling a familiar sinking in my stomach.

"Well, by my teaching dancing to young girls, other people might look at those girls, and the girls might teach the dances to other girls. . . . The more that I thought about it, the more I realized that it was not Islamic for me to be teaching dancing. It's just better that I don't do it."

"But we've always had dances at family weddings," I say, remembering that just yesterday I had joked that if I got married in the U.S. I would fly Aliyah out to teach my American friends the steps.

"I know, Sadia Apa. But it's better this way. It really is."

I remind myself that traditions like this one were never part of Islam to begin with. Dancing at weddings, wearing red and gold to your *nikaah* ceremony, decorating your hands and feet with henna, marrying a first cousin—these traditions are indigenous to South Asia, regardless of what religion you are. But it's the cultural traditions that are associated with faith, not the faith itself, that I feel the strongest connection to, and it's their loss that I miss. I am reminded of my conversations with the Bene Israel in Bombay. I admire their resolve to become more observant Jews in Israel, but it is the customs of the Bene Israel in India that have pulled me to India. The more time goes by, the more I believe those are the traditions that Nana wanted me to learn about, to feel connected to.

"Don't worry, Sadia Apa," Aliyah adds cheerfully. "I'm going to be a choreographer in heaven."

"In heaven?" I repeat, confused. "Why are you going to be one in heaven?"

"Because in heaven, Sadia Apa, everything that is forbidden on earth will be provided. *Allah mian* has promised to make all of our dreams come true."

I notice a group of people in their mid- to late twenties, four or five young men in suits and a handful of young women in salwar kameezes, standing at the back of the gathering, talking and laughing, and go to join them. As I near them, I hear the reassuring sound of their American accents.

"Sadia!" one of them says, and I recognize my cousin Rehana.

Rehana and her sister, Ameena, grew up outside of San Francisco. I have met them only a handful of times, at other family weddings, but I find them interesting. Instead of following the paths that most Pakistani Americans pursue—medicine, law, or finance—Rehana works in a graphic design studio, and Ameena as a real estate developer. Both are stylish, always outfitted in the latest Pakistani wedding fashions, and seem completely comfortable both in the U.S. and in Pakistan. Rehana strikes me as a thoughtful sort, whereas Ameena comes across as spunky. She is the only Pakistani American I have ever seen who wears her hair in a pixieish, close-cropped style, which suits her. Hair is considered to be one of a woman's finest attributes here, and when I compliment her new look she jokes that all of the

Pakistani aunties are staring at her head, wondering why she would do such a thing.

As I enter the conversation, I gather that the group is teasing one of the young men, Asif, who has expressed some interest in a young woman who is sitting on the other side of the room.

"If we were back home, I'd go talk to her, you know? But here it's like, sheesh, everyone is looking at you, and then you talk to a girl, and—boom—you're married!"

The group laughs, and an older boy claps him on the back.

"Oh, don't pretend you're not looking for a wife, Asif!" he says congenially. "Don't pretend your dad isn't doing the rounds right now, finding out about all of the single girls at this function!"

I look over at the buffet table and see Asif's father filling up a plate with samosas. As if on cue, he walks toward the group and offers us the plate.

"So," he says, in Asif's general direction, "see anyone you like?"

The group laughs again.

"Here we go again." Ameena rolls her eyes. "Another wedding, another HMM."

"HMM?" I ask.

"Halal Meat Market," Ameena says with a smile.

"Happens every time," Rehana adds.

I look around at the group and am reminded of my teenage resentment at my mother because we didn't live in a Pakistani American community. Many of my cousins went to Sunday school in their local mosques, fasted for all thirty days of Ramadan each year, socialized with other Pakistani families on a weekly, even daily basis. Some of them are more religious than others; one cousin, Aadam, has become a kind of unofficial youth leader in Islamic societies along the Eastern Seaboard. I wonder if he finds time during his day as a banker in Boston to pray. I wonder about how my cousins' teenage and college years and young adulthoods have been different from mine, and why. I am drawn to the sense of belonging I feel as I stand with and near my cousins; for a little while, I am part of the club—Pakistani American, Muslim American, and nothing else—but only as long as I am standing here.

Aliyah doesn't join me in spending most of the evening joking with my cousins.

"Why don't you come and meet them?" I ask her toward the end of the night, and she walks over to exchange a few greetings with some members of the group. I can't tell if she's shy or reluctant to join in the conversation for other reasons.

"They're your cousins, too," I say.

I TELL MY MOTHER on the telephone that her family in Pakistan no longer approves of socializing between men and women who are not related. The picture I paint for her in my descriptions is a culture she doesn't recognize, far removed from the pluralism of Karachi in the 1960s, when she was a teenager. Hearing my stories exasperates her.

"My father used to recite a hadith of the Prophet Muhammad: 'Difference of opinion is a mercy for my community.' That's the way we were raised. He put his children in different kinds of schools—Catholic schools, British schools—just so that we would have different opinions. So that we could debate! That's the way that I was raised. That is the faith that I know, that my father practiced. . . ."

"I know, Mama," I say. "But it's different now. It's different here."

"Have you been to Siddiqi House?" she asks. "Have you seen Nana's flat?"

"Not yet," I say. "I'm going tomorrow."

"Remember to visit Bibi first—she's the eldest, so that's protocol. Then Zaitoon."

"Right. Thanks."

BATH ISLAND, once a desirable residential district for British officers, became prime real estate in the late 1940s for wealthy families, many of whom had recently relocated to Karachi from India. The houses of my grandfather's

Parsi friends remain, isolated oases behind tall gates, but gone are many of the grand villas that transplants like my grandfather built to replace the homes they left behind in India. Siddiqi House is now a relic, an anachronism, and people say it's only a matter of time before it, too, is sold and demolished, and a tall, lucrative tower built in its place. My mother hopes that her family will hang on to the house, but she knows it is not practical. Though there is still a flat in Siddiqi House in Nana's name, it is only one-sixth of the property, hardly even a voting share. People say that, by virtue of its location, the house might sell for as much as two million pounds sterling.

I ask my hired driver to drop me at the one of the two main entrances, and look up at the house, shielding my eyes from the sun with one hand. I had expected Siddiqi House to appear diminished, to exist in contrast with the magnitude of how large it seemed to me as a child. To my surprise, it feels as big and impenetrable as it always has; as tall and wide as it exists in my memory. But when I move closer, I can see where a recent paint job was started and then abandoned, where the two shades of yellowish cream don't match. Cracks in the exterior have been filled in with plaster but are not yet smoothed over. I think of all the people who used to live here and have long since departed for other houses, other countries. There is no longer the sound of music coming out of the windows, my aunt Farida's dogs barking and playing in the yard. There are no children growing up here. Outside each front gate of Siddiqi House, according to my grandfather's standing instructions, a large clay urn was to be filled constantly with fresh drinking water, so that any thirsty traveler could find refreshment. Instinctively, I peer inside, expecting a deep, reflective pool, and find nothing but dried mud.

All six flats have separate doors on separate floors, large imposing blocks of wood with brass knockers, and brass plates bearing the name of each flat's owner. Which door you consider the main entrance of Siddiqi House depends entirely on whose child you are, and whom you have come to visit. Two open stairwells where servants run up and down between flats form the axis of communication—that is, between the residents of Siddiqi House who are talking to one another. There always seems to be some kind of strain in the house between different factions of the family. These feuds hang like uneven strings from my grandfather's children, even now, more than forty years later. I have heard the stories. During my grandfather's lifetime, the different branches of the family lived peacefully together, maintained harmony. In the years since he died, it has been harder and harder to remember a time when the Siddiqis were one united family.

"*Joint* property," I can hear Nana saying in my mind, by way of explanation. "*Joint* family."

As a child, I thought the fault lay with the word itself; I thought the "joint" Nana referred to was a faulty junction between multiple parts. Now I understand that Nana was trying to make sense of how she ended up where she was, the young widow with five small children, trapped in a crowded, jealous house, with no resources of her own.

While my grandfather was alive, Nana was the favored wife. She had three more children in Karachi and enjoyed a special status in the house. It was Nana who shared a bedroom with her husband, who accompanied him when he attended formal functions, who oversaw the construction of his real estate holdings. Nana carried the keys to his properties on a chain around her waist; my mother remembers the announcement of her mother's step by that unmistakable jingle. Each day, Nana visited the properties and made sure that construction was proceeding according to plan. Her husband built her Rahat Villa, near Siddiqi House, to replace the house she had lost in Bombay. This tall concrete structure looked nothing like the original; it was meant as an income property, something that she would keep in her name and pass on to her children. He was building others—he had an empty lot in Housing Society, a large duplex on Tipu Sultan Road. He was constantly investing in new schemes and new businesses. Then he had a heart attack.

In the hospital, he held his three wives' hands together on his chest.

"I have left a property of equal value in each of your names. Promise me that you will divide the assets equally. Promise me that you will live as one family, united, and act in the common good of our family, of all of our children."

The women nodded, quietly sobbing, and Ali asked for a moment alone with each of them. When it came time for him to see Nana alone, he touched her cheek briefly.

"I had always planned to give each of you two flats in Siddiqi House, for your children—"

"Never mind, never mind," Nana said.

"No, listen, sweetheart—the house remains in Choti Amma's name. But you have the new Rahat Villa; it's a property of equal value. I haven't given you the life you wanted," he said quietly. "And I have not been able to provide for you in the way that I had hoped to."

"Shh-shh—" Nana said.

"Promise me that you will help the family to stay united, to stay together. They will need your strength."

"I will. I promise."

What had been assets while he was alive—her youth, her beauty, and her five bright children—were liabilities for Nana once he was gone. Suddenly the financial situation of the family had changed, and with it the rules. Everything Nana had came now out of a collective pot, which was managed by Bari Amma, my grandfather's first wife. The household duties were divided among the three women; Choti Amma managed the grocery shopping and food preparation, Bari Amma supervised the funds and the household staff, and Nana's job was to get all of the children ready for school and organized when they came home. But without a breadwinner, there was no car and driver so she could visit her family on the other side of Karachi, no extra money for music lessons or new clothes. Not long after Ali's death, it became clear that the family was in debt. If they were to retain Siddiqi House and keep the family together, something had to be sold. It was decided that it made the most sense to sell the new Rahat Villa, and there went the first of Nana's properties. Though the other wives retained their holdings, Nana willingly ceded hers, acting in the common good as she had promised her husband. In compensation for Rahat Villa, Choti Amma gave her one flat of Siddiqi House in her name, and Nana leased it to a Parsi family, the Mehtas, painstakingly saving the rent. Each month, she put aside a small amount of money. Once a week, she walked to the market at the end of the lane to buy fruit, eggs, and imported luxuries. She kept these things safely in her bedroom, her private stash. When her five children came home from school, she prepared thin slices of apple, cold milk with Bournvita chocolate drink, toasted sandwiches made with Kraft cheese from a can, and they pretended for an hour or two that nothing had changed. She dreamed of living in her flat by herself, with her own children, a modest approximation of the life she had lived in Bombay before Partition. But with her other properties sold or held collectively, she was reliant on the meager income of the rent to have some degree of financial independence.

Years later, the flat eluded her still. When Nana finally convinced the Mehtas to move out, just two years before her own death, she did so with the dream of fixing up the apartment—finally—and having a place of her own again. She had new wiring, air-conditioning, and curtains put in, and installed Bibi, the widow of her late brother-in-law and the last member of Nana's generation of Siddiqi women, to stay there as a kind of caretaker. Bibi needed a place to stay, and Nana thought of her as a kind of place-holder, until she could make the trip herself. While moving between her children's homes in Europe and the United States, Nana began to frequent outlet sales and collect towel sets, picture frames, and other miscellaneous household items to bring back to Karachi. She would describe the details of her purchases and home improvements to me on the phone in detail, and I would listen with curiosity from graduate school in California. At the time, I could not understand why she was doing it.

"But Nana, what's the use of fixing it up now?"

"It's mine, too," she would say quietly. "It was my husband's house."

When it came time to vacate the apartment in anticipation of Nana's arrival, Bibi was reluctant to let go of the flat. After Nana had spent so many years in the United States, Bibi couldn't understand why she would want to return to Karachi now, and accused her of ill treatment. Months passed, and the disagreement persisted. Nana died without seeing the apartment complete.

. . .

I SPEND THE NEXT HOUR photographing the house from all angles, try-ing to understand its shape and presence. I cover the house from both sides, standing on the lawns, on balconies looking up and looking down. I imag-ine the stories I have heard and play them out for myself, imagining where they took place—there the gate my mother walked through when she came home from convent school, there the driveway where Uncle Salman entered on a white horse for his wedding. But my camera can't capture these invisi-ble moments. The house, through my viewfinder, seems both too big to convey and too ordinary for what it really is.

"You there, what are you doing?"

The jagged voice comes from an upstairs window, and I look up to see my aunt Zaitoon, a small woman with a fearsome presence whom I have always found intimidating. She is the one I am supposed to visit second, according to family hierarchy, but I see that that is impossible now.

"*As-salaam aleikum,* Zaitoon Auntie," I call out. "It's Sadia."

"*Kaun hai?*" she calls. Who is it?

"Sadia," I say, "*Samina ki beti.*" Samina's daughter.

"*Accha,*" she says, I see. She retreats inside the window.

I walk upstairs and knock on her door. Zaitoon comes to the door and cracks it open just wide enough to wedge herself in the doorjamb, but not wide enough for me to come inside. I am reminded of my childhood im-pression of Zaitoon. Her thinning hair and the unfortunate placement of a large mole on her cheek have always reminded me of a witch.

"*As-salaam aleikum,* Zaitoon Auntie," I repeat. "It's Sadia." But she doesn't move.

Zaitoon was married to my mother's half brother Irfan. When she was a child, her father was the manager of my grandfather's agricultural lands out-side of Karachi, and she played with the Siddiqi children when they were all young. My mother remembers her as a small, scrawny kid, neither bright nor pretty, and most of the family were surprised when Choti Amma arranged for her to marry her son Irfan. He died young, and left her with a respectable inheritance. Zaitoon was now left to manage Siddiqi House, and in recent years she has seemed determined to move most of her immediate family into the house. When my mother's half sister Farida died without a will, Zaitoon was the next of kin, and she now had two of the six flats of Siddiqi House in her name. She began to inquire discreetly about buying out other members of the family. If the property was ever to be sold, she stood to gain the most.

"I didn't recognize you," she says, and I smile, expecting to be asked inside. "I heard that you were in Karachi." She does not ask the customary questions about my parents' health.

"How are your sons, Auntie?" I ask.

There was a time when her sons and Cassim and I played together for hours in the garden, when we were all friends. I haven't seen them in years, and know only scattered rumors about their whereabouts.

"They are fine," she says.

It seems that I am not going to be offered tea, and so I shift my attention to the purpose of my visit.

"Do you have the key to my grandmother's flat?" I ask. "My mother wanted me to look in on it."

"There's nothing there."

"I know, but I'd just like to see it. . . ."

"Don't bother."

"I'd just like to take a look, if I could. Do you have the key?"

Zaitoon closes the door and goes back inside. She returns a few minutes later with an old-fashioned long metal key, which she hands over reluctantly to me.

"I don't know anything about it," she says as I am walking up the stairs. "I wasn't the one in charge."

When I reach the door of the flat, I extend my hands to feel the embossed letters of my grandmother's name. I turn the key, trying to budge the difficult lock. After several tries, it opens with a soft click.

Later, I will ask myself what I'd expected to find, and I will admit that I had irrationally hoped for a semblance of home, of Nana's presence, as if somehow the boxes of pink dish towels and discount soap sets that I'd found in her Miami bedroom after she died could have made their way here. I am not prepared for what I see when I walk inside: an empty, desolate space crusted with a thick layer of pigeon droppings. Gone are the air-conditioning units she'd had installed. In their place are gaping holes, the new wiring she had so proudly described to me on the phone ripped out. It looks as if some-one took a hammer to the walls and pulled the cords out with his or her bare hands. A few scattered curtain rings lie on the floor, and I wonder which house those curtains now hang in.

Nana's flat has the same dimensions as the other flats of Siddiqi House— it's grand and airy, with tall ceilings, fireplaces with marble mantels, and French doors on either side of the main living room that open onto a long, cool veranda. I remember Nana describing the indoor gardens she'd planned to grow.

I walk through the wide-open space in disbelief. No wonder Zaitoon was reluctant for me to see the apartment.

Nana's flat has been emptied of all its furniture, with the exception of two dark Art Deco–style pieces too heavy to move—a tall armoire and a low table with drawers. I feel a pointed sting of recognition, the same feeling I had in the original Rahat Villa in Bombay. This is the other half of her fur-niture set—the pieces that came by ship to Karachi after Partition. I feel the same impulse to lay my hands on them; after all these years, in both places, these blocks of wood are like anchors.

Who did this? I wonder, feeling a sharp rise of anger. Why would some-one steal curtains and air-conditioning units? Why would someone rip wires out of the wall?

ON THE PHONE THAT EVENING, Mama sounds resigned.

"This is an old story," she tells me. "Probably it was no one person but a series of people, and people who work for those people. Everyone knows that none of Nana's children are coming back to live there, and so they think, why not help themselves?"

"Aren't you angry?" I ask her, trying to keep my resentment in check.

"I'm sad. I'm glad that my mother and father are not here to see this."

THE NEXT DAY, I return to Siddiqi House to visit Bibi, my great-aunt, who is now in her mid-seventies. When Bibi opens the door, I smile and introduce myself, embracing her and kissing her on both cheeks. Even now, it's clear that Bibi was once a beautiful woman. She still keeps her hair long and brown, and when she is fresh from her bath, like now, her braid hangs down her back like a girl's.

"*Beti! Beti!*" she says, smiling broadly and clasping me to her chest. I am more than a foot taller than she, and so I stoop down, accepting her warm hug.

She ushers me inside and insists that I stay for lunch. From what I can tell, she says that she wishes she had known I was coming, because she would have prepared something special for me. What is my favorite dish?

I tell her brokenly that I like everything, *sab kuchh,* but she insists on my naming a specific dish.

"*Murghi,*" I say finally, figuring that chicken is a safe choice.

She tells me enthusiastically that in that case I must return to her home to eat chicken curry. I tell her not to go to any trouble, but privately I feel delighted at being fussed over like a beloved grandchild. It reminds me intensely of Nana, of what she would do.

Bibi is now living as a kind of caretaker for Uncle Salik and Auntie Sheynaz's flat, which they visit once or twice a year from their permanent residence in London. Bibi has, at one time or another, lived in almost all of the Siddiqi House flats. She is the very definition of a grateful beneficiary of the extended family structure, and she has learned, over the years, how to make this system of favors and complex hierarchies work to her advantage.

I want to ask Bibi about Nana's flat. It was she who lived there once the

renovations were complete two years ago; she must know more than anyone. But my Urdu can only get me so far. Apart from the topics of food and
weather, my language skills are almost useless.

As Bibi bustles between the dining room and the kitchen, retrieving
dishes and heating up leftovers, I follow after her, trying to offer my help.
There is so much that I wish I could ask her.

Why was Nana so uncomfortable with Bibi? I wonder. "Never trust a
milkman's daughter," I can hear Nana say—the only unkind words I ever
heard her utter. That night, I call Mama and ask her about it.

"There's a long history there," she says, and then she tells me a story that
I have never heard before.

"I was seven years old, and I had a nightmare. I don't remember what it
was, just this terrible sense of dread. And I ran into my mother's room to
find her—she and my father slept in separate rooms then. And I found her
sitting at her vanity table; it had a long, narrow mirror in the middle and
two sets of drawers on either side, where she used to keep her medicines.
And she was sobbing uncontrollably, and in her hand she was holding an
open bottle. I remember that it was dark blue glass and it had a label on it
with a skull and crossbones. I learned later that it was tincture of iodine,
standard in first aid, fatal if it was swallowed. And I ran as fast as I could to
the room where my father was sleeping, and I woke him up and made him
come to my mother's room, with me. He took her in his arms and he said,
'What have you done? What have you done?' over and over again; he was
sure that she had swallowed it. And she looked at him and she said: 'I have
done nothing. The bottle was empty.'"

"What made Nana so unhappy?"

"I think I was too young to understand it then, but it made me aware
that there was some way that my father made my mother very sad, something more than the fact that she had to share him with other wives and
childen. Later, when I was about twelve, I came into Bibi's room and found
her ironing my father's undergarments. He used to wear white undergarments, made of pure white cotton, and he was the only person in the house

who wore them. I got very angry. I grabbed a pair of his shorts and I stormed into my mother's room, where she was alone. 'This is *your* job!' I said, flinging them at her. 'Why do you let Bibi do what you should do?'"

"What did Nana say?" I ask.

"She looked at me and said, 'Don't you think I want to?' and I understood for the first time that my father was not faithful to my mother, whom I know he loved. 'How can you stand it?' I remember I asked her. She told me that she would retreat inside herself and imagine that she was standing on the balcony in Rahat Villa, looking at the ocean. When I learned that, I think I understood something about my mother. In order to exist in that house, she had to pretend she was somewhere else."

Mama lets out a long sigh, like air being released from a balloon, as if she has not thought about this in a long time. "Go to the bank tomorrow for me, if you can," she says. "Ask for Tariq Ali; say that you're my daughter and you're there to close your grandmother's account. Call me tomorrow night and let me know how it goes."

IN RETROSPECT, it seems logical that Nana's bank account was closed, emptied, more than a year before my visit. Tariq Ali, her account manager, looks apologetic, but he does not seem concerned. I hold my grandmother's old-fashioned long check register in my hand. In it, she calculated each month what her expected earnings would be from the rental of her flat, and I have guarded it carefully in India, always remembering to carry it in my handbag, not to check it in my luggage. It is now a meaningless document. Standing in the bank, watching Tariq Ali's mustache move up and down as he speaks, I have the absurd sensation that I am in a tunnel; I can see him speaking, but I cannot understand what he is saying. I try to concentrate. The milky tea in front of me, almost orange, is growing a thick skin from the powerful fan pulsing above me. I hear Tariq Ali claiming that my grandmother authorized the action herself.

"See here, her signature." He points to an unfamiliar scrawl on documents that I can't read and don't understand. "I have known your family a long time," he says calmly. I watch the brittle shoulder pads of his jacket buckle and fold as he shrugs. "It was a long-standing account," he says, "and then it was closed. Nothing to be done, really."

I walk outside into the hot, bright sun of the early afternoon and feel myself welling up. The money seems unimportant. But the knowledge that Nana has been stolen from, time and time again, upsets me deeply. I feel foolish, thinking that I was going to go to the bank and rescue my inheritance, withdraw Nana's money, and return it proudly to my mother. How silly of me to think that someone hadn't thought to retrieve it already.

I call Mama, waking her up.

"Mama, Nana's money is gone."

"Gone?" she says, sleepily. "What do you mean, gone?"

"The banker said that someone, a family member, closed the account more than a year ago."

There's silence on the other end of the line.

"More than a *year* ago. Are you there, Mama?"

"Closed the account . . ." she repeats, trying to find meaning in the words.

"Emptied. They emptied the account."

"Do you know what that money was for? She asked me to make a piece of jewelry for each of her grandchildren, for each of their weddings. I was supposed to design them and have them made in Karachi. That's what that money was meant for."

"Who took it, Mama?"

"It could be any number of people. I don't know that I care to find out."

"But don't you want to know?"

"I need to leave this behind," she says. "It's not useful. I just think of my father, and how sad he would be to see his children stealing from one another. It makes me terribly, terribly sad."

• • •

UNCLE WARIS is giving me a history lesson.

"The trouble between the Jews and the Muslims has nothing to do with the Jews or the Muslims, sweetheart," he begins. "It's all the fault of the Christians. . . ."

I'm not sure how I can continue to keep all of these theories straight. I write in my notebook: "Christians?"

"Sadia Apa, do you really have more questions for my grandfather?" Aliyah asks, bursting into the room and seeing me with my head in both hands. "Because we are going to Paradise Stores, and my mother said that you can have any kind of snack that you want, if you want to come."

"No, thank you, Aliyah. I'll stay here," I say. "I want to make sure and say goodbye to Sartaj and Fatima before I go."

"But it's your last day!" Aliyah frowns. "I really just can't believe you are going to leave so soon!"

"I know, but I'll come over to your house in a little while, I'll be right over."

"You get the watchman to walk you," she says sternly.

Her house is next door, separated by a wall and a short driveway, and I can't really fathom that it's necessary to be escorted fewer than thirty feet. But I still don't know the rules here, I remind myself. This isn't Bombay.

Fatima enters the living room, wearing a pressed black salwar suit and matching black headscarf.

"You're going somewhere?" I ask.

"We're going to see the Imam," Fatima says. "He's someone we know from the U.S., actually. He's here visiting."

"He's a very important man," Uncle Waris says, walking back to his bedroom to lie down. "They are going to pay a call on him."

"Oh, I see," I say.

"I was sorry not to be able to spend more time with you this visit," Fatima says, resting her hand on mine.

"Me too," I say, feeling suddenly nostalgic, the way I often do at the end of short journeys. "I was hoping to talk more with both of you."

"What about?" Sartaj says, entering the room.

"About Nana, actually. My mother told me . . ." I begin. I am not sure how to phrase what I want to ask. So much gets left unsaid with this side of my family, and I am not accustomed to speaking candidly.

"My mother told me that the day Nana died she asked to speak with you."

The moment I have spoken these words, I realize that I have questions, things that only Sartaj and Fatima might know.

"That's true," Sartaj says.

"I want to know if she converted, if she accepted Islam, with your help, that day, before she died."

"Ah," he says, "that." He nods to Fatima to indicate that they will leave in a few minutes, and sits down. "The family was all gathered there in her hospital room, and then your grandmother said that she wanted to rest, and so we all said our goodbyes. Fatima and I weren't sure if we would see her again; it's a long drive from Atlanta to Miami, and we weren't sure how much longer she would be with us. But just when we reached the parking lot, your mother called and said, 'Sartaj, she wants to see you again. Alone.' So I went back upstairs, and I went into her room, and I said, 'How can I help?'"

"Did she have questions for you?"

"She had . . . concerns, as you know. She was mainly worried about her parents—how she would face them if she no longer shared their religion. But she was also very worried about God, whether God would accept her. 'Sartaj,' she said, 'I was born a Jew, but I do not know the Jewish prayers. I only know the Muslim prayers. I only know how to pray in Arabic.'"

"What did you tell her?"

"Some of what we discussed that day we spoke about in confidence, and I cannot reveal it."

"I understand."

"And some of it, some of it is between your grandmother and God."

"I understand."

"There is some of it that you and I will never know."

I nod, hoping that he will continue.

"But, yes, your grandmother said her *kalimah*, the Muslim prayer."

Sartaj gets up, smoothing out his kurta with his hands. "I believe that she died a Muslim."

I get up, putting my hands on the table, not sure of what to say and conscious of trying to make my voice steady.

"Thank you," I say. "For telling me that."

Sartaj raises one hand in a wave of farewell and walks out the door and toward the car. Fatima lingers, sensing that I am about to cry, and puts her arm around me.

"Sadia, I want to tell you something," she says. She smiles tentatively. "I dreamt of your Nana, after she died."

"You had a dream about her?"

"It's strange, I never have dreams like this. But in my dream, your grandmother was wearing a white sari, and she was standing on a curved balcony, overlooking the ocean. She was standing there with her arms on the railing and talking to me, and she said, 'I'm so happy, Fatima. I'm so happy here. I'm home. I'm in my own home.' And somehow I knew that she was in her old home place, her original home."

"You mean in India?"

"In India. The ocean was behind her, and there were other people there with her in the house. . . . I didn't know them. . . ."

"Her family . . ."

"I don't know who they were, but they told me that she was happy, and I could tell that she was."

"Fatima, that is her house in Bombay, that's Rahat Villa."

"I don't know anything about that house—we never discussed it—it's so strange that I would dream of it. But you know, they say that when you dream of someone after they die, and if they look well, then their spirit is in a good place, they are at peace. I think your Nana is at peace."

"She's in Bombay," I say. "Nana is in Bombay."

. . .

BEFORE IT'S TIME for me to leave for the airport, I go to visit Nana's flat one last time. This visit has a feeling of inevitability, of memorization, like the last time I saw my childhood home in Massachusetts, before my parents moved to Miami. I walk through the gate. It seems likely that this will be the last time I will do this. I don't know when I will be able to return to Karachi, how I will be different then, how this house and its inhabitants will have changed. I don't want to imagine a high-rise standing in place of this house, the last chip of my grandfather's dream of a unified family pulverized. But this outcome seems likely enough so that I have to push the thought, sharp and crystallized, out of my mind.

I turn the key in the door of Nana's flat and enter, prepared now for the sight of pigeons making a nest. I place my hands on the armoire again, and recognize the feeling of my hands on this wood as if I have stood here a million times. I have the sense that I am walking through someone else's memory, Nana's memory. Then, as if I have done so a million times, I take off the chain around my neck and remove the key. I don't know how I didn't realize it before. I am suddenly sure that the key is going to open the armoire, and that whatever I am looking for will be hidden there.

I am unsurprised to find that it is a perfect fit. I feel that Nana has guided me here, that she somehow knew all the time that I would come. The door is jammed, and I feel a slight panic. What if I can't get it open? I wrap my arms around the armoire and pull, and the door swings open with a thud, the latch popping open. There are three shelves inside. On the top shelf are tablecloths. I open them eagerly, releasing clouds of dust that make me sneeze. The middle shelf is empty. The bottom shelf is empty. I feel a sinking feeling of disappointment.

Then I notice a small drawer, just underneath the middle shelf, and pull it open by its small brass handle. Inside are sheaves of paper and two crumbling books. My heart skips a beat, tripping over itself. All of this time, I think. This has been right here.

I sit on one side of the armoire, spreading the contents of the shelf before me. A deed to Rahat Villa, in her original name, Rachel Jacobs. Three IOUs from Choti Amma to Nana, stamped and dated, all from the 1950s. An English translation of the Talmud. A stack of letters, written in both English and Devanagari script. Holding these remnants of my grandmother's life feels eerie. It's as if she left me signs, a map to follow.

I fold these precious objects carefully inside my dupatta, cradling them to protect them from questions. I place the key inside the cupboard, and shut the door.

This time, my trip back to Bombay is maddeningly slow.

Matar.

Dist.Kaira.

13th.May 33.

My dear Rachel,

It is strange that you have not written
to me all these days. I am anxiously looking out for your
letter. I trust you are quite comfortable.xxxxxx Do let me
know if you want anything. I am busy these days. Any way,
I will give you a look up on hearing from you.

Give me all the details of your work and
the time that will be convenient for you to see me.

With best wishes,

P.S.   Very sincerely yours,

I had a letter from

Papa. He too was complaining   *ali*

of not having received a letter from

you. I have given him xxxxxxx your news.

Write soon.

Address.   Inspector of Customs,

Matar. Dist.Kaira.

20

NANA'S PAPERS

BOMBAY, JUNE 2002

On my first evening home in Bombay, I start with the Talmud. It's a fragile leather-bound volume with a tooled cover and embossed gilt letters, and I open it gingerly. The flyleaf is loose and nearly falls into my lap. I hold it carefully between my thumb and forefinger and see that it is stamped, in fading purple letters: "Property of Ralph Jacobs."

So this was Nana's father's book, then. I've never before touched anything that he owned. Underneath his name it reads: "For my children and their children after them."

The book is an English translation of portions of the Talmud, most of which are organized around themes—love, family, faith. I can imagine Ralph reading this book aloud to his children. Like her mortar and pestle, this object made the journey with Nana from India to Pakistan, from her girlhood to adulthood. Now these papers travel back to Bombay, with me.

I open the bundle of letters, which are threaded on a crumbling piece of string. They vary in color and weight, from a sepia scrawl on parchment to heavy rag paper nearly perforated with type. Pieces of the fragile paper, perhaps untouched in decades, break off in my hands. Carefully, I begin to make sense of their order, laying them gently on my round glass table. I chart their progression from 1933 to 1940, making rough notes and calculations in my notebook as I muddle my way through the unfamiliar handwriting. The first folio of letters is from Nana's father, Ralph, to his twenty-five-year-old friend Ali, the man who would become Nana's husband. The second is a series of letters from Ali to Nana. There are no letters from Nana to her father, or to her husband, so I have to imagine what her replies might have been.

I recall that Nana's father and husband were business partners in a mining venture in remote Castle Rock, the town where Nana and her siblings spent some of their childhood. Uncle Waris told me that the preceding generation of the two families had known each other, but the correspondence surprises me; Ali describes how much he misses the times he spent in Castle Rock with the Jacobs family, where "our two families lived as one," and details the various remote postings he has received as an inspector of salt and customs in Gujarat. Ralph asks after Ali's two wives, who are now managing separate households in different parts of the state. Ali asks Ralph to send his "salaams to everyone at home." The substantive part of their exchange is about Ali's help in arranging for Nana to enroll in nursing school a few hours from his government posts in Gujarat. Ali instructs Ralph on which letters and certificates Nana will need, and in one letter suggests that she obtain a letter that states her age to be "about 18 years." But the postmark tells me that at the time she is only fifteen.

Ali's letters to Nana are in a second folder. The first ones are typed, circumspect. They are addressed to "My dear Rachel." He asks after her family, and assures her that she will be happy at the Female Hospital in Ahmedabad, where "you will be quite close to us. . . . I will write and tell you all about it. In the meantime keep on studying hard. . . ." He closes his letters by saying, "Reply soon, will you? Very sincerely yours, A. Siddiqi."

Once Nana reaches Ahmedabad and settles into the nursing school of the hospital, Ali seems to grow more anxious that she is not responding to his letters.

My dear Rachel,

    It is strange that you have not written to me all these days. I am anxiously looking out for your letter. I trust you are quite comfortable. Do let me know if you want anything. I am busy these days. Any way, I will give you a look up on hearing from you.

    Give me all the details of your work and the time that will be convenient for you to see me.

    With best wishes,

Very sincerely yours,
Ali

Ali occasionally refers in his letters to things he has obtained for Nana that she misses from home—mango preserves, a fountain pen, a packet of sweet limes. He advises her on how to handle her housing arrangements at the hospital, and worries about whether her blanket is keeping her warm enough in the cool weather. Then, three months after Nana arrives in Ahmedabad, the tone of the letters changes.

My dear Rachel,

Dear, you were one day late in writing to me. I expected you would write on 12th. Why so? This letter should reach you on 16th and if you reply the same day I will get it on 17th. Let me hope you'll do so.

I have started counting the days and within eight days I'll be there.

I'll ring off my dear with an X.

Yrs as B/4
Ali

With each letter, Ali seems to grow more persistent. The letters now address her as "darling," or "dear-heart," and in them Ali worries about Rachel's feelings toward him.

I find you indifferent toward me these days. Why so my love? Am I to understand that you do not care for me or is it that you are so busy that you do not find time to think about anything else? Anyway, I hope you are comfortable and happy. Have you been able to get a cot with mosquito netting? You must sleep under a net. . . .

I feel very lonely. I do not know what to do.

Since I am missing Nana's half of the correspondence, there is no way to know what her feelings were toward this man—her protector, her guardian, perhaps her lover, soon her husband. From his references to her replies, Nana seems by turns reluctant and responsive. But, judging by the tone of the letters after Nana turned sixteen, I am convinced that Ali has seduced her.

My darling Rachel,

When would it be possible for you to take leave and come here? Do inquire and let me know. You must come on 7 days leave at least . . .

I cannot help thinking of you the whole time. So much so that I always dream of you at night my young darling. . . .

Ali's letters continue, with increasing passion, through the next five years, while he continues to send money and gifts and to complain that she does not write often enough. Once Nana moves back to attend nursing school in Bombay, he begs her not to go unaccompanied on trains, or to attend movies at night, where she "might be followed, or worse." I remember Nana's story about her friendship with the Sikh doctor Mr. Singh, which must have taken place during this period. Then, in 1938, when Nana is about twenty-one years old, the letters take another abrupt shift.

Honey, my Love,

I know my people will have and do have a lot to say. The same will be the case with your people. But so far, your mother has been kindness itself. She has, as it were, given you to me. And I must say I am lucky. Sweetheart, are you going to eat your heart and mine too for other people's sake? If you really love me then you will have to put up with everything and that too cheerfully. . . . If I cannot smile at looking at your pretty eyes it is not worth the trouble. I want you. It is for you to choose.

I do not want you to love me because you loved me once and you feel you have to now. Whatever you do dearest, you do with a free will. Neither of us have any control over our people so what cannot be cured must be endured. Do you agree, Sweetie?

Be good and write soon.

Xxx
Hubby

This letter startles me the most. It seems that Nana considered leaving her husband for fear of what their families and communities would think. At this stage Rachel and Ali had no children; had she left him in 1938, she might have gone on to live an entirely different life. Instead, he must have persuaded her to stay.

When I reach the end of the folder, I am exhausted. I look outside and realize that I have been poring over Ali's tiny script for the better part of a day. Julie arrives, and is concerned to see me sitting in the dark.

"You will ruin your eyes, I think so!" she says, opening up the shuttered windows, letting in the afternoon light.

There is one last letter, dated January 11, 1940. I do a rough calculation; in 1940 Nana would be twenty-three, living in Bombay. Ali would be living in various parts of Gujarat and visiting her every few months. From what I can understand from the letter, they must have had a fight on his most recent visit.

My darling wife,

I am really and truly sorry for what happened on the eve of my departure. You are a wise girl, you can realize the depth of my feeling for you. After the clouds disappeared I saw the moonlight and by Jove, what a silver lining. Your sweet kisses I will always miss till we meet again. I have discovered something—Darling, why did you not kiss me like that all these years? Is it that you too have a weakness like me to want to be kissed? X. Here is one from me.

Fond love and true kisses on your sweet lips
Yr Hubby

I close the folder, my grandfather's words spilling through every impression I had of him as a child: the tall, magnanimous provider; the eccentric; the heartbreaker. I lie down on my slim bed, closing my eyes and trying to imagine how it would feel to receive letters like these from a man. I think about what Nana might have felt, reading these letters for the first time. Such extremity bound into one relationship. The gaps and the silences he complains of remind me powerfully of her, of how quiet she could be, of how prodding her to talk could provoke her to say nothing at all. I feel the familiar pull of missing her.

THE NEXT MORNING, I wake up early and read the last letters again. Then I flip the pile over and see something new, a thin stack of pages tucked into a pocket of the folio.

The pages are in Nana's handwriting and seem to be ripped out of a diary. I run my fingertips lightly over the deep impressions of my grandmother's fountain pen as if it were Braille, wondering what the unfamiliar Marathi characters mean. Pages and pages of text, written on a discarded date book: "Friday, January 28, 1949." "Saturday, January 29, 1949." I have to find someone who can decipher this for me. Instantly, I think of Shoshanna Auntie. Shoshanna Auntie is the head cook of ORT India and matron of the girls' hostel. She has a soft, rounded appearance and a gentle way about her, and I like to drink tea with her in the afternoons when I'm waiting to meet with my cousin Benny Isaacs.

That afternoon, I find Shoshanna making lunch for the staff of the school. My request confuses her.

"You want me to read some Marathi for you?" she asks. "But you won't understand what I am saying!"

True, I tell her, but you can tell me what it means, what my grandmother wrote in this book. I am slightly fearful, and hopeful, that Nana has revealed her secrets in this diary, and my thoughts leap to my most private questions about her life—if she was ever officially married to my grandfather, if she regretted her choice to leave her religion, what it was like to live as the third wife in a joint family in Pakistan. Shoshanna shrugs and says cheerfully, "As you like." She washes her hands and wipes them on her apron, then sits down at one of the lunch tables and puts on her bifocals.

She spends several minutes looking at the pages, turning them over, studying them carefully. She seems to be having trouble making out the letters; some of them have bled into one another with age. I become more and more anxious, sitting on my hands like a child. Finally, she looks up, smiling with recognition.

"These are recipes!" she says. "These are very, very old Bene Israel *lady* recipes! Sweet *ladhus* to feed the woman after birth, *halva* to celebrate Rosh Hashanah. I have not seen these foods for so many years—my grandmother, no, my grandmother's grandmother, she used to make these sweets, but no one makes them anymore!"

I'm crushed that the pages aren't diary entries. I had wanted so dearly to have some words that Nana had written in her own hand. But then Shoshanna Auntie begins to speak the recipes aloud, and we begin to work on translating them.

A Treat for a Coconut Day

Coconut Halva

Take 2 coconuts; 2 cups of sugar; 1 ½ cups of mava, 4 of almonds blanched and sliced.

½ teaspoon of minced nutmeg and cardamom powder; ghee.

Grate the coconut. Make a thick syrup with the sugar and then add all the ingredients and mix well. Remove from the fire when quite thick and spread evenly in a deep dish which has been lined with ghee. When cold and firm, cut into squares and serve.

Coconut Blancmange

Take 2 coconuts; 4 spoonfuls of corn flour; 4 spoonfuls of sugar; essence of rose.

Grate the coconut. Soak half in two pints of boiling water and after ten minutes, squeeze out the milk. Keep half a cup of this milk aside. Heat

the rest till it boils, then dissolve the corn flour in the cold milk and add
it to the pot with the sugar. Throw in the grated coconut and stir con-
tinually till it thickens. Add the essence, mix well, and when slightly cold,
pour into wet molds. Chill and serve.

I hear something of Nana's cadence in Shoshanna's recitation. In this
litany of ingredients is a song of portions, one that traveled with Nana from
her mother and her mother before her, and now finds me. I remember
something that Nana said, many times: that recipes don't just make food,
but teach you patience and care. Among the recipes are things that she made
when she was happy, to celebrate—my favorite is a dessert called *sheer
khurma,* made of vermicelli noodles, cardamom, and cream. Then there are
also recipes for things she made when she was sad—I remember watching
her at the stove stirring a pot of shredded carrots, almonds, and sugar to
make carrot *halva.* You have to be careful, she told me, that you don't feed
anyone else with the food you have made in sadness.

I try, unsuccessfully, to make coconut *halva* on my two gas burners, and
I think of how Nana would scold me for trying to cook the coconut mixture
over too large a flame. Hearing her small voice chiding me makes me laugh.
I say a prayer of thanks for the window in my mind that Nana's papers have
cracked open.

I WAKE UP AT four every morning like clockwork, wheezing and cough-
ing, the previous day's exhaust printed on my lungs. Lately, in the silence of
these early hours, I feel something else, the beat of my heart in my throat
like a drum. I put two fingers underneath my jaw and I count. *One . . . two
. . . three-four . . . five . . . six . . . seven . . . eight-nine.* Sometimes it feels as
if my heart is skipping a beat. I've now been in India almost ten months,
and I feel the winding down of my year abroad. It's a tidy thought, to spend
a year away, to return with vivid stories. But it's too soon to go back, I know
that now. I'm not ready to go home. The truth is that I've barely started
what I came here to do. I have pages and pages of notes about ceremonies,

rituals, and traditions that I have barely begun to document. There are so many more people that I need to interview, so many more places I need to visit. I understand now why some people devote entire lifetimes to one subject. My fear of failing knocks on the door and begs to be let inside.

"When do you think you might come back?" my mother asks over the phone. She wants to be supportive, but I can hear the concern in her voice. There has been rising tension between India and Pakistan in recent months, and now the international news is full of talk of war. India has withdrawn its high commissioner from Islamabad and suggested that Pakistan's high commissioner leave New Delhi.

"I can't come back until I make a success of things."

"What would be a success?" she asks gently.

The truth is that I want to be accepted here more than anything. I want to understand the story of the Bene Israel and find a way to tell it; I want Rekhev's approval; I want the grocer and the vegetable man in Bhaji Gali to recognize me when I approach. I want to make myself understood in Hindi. I want to fit in, to live here and feel at home. I want to like myself in this place. Some days, those goals feel within reach. Other days, they're more elusive than ever.

ONE AFTERNOON, I'm in a taxi on my way home, stopped at an intersection near Haji Ali Mosque. Scrawny boys of about twelve or thirteen press magazines and books to the windows of the cars, shiny copies of *Cosmopolitan, Time,* and *Popular Mechanics,* bootlegged copies of books written in English and set in India. A boy comes to my open window, and I shake my head pre-emptively to say: No, thank you, I'm not interested. But he persists, keeping his chin on top of his stack of books while he shows me the covers and quickly recites the titles:

"*Indepreter of Maladees?*" he says hopefully. "*God of Small Tings?*"

I shake my head. No, no. Not interested. But he sees my eyes alight on his copy of *Midnight's Children.*

"Want, madam?" he says, holding the book inside my taxi and raising his eyebrows for emphasis.

No, no. I shake my head. No.

He quickly looks over his shoulder to check if the light is changing. Just as it does, he drops the book into my lap. The taxi speeds forward.

"Wait!" I call after the boy. "Your book!"

We lurch into the chaos of several lanes of traffic merging into one, and I watch out the back window as the boy hands his stack of books to another boy and runs at breakneck speed to keep up with my taxi. I hastily ask the driver to pull over to the side of the road, where we meet the boy, panting, on the other side of the intersection.

"I can't believe you did that," I say in English as the boy wipes his brow, still panting with exertion and looking very proud of himself.

I shake my head in exasperation at his stunt. I give the boy three hundred rupees, twice what the bootlegged book is worth. The boy looks at the money and asks me if I need change; I tell him to keep it. My driver clucks his disapproval.

"Be careful!" I call out to him as we drive away. As I look back, I see the boy waving to me in sheer delight, his right hand flopping from the wrist like a little bird.

"Bye, madam!" he calls after me. "Bye-bye, madam!"

A few days later, I see the same boy across the street from my house. This time he's selling a series of neon-colored plastic watches, and his eyes brighten when he sees me.

"Madam!" he says, running over to me. "Want watch?"

I thank him and tell him I'm not interested. I learn that his nickname is Rintu, and that he lives near Grant Road Station with his mother, who is not in good health.

"What kind of sick?" I ask, trying to practice the Hindi I have been learning with Mr. Shukla.

He shrugs, not sure what to say. All of the street kids have a story, but maybe his mother really isn't well. We're standing in front of the bus station.

There's a tea shop there, which sells glass cups of hot, steaming liquid drawn from a large cauldron in the back, and grills simple sandwiches over a large, flat griddle. I've been tempted by both the tea and the sandwiches, but the stares of the silent men who sit watching me from the road have prevented me from going inside.

"Do you want a sandwich?" I ask Rintu, gesturing inside.

His eyes widen in disbelief. He looks hopeful and reluctant at the same time, unwilling to believe that my offer might be genuine.

"Come," I say, and bound up the stairs.

"One sandwich," I say to the man standing attention at the grill.

The man looks at me and at Rintu, sizing up the situation and smirking at me.

"What kind of sandwich?" he asks.

"Rintu? Tell the man what you want." Rintu looks at the menu in utter amazement. Then he orders a sandwich with every possible item on it.

"Cheej?" the man asks me, indicating that Amul cheese, the canned delicacy of India, will cost extra.

"You want cheese on your sandwich, Rintu?" Rintu looks embarrassed, then excited. "Yes, madam," he says, smiling.

The cook gives me a disapproving look, sprinkling shredded cheese on the bread and grilling everything Rintu has asked for—sliced cucumbers, onions, tomatoes, potatoes.

Rintu inspects the sandwich making, and begins directing the cook on how he'd like his meal prepared. Suddenly Rintu's become a gourmand.

When the sandwich is complete, we sit in the shop and I watch Rintu eat it, his eyes getting larger as he devours the vegetables barely contained between two flimsy layers of bread. Our fellow patrons sit and watch us furtively. We leave the shop and walk toward the bus station, Rintu following behind me.

Rintu looks up at me as if he's expecting me to deliver a final word. "What do you say?" I ask, feeling like a schoolteacher.

"Thank you, madam," he says shyly.

•   •   •

THE SHARP RING of my phone punctures the morning. It's the Bombay coordinator for the Fulbright. "Have you been following the news?" she asks.

"Yes," I say, but I'm not sure what she means. I worry that there's been another terrorist attack.

"The U.S. Department of State is encouraging American citizens to leave India."

"Has something happened?"

"Because of the threat of war," she says.

"With Pakistan?"

There have been recent exchanges of mortar and artillery fire across the Line of Control in the disputed region of Kashmir, and the news is filled with talk of disintegrating relationships between the two governments. But it is hard for me to imagine that India and Pakistan would fight a third war now. It seems far worse when I read the Western news, which makes it seem as if the two countries are on the brink of launching nuclear attacks, than when I read the Indian press.

"The State Department would prefer that Fulbrighters go back to the U.S."

"But I can choose to stay. . . ."

"They would prefer that you didn't."

"I see," I say, and thank her before hanging up.

When my irregular heartbeat wakes me up the following day, I make an appointment to see a specialist at Breach Candy Hospital. He gives me a Holter monitor, a mass of wild-looking colored wires coming out of a box. The contraption is strapped to my skin underneath my salwar kameez.

"What's that you have on your chest?" Julie exclaims when I walk in the door and she sees the surgical tape peeping out of my collar. I explain that it's a monitor to show the beating of my heart, that the doctor is worried about me.

"You are only too sad, Miss Sadia, this is the problem with your heart," Julie says. "You are trying to find your place, that's all."

21

Travel Advisory

BOMBAY/SOUTH DARTMOUTH, JULY 2002

Before I leave Bombay, Rekhev comes to visit. When I go out to retrieve my mail from the mailbox, I find him smoking a cigarette at the edge of my driveway, having an animated conversation with the man in the checked shirt, the one who talks to himself. When they finish, the man wanders off absentmindedly, and Rekhev turns to me.

"It's quite amazing," he says. "It seems that he received some sort of scholarship to go to France, many years ago, to get a doctorate in math. I believe he thinks that he's in Paris half the time. He asked me if I could help him get a map of the city, because he keeps getting lost. Incredible. I'm fascinated with characters like this."

I laugh, happy to see him again.

"You're going somewhere," he says, noting my jeans.

"I have to go home to Massachusetts, for a few weeks," I explain. My parents have finished their assignment in Miami and are now renovating an old farmhouse in South Dartmouth, about an hour and a half south of Boston. I tell him about the travel advisory. I don't tell him that I want to get a second opinion on my strange, irregular heartbeat, that the test my doctor in Bombay conducted was inconclusive. I feel strange telling him that I'm leaving, like I'm cutting something short. I'm not sure what.

"I don't understand it. How you travel," he says finally, looking at the street.

"What do you mean?"

"Moving so quickly between different realities. I can't do that."

Rintu approaches, carrying some incongruous plastic objects: cheap toys made in China—spinning tops, noisy rattles, things that it seems no sensible person would ever buy. He shakes his wares at us, trying to gauge whether we're impressed.

"Rekhev, this is Rintu," I say.

"You're making new friends, I see," Rekhev says. "What is this stuff?" he asks Rintu in Hindi, picking up a long spindle with silvery threads hanging off of it.

Rintu shrugs, looking noncommittal. He offers me a rattle.

"Want one, madam?"

"No, thank you," I say.

"It's terrible stuff, isn't it," Rekhev says to me dryly, inspecting a shiny top.

"Hus-band?" Rintu asks, jerking his thumb in the direction of Rekhev.

"No," I say, shaking my head and feeling a little embarrassed.

"Where is hus-band?"

"No husband."

"*No* husband?" Rintu says, raising both eyebrows and looking shocked. "Why not?"

I shrug. I can't believe I have to defend being single to my local street kid.

Rekhev and I go inside my apartment, and I set about the business of making tea, measuring spoonfuls of sugar, tea, and cardamom into a pot and bringing it to a boil. I'm not very good at it yet; my results are inconsistent.

Rekhev sits down at my round glass table. "The trouble with you is, you do want to get married."

"Why do you say that?" I ask, laughing.

"You're very Indian that way. Not American." He thinks for a moment.

"You should have married that Tony," he says finally. "That was your mistake."

I told Rekhev about Tony once, about how he and I had once talked of getting married and how he asked me if I was ever going to stay in one place. Despite how strongly I felt about him, I knew then that we weren't right for one another. I feel a welling up of resentment that Rekhev would bring this up now. I disagree with him, but I don't feel like fighting on the eve of my departure. I let his comments hover in the air. At this moment, I am too full of all of the possibilities laid out before me, and all the things I could not have done if I had stayed in the U.S. I look over at my open suitcase on the floor. I left that life so that I could stand here, with this wide expanse of not-knowing before me.

Going back will be temporary, I remind myself, just a chance to be there and see a doctor, and then I'll return to Bombay.

MASSACHUSETTS SEEMS impossibly strange, its patterns too tidy, the streets that surround my parents' house too green. I wake up to an unfamiliar quiet; from my bedroom window I can see a silo and fields of corn, the patch of blue of a nearby river in the distance. I watch with amazement at how sheets of hot water come out of the bathroom shower at all times of the day; it feels excessive to me. I walk to the country store, a yellow clapboard house where an elderly couple sells groceries and candy. "Hear you've been to India!" the man says when he hands me the mail from our post office box. I'm thrilled to see my mother and father and Cassim, but I feel out of place, as if I am watching my arrival from afar. I visit my friends in New York and find that I am unfamiliar with the new details of their daily lives, with the shorthand we used less than a year ago. I don't know how to summarize what I have been experiencing in Bombay. I don't know the words to explain how I spend my time, the work that I am doing, how strangely exhausting it is. I don't know how to explain my friendship with Rekhev or what it means. This is the first time that I encounter the split-in-two feeling of dividing a life between multiple places.

Even though I know better, what Rekhev said about Tony sticks in my mind. I trace Tony's number on the keypad of my phone and give in to the temptation to call. The phone rings and rings, and I decide that I will leave him a message. I'll just let him know that I am back. Then he answers.

"It's Sadia," I say, rushing my words in my excitement to hear his voice. "I'm home from India."

Then I hear him speaking to someone else in the room, in the warm, hushed voice that he used to use with me. There's a long silence, and I wonder if I should repeat myself.

"It's Sadia. Sadia is calling," I hear him explain. I feel the knowledge sink in that he is no longer mine to tell my news to. I should have realized it earlier.

We exchange a few clipped greetings, but he sounds strained, very far away. It's clear that he wants to get off the phone.

"Can we talk later?" he asks.

"Of course. Call me anytime." I hang up.

I sit, looking at the receiver, knowing that I won't hear from him again.

My doctor in Boston tells me that ten months in India have given me the lungs of a smoker. My strange heartbeat is more mysterious. Tests reveal that I am experiencing something called ectopic beats: some of my heartbeats are appearing prematurely, others in what sound like pairs. He asks me if I find India stressful.

"No one knows where they come from exactly, but they are called PVCs, premature ventricular contractions. We did a study once with medical students. One fellow had them, and we had him wear a monitor as he went about his daily life. Every time he went home and saw his wife, he had the ventricular contractions. No one could explain it exactly. But a year later, they were divorced." He chuckles slightly at the memory. "If you ask me, I would say that something in India is causing you anxiety, and I would think about how long you really have to be there. But will it kill you? No, it won't."

*   *   *

ON MY MOTHER's bedside table, I notice the small Qur'an that she's kept there as long as I can remember. I don't know that I've ever examined it closely. I pick it up, studying the dark green Arabic script.

When she comes into the room, she finds me looking at it and lies down next to me on the bed.

"How long have you had this?" I ask.

"Since I was small," she says.

"The same one?"

"We had a lady Qur'an master, Ustaaniji, who used to come to the house and teach us, my sister and me. When we learned to read the entire Qur'an we had a ceremony and a celebration. I remember I stood with the Qur'an on my head, and my father took my picture with his Brownie camera."

"How old were you then?"

"About nine, I think," she says, trying to remember. "My sister was six years older, but we were at the same level. She always resented me for it," she adds, chuckling. "But it was so much easier for me because I had a photographic memory—I could literally see the shapes of the letters in my head, and Arabic is a phonetic language."

"How often do you read the Qur'an now?" I ask her, thumbing through the pages.

"I read the Pansura every night," she says. "The most important sura of the Qur'an. And I keep a copy of it in my purse. Then there are my *duas,* the verses that I say and read to comfort me when I am worried about something. It's an eclectic kind of practice, I suppose. Since Nana died, I've read it more and more. It gives me comfort."

"Do you ever feel tied to Judaism, Mama?"

She thinks for a few moments before answering.

"When I was a baby, they recited the *azaan,* the sound of the call to prayer, in my ear. I am interested that Judaism is a part of my DNA, but I know that I am a Muslim. It's the faith I was born into, raised into, it's the faith that I practice. Those are the rituals I have followed all of my life. My mother made a promise to my father that she would raise her children as Muslims, and I am that. I am the fulfillment of that promise."

"I miss her so much," I say.

"Sadia, you can pray in whatever language you feel like," she says, reaching out to rest her hand on my shoulder. "You can always talk to God, to ask him for guidance. I'm concerned that you feel that you have to fix everything yourself. That's a kind of arrogance, you know, to think that everything is within your power. . . . Your father and I, we've never wanted to push any one thing for you kids, but I don't want you to feel unanchored, either."

"Mama, did you and Abba talk about choosing one religion to raise us in?"

"When you were a baby, we were very torn about baptism—we thought seriously about it, but we felt that we didn't want to choose for you, to say, 'Now you are a Christian. . . .' There is more than one path to God, it says so in the Qur'an. My father used to recite, 'Unto every one of you have We appointed a (different) law and way of life. And if God had so willed, He could surely have made you all one single community.' I taught you about my religion, and your father taught you about his. . . . Nana taught you what she knew, and now you are learning so much more. I believe that we're saying similar things in different languages."

"Do you think I have to make a choice, the way that Nana did?"

"I don't know," she says, thoughtfully. "Muslims believe that each faith contains the essential truth that God is unified and singular. My father used to tell me that Muhammad was the last prophet, but that all prophets are only messengers. Our first duty is to God. That's what I believe." She picks up the edge of my sleeve, playing with it. "Sweetheart, I wish you would come home."

"I know, Mama."

"How much longer are you going to stay in India?"

"I think I need seven or eight more months to finish my work there."

"Seven or eight *months*?" she asks. "That'll be March. . . ."

"Or maybe April."

"Promise me that when you're done you'll come back."

"I will, Mama."

22

HIGH HOLIDAYS

BOMBAY, SEPTEMBER 2002

The threat of war between India and Pakistan has diffused, and I arrive back in India the day before Yom Kippur, the Day of Atonement. Several weeks have passed, and I am shocked to find myself reassured by the wave of heat that envelops me as I step out of the airport, by the long queue of waiting relatives and drivers, by the familiar way my clothes stick to me on the winding drive back to Gamdevi, where I'm greeted by my familiar belongings. It strikes me that this is the easiest homecoming I'll ever have in this part of the world—my apartment established, my clothes folded, my drawers filled with rolls of film. I have received a grant from a foundation in New York that will allow me to continue my work after my Fulbright funding runs out in the next two months. My aim is to spend my remaining time here creating a photographic record of the Bene Israel, to make something tangible that Nana would have appreciated.

I begin my fast for Yom Kippur at sundown, dressing in an all-white salwar kameez, according to Bene Israel tradition. I take a taxi to an area of the city once known as Jacob's Circle, where Magen Hassidim Synagogue is located. This year, the Jewish High Holidays overlap with Ramadan, the Muslim month of fasting, and as I walk through the Muslim area surrounding Magen Hassidim, I hear the call to prayer and instinctively place my dupatta over my head, the way my mother does when she hears it. I have trouble finding the synagogue and walk in circles, getting frustrated, until I finally see the building—that large familiar boxlike structure set back from the road and separated by a gate bearing painted blue Stars of David.

When Cassim and I were growing up, we typically kept the first and last fasts of Ramadan, occasionally one in the middle. We fasted as a family, when it was possible on a weekend, and we made a day out of it, going to the movies to distract ourselves from hunger, talking about the things we were thankful for. During our fasting days, my mother would tell stories about what Ramadan was like when she was a child, what it was like to fast in a country where it's the rule, not the exception. At night, Nana would give us dates, which we ate to break our fast, saying a prayer and drinking a glass of water. Then we would eat our *iftari* meal, usually Nana's kebabs followed by her handmade pastries, light sheets of dough layered with a paste of coconut, honey, raisins, and pulverized nuts, folded into pockets. I have not fasted in recent years, and just two hours into my first Yom Kippur fast I am aware of a slight panic that I will not be able to eat anything for twenty-five hours. But as I enter the main hall of the synagogue, I look around and see what seems like the entire Bene Israel community in quiet, contemplative prayer, and I feel reassured.

The synagogue's marble gleams with fresh cleaning; the floors of the hall are lined with new white sheets. The men's bowed shoulders are covered in prayer shawls. Upstairs, I join the assembled women, dressed all in white, their heads covered with white handkerchiefs, and look for a place to sit. I have been reading about Yom Kippur, the holiest day of the Jewish calendar, a day when one is meant to atone for all of the sins of the previous year. These are sins between a person and God, not between people, and I begin to consider the difference.

As I search for a place, I spot Shoshanna Auntie from ORT India. She looks up and waves. She gestures to the space next to her and shows me where we are in the prayer book. The prayer books are in Marathi and Hebrew, neither of which I can follow, but I take the book gratefully and smile at her, thankful for her welcoming presence. She explains to me about the Kol Nidre, the prayer in which we ask God to annul all vows that we might try to make in the coming year. Then she explains the confession of the sins of the community, in which the group confesses as a whole and takes responsibility. Interspersed with these prayers are petitions for forgiveness. It is a powerful feeling to be surrounded by the strength of these shared thoughts. I close my eyes and think of Nana, who must have sat in these same benches as a girl. I atone in my own small way.

I spend most of the next day back in Magen Hassidim, resting my head from time to time on the banister in front of me, asking for God's forgiveness for the sins I have committed in the last year, knowingly and unknowingly, as I have been instructed. Since this is the first time I have observed Yom Kippur, I also ask him for forgiveness for the other years of my life, and for guidance through the next few months. I begin to feel faint in the early afternoon, but my hunger gives me clarity as well. Toward the end of the service, I watch as the congregation rises and laments together. Several men approach the Ark, placing the Torah scrolls back in their protective enclave. As the men slowly begin to close the doors, the women around me intone their prayers with greater fervor, the pitch and intensity of their voices rising. This is their last chance to make reparations and face the new year with open hearts.

Outside, the service completed, Shoshanna puts an arm around me and tells me that she's proud of me. She opens up a small paper packet from her purse and takes out two dry moon-shaped pastries with crimped edges.

"This is *saath padar,* traditional Bene Israel lady sweet. For breaking fast," she says, handing one to me. "Like your grandmother used to make from the recipes. Eat."

I take a bite out of the pastry, and it crumbles in my mouth; inside, I taste the sweet filling of coconut, raisins, and crushed nuts. I recognize it instantly. It's the same sweet Nana used to feed us during Ramadan.

. . .

I CALL REKHEV to tell him that I'm back, and he comes to visit the next afternoon, holding in his hand a curious-looking instrument peeking out of a plastic bag. My sojourn in the States has made me forget that we never touch. When I see him, I throw my arms around him impulsively, crushing my cheek against the starch of his shirt, startling him. The instrument is a kind of horn made out of a gourd and wrapped in string, which he explains was made for him by the indigenous Warli people of Maharashtra. In the weeks I've been in Massachusetts, Rekhev has been making his first documentary, a film about the Warlis, and has been living in one of their villages, several hours from Pune. He is filled with tales of late nights of singing, campfires, and the stories that the village elders have told him. I listen to his adventures in wonderment. Though he says that he resists making friends, he draws out people's life stories easily, as my mother does. It's one of the contradictions about him that I find most interesting.

"I thought about your work while I was there," he tells me. "I've been reading this essay by A. K. Ramanujan which asks if there is an Indian way of thinking. He argues that we may think of space and time as universal contexts, but that in India they have properties, varying specific destinies. The soil in a village produces the crops, which are eaten by the people—and those crops, the soil, the vegetation around them, affect their characters. Houses here have mood, they change the luck and experience of those who inhabit them. My interest is always in the story, in the myths that I grew up with, in translating those into images. But I thought about how you research and frame your photographs, about how you allow people to pose for you, to suggest what you should photograph. I adopted this strategy with the Warlis, and the results were very interesting. I don't know if I would have been interested in making a film like this if I hadn't met you."

He pauses for a moment. He hands the horn to me, telling me that he'd like me to have it, and I think that it might be one of the most wonderful things that anyone has ever given me.

. . .

WE GO ACROSS THE STREET to the tea shop, and then for a long walk down the leafy lanes behind my house, peeking into a Hare Krishna temple. We visit Mani Bhavan, the Gandhi museum, where I stand on the balcony and imagine Gandhi writing. It has been a long time since I have spent a full day in Bombay without working on my project, and it feels like a vacation, an unexpected chance just to observe the city. We continue down Laburnum Road to the park, where Rekhev tells me the Quit India movement held many meetings. There I'm thrilled to discover a wonderful old playground slide shaped like an elephant, where children clamber up a ladder on one side and swish down the other. We resolve to return another day with my 16mm movie camera. I feel comfortable with Rekhev, and grateful for his company. I'm surprised at how much more at ease I am with him now than with any of my friends in New York. The thought makes me feel very far away and right at home at the same time.

"Tell me," he says, after we've walked in silence for three-quarters of an hour. "You didn't have to come back. What is it that you have returned to do here exactly?"

"Well . . ." I begin, "so far I have photographed each of the synagogues of the Konkan Coast and Bombay. I've gotten to know the Bene Israel a little bit, through teaching and through interviewing people and taking pictures."

"Yes."

"But I don't know what the story of the community is yet, what the story is that I came here to tell."

"Ah," he says. "You want my help."

"Yes," I say, "if you have time."

"I have time."

"The Jewish festivals of Sukkot and Simchat Torah are in a few days," I say tentatively, as we round the corner and walk back to my house, and as soon as I say it I realize how much I hope that Rekhev will accompany me.

Truthfully, it would be difficult for me to go to Revdanda alone. But there is another reason I hope Rekhev will come. I feel as if I have embarked on the journey that he sketched out for me in the library, and I want to experience part of it with him. I try to keep my tone light, so as not to betray how badly I want him to join me. "It's the harvest festival that David told you about, where the community finishes the annual cycle of Torah readings and begins again."

"In Revdanda?"

I nod. I'm prepared to start convincing him, but it doesn't prove necessary.

"Let's go," he says. "I'll come for you tomorrow."

REKHEV AND I retrace our steps from Bombay to Revdanda: a boat to the port of Mandwa, a bus to Alibag, a six-seater rickshaw to Revdanda. We each have a shoulder bag with a few changes of clothes, and we take turns carrying the video camera, tripod, still camera, and case of sound-recording equipment. I feel self-consciously tall. I'm aware of people looking at us, at our city clothes and behavior, at a foreign girl and a young Indian man traveling together. I watch as the omnipresent neon lights, car horns, and loud music of urban India give way to forests, houses set back from the road, and winding paths. Every so often there is a stall selling tea or cigarettes or soft drinks. We share the last leg of our journey, the rickshaw from Alibag to Revdanda, with a young woman and her small daughter. The woman looks at us furtively through her hands, clearly curious as to the purpose of our journey. The little girl stares at us openly. She reaches out a small hand and touches my hair, then frowns instantly, as if she has tasted something sour.

We reach Revdanda before dusk. It is a Friday evening, and Shabbat must be about to begin. I have several loaves of challah bread from the ORT bakery to give to the Waskars, but I hate to arrive unannounced. Rekhev assures me that I'm worrying for nothing.

We hike the last section of road, from the outskirts of the town to the center, and after a bend in the path I notice a sign for something on our right hand side called the Sea Side Holiday Home.

Rekhev stops in front of it. "David Waskar mentioned this place to me the last time we were here—this is where people from Bombay come to stay when they come to see the synagogue."

"Really?" I ask, relieved that the place has been vouched for. "Shall we go inside?"

It feels slightly uncomfortable to ask for a hotel room with Rekhev standing beside me. We find the innkeeper, who shows us around his pleasant guesthouse. His large rooms contain rows of cots lined up such that an extended family can easily stay comfortably together. The innkeeper assumes that we will take one room, and I correct him quickly by asking to see another one across the hall. Rekhev and I don't discuss the strangeness of the fact that this evening we will sleep in rooms a few feet from one another.

AT THE SYNAGOGUE, we find David and his sons Ellis and Benjamin preparing for a weekend of festivities, cleaning the main hall of the synagogue, laying down white sheets on the veranda for guests to sit on, and hanging strings of flowers and colorful crepe paper from the ceiling. Like their co-religionists around the world, the Waskars have constructed a sukkah, a temporary dwelling, to remind them of the forty years that their ancestors spent wandering the desert. They have made another one that they keep outside their home. The sukkah, made of saplings and long reeds and thatched with palm leaves, looks sturdy and well packed, as if someone could camp there comfortably. Tonight there will be prayers for Shabbat, and Simchat Torah will begin. Simchat Torah is a joyous holiday, a celebration of the Torah, and I've been told that young men and boys sing and chant songs and prayers in the synagogue, the festivities lasting late into the night.

In the back of the synagogue, we meet a young man who is mashing small dark purple berries into a pulp to make the kiddush wine for this evening's Shabbat prayers.

David greets us enthusiastically, throwing his hands into the air, exclaiming his happy surprise to see us again, and I feel endlessly glad that we came. Rekhev explains to David that we would like to shoot the preparations for the holiday and the ceremonies on video, which makes David laugh uproariously.

"You want to put me on the movie camera?" he says. "Ha! Why not?"

REKHEV HELPS ME UNPACK and organize the equipment. We begin by shooting the synagogue: long shots of the exterior courtyard and garden, then the interior spaces, where the men are working. Rekhev is fascinated by each ritual, by the reasons behind each decision, and asks David and his sons numerous questions. I tease him that he will be a documentary filmmaker, instead of a fiction filmmaker, before long. As we are shooting, a sprightly young woman in a bright green sari comes up behind us and peers inquisitively into the viewfinder.

"I have a video camera also," she says proudly, in Hindi. "From the Gulf."

We say hello to her and begin to shoot Benjamin polishing the ornate silver casing of the Sefer Torah, which is kept carefully in the Holy Ark of the synagogue.

"My camera is very advanced," she boasts, smiling.

I nod and smile at her, but she seems determined to interrupt us.

"It's smaller than yours. Probably lighter, too."

Rekhev takes a long look at the woman, and I think that he must be about to scowl at her.

"What can you do on that camera? Special effects?" she asks.

Rekhev explains that we don't use special effects with this camera.

"No special effects?" she asks incredulously. "That's too bad. I have many different special effects on my camera."

She sticks her hand out to shake our hands and introduces herself as Sangeeta Roi, smiling broadly again. Sangeeta is an attractive, affable woman with wavy black hair who appears to be in her late twenties. She pronounces the "S" in "Sangeeta" with a "sh" sound, so that her name sounds like "Shangeeta." Sangeeta explains that she rents an apartment across the street from the synagogue. She doesn't have the light coloring or the rounded features of most Bene Israel, and I note the *bindi* on her forehead and her *sindoor,* the part in her hair colored red to indicate that she is a married Hindu woman. Before I can express to Rekhev my curiosity about Sangeeta's origins, Sangeeta explains herself.

"I'm from Calcutta," she says proudly.

"Calcutta se?" asks Rekhev in surprise. Calcutta is clear across the country. How on earth did she end up in a tiny place like Revdanda?

"Do you have family here?" I ask, suddenly curious.

"Just me and my daughter. My husband is working on a ship. In the Gulf," she says proudly. "A very big oil ship."

"Why do you live here in Revdanda, instead of in Calcutta?" Rekhev asks, his curiosity clearly getting the better of him.

"I may look stupid, but I'm not stupid," Sangeeta responds brightly. She holds out her hand. "This is India, *na?*" she says, offering her palm as a map. "The Gulf is here, *na?*" She points to one side of her hand. "And Calcutta is here." She points to the other side of her hand. "So, when my husband comes home from the Gulf, where is he going to go first?" she asks us. "Obviously, he is going to come to this side faster, *na?*"

She turns to me, taking in my cotton salwar kameez, and then looks back at Rekhev, concerned.

"She's not going to wear that to the festival, is she?"

Rekhev translates her question for me.

"This or something like it," I tell them. "Why?"

"No, no, no," she says firmly, making a clucking sound with her tongue, "She has to wear a sari."

"Sari?" I say, picking up the familiar word. I don't have a sari.

"Come with me," she says, pulling on my arm and leading me outside. I look over my shoulder at Rekhev, who raises an eyebrow at me in amusement.

I go with Sangeeta across the street to her apartment, a bright, whitewashed room on the second floor with one bed, three plastic chairs, a big tin trunk, and a large television.

"From the Gulf," she says, patting the television with admiration. "Come, sit over here."

We sit on her bed, and she instructs me to undress. She pulls her belongings out of her trunk and finds a white sari petticoat for me to wear. She finds a dark purple sari and begins to wrap it around me. But my arms are far too big for the armholes. She can't understand why the blouse won't fit.

"It's because you're so much smaller than I am. . . ." I say, resorting to English. "There's no way it will fit. . . ."

"*Arre . . .*" she says, rolling her tongue in exasperation.

She goes to the window and starts yelling at Ellis, working in the courtyard of the synagogue. She motions for me to come to the window, and I hastily pull on my kurta so that I can stand beside her.

She points to me, says something I can't understand, and throws her hands in the air. Ellis nods as if to say that he understands and gets on his motorbike. What on earth is going on? I wonder.

Sangeeta instructs me to sit down, and pulls out a box from her trunk. She pulls out thick black eyeliner, a pot of bright red rouge, a crimson lip pencil, and a dark shade of lipstick, and asks me to close my eyes. She moves slowly, drawing a line with the lip pencil around the perimeter of my lips, and then fills in the empty space with the lipstick. She takes the eye pencil and draws a bold line across each of my eyelids and, finally, pats my cheeks with the rouge. I shudder to think of what all this must look like. Another box reveals the gold earrings and gold chain that she must have worn for her wedding. As she begins to place the earrings in my ears, I stop her.

"Are you sure?" I ask her, and she nods emphatically.

There's a knock at the door, and Ellis's wife, Noorit, arrives, with a white parcel of cloth in her hands. I finally understand what's going on. It seems that Sangeeta dispatched Ellis back to the Waskar house to bring Noorit with a sari that might fit me. But Noorit, though slightly larger than Sangeeta, is still tiny. I don't want to disappoint these ladies, but I can't imagine this working.

Together, the three of us struggle to fit my arms into another blouse. Noorit takes the blouse in her teeth and breaks the stitches to make more room. We push my arms into the holes and begin to try to make the sari of a woman half my height wrap around my much taller frame. We have to keep the ill-fitting blouse together with large safety pins, which we cover with the *pallu,* the decorative border of the sari.

When we are finished, Sangeeta combs and braids my hair and pronounces my transformation complete. Then she instructs me to sit, stand, and wave while she shoots me on her video camera. She asks Noorit to hold the camera while she sits next to me, holding my hand. I look at myself in the mirror. I have dark, thick lines of lip liner around my mouth, and two large circles of rouge on my cheeks that make me look like an old-fashioned porcelain doll.

"Is it too much?" I ask, looking at the women.

"No, no, no," insists Sangeeta, proud of her work. "Bee-yootiful."

When we go downstairs and into the synagogue, I feel shy to see Rekhev. He looks startled by my appearance.

"Someone really ought to take *your* picture," he says. "I've never seen you look quite so . . ."

"Strange?" I say.

"Really strange," he says, and we both laugh.

PEOPLE BEGIN TO ARRIVE at the synagogue for the evening Maariv service, mostly young men and teenage boys and a few women from nearby villages. The men are wearing *kippahs* and prayer shawls over their pressed shirts and pants, and the women are wearing their good silk saris. The women look approvingly at my outfit, and don't seem to be alarmed by my makeup. From time to time I catch Sangeeta looking at me and smiling with approval. Benjamin leads the recitation of the Amidah prayer on the *bimah,* the dais in the center of the synagogue, which is followed by Attah Hareita, a collection of Biblical verses in praise of God and the Torah. After Benjamin reads each verse, the verse is repeated by the other worshippers. It seems it would be disrespectful to videotape such a private experience as the congregation in prayer, but Benjamin and Ellis remove all of the Torah scrolls from the Ark and are joined by the men of the congregation, and I begin to shoot again. Benjamin and Ellis begin to walk around the interior of the synagogue, holding the Torah scrolls and leading a small procession that orbits the room, seven times. Benjamin calls out a line, and his words are repeated, like a call and response, by those walking behind him, who clap their hands in time to the music. As the group moves about the room, the procession gains greater momentum, their voices rising in pitch and volume. The men are sweating and look jubilant. Some pick up their small children and dance with them in their arms. David Waskar sways in time with the music, laughing, his grandson Israel perched on top of his head as if riding a wave. When the group reaches the crescendo of the song, seven men throw their arms over each other's shoulders to create a tight, revolving circle and spin faster and faster, like a top. Benjamin calls out, "Simchat Torah!" and the men shout, "Hai! Hai!"

Exhausted, Benjamin begins another orbit around the synagogue, slower this time.

The women reach out two fingers to touch the Torah as it passes, then place the fingers to their lips. I watch through my viewfinder as Sangeeta reaches out a hand and mimics the motion, then closes her eyes and says a small prayer of her own. I wonder for a moment what language she prays in.

At the end of the service, the group pile into rickshaws and onto motorbikes and drive in a long caravan to the Waskar home, where another sukkah has been set up in the yard. The inside of the hut is ringed with red plastic chairs. With some surprise, I notice a rented sound system and a young man with a microphone acting as the DJ. I look up and see that fresh vegetables—long cylindrical gourds and round melonlike fruits—hang from individual strings all over the ceiling, just out of reach. David takes the microphone from the DJ and asks all the young men to gather in the hut. They assemble eagerly, watched closely by the young women of the group. This is clearly the part of the night that everyone has been waiting for. David calls out a countdown, and when he reaches zero, the young men begin leaping into the air. They shout and laugh, reaching over one another to hit the fruit and vegetables and try to knock them free from the ceiling. The women watch, covering their laughter with their hands, slightly alarmed and amused by the show.

Out of the corner of my eye, I see Ellis's wife, Noorit, and Benjamin's wife, Shoshanna, the younger generation of women in the Waskar house, tying up their own stash of fruit and vegetables in a separate, smaller tent, and go to investigate.

"Want to play?" Noorit asks me, and I smile, glad to be included and to see that the women do not intend to be left out of the festivities.

We gather the women and girls, including the elder Mrs. Waskar, and huddle together in the room. Noorit counts down in her small but strong voice: *"Panch! Char! Theen! Do! Ek!"* We reach up our arms, raising them to grab the fruit and bring it to the ground, where we stomp on it with glee. Though I'm a full head taller than any of the women, I'm the least coordinated and the worst at the game. We return to the main tent, panting with the exertion and laughing among ourselves.

The DJ makes some kind of announcement, and four young children, clearly siblings, get up from their seats and walk toward the front of the tent. I notice a large man in the background who must be their father. He waves his arms as though he is conducting them, and the children begin to sing the traditional Shabbat song, "Shalom Aleichem," to a tune that strikes me as both familiar and slightly Indian.

Shalom aleichem malachei ha-shareit malachei elyon,
mi-melech malchei ha-melachim Ha-Kadosh Baruch Hu.

Bo'achem le-shalom malachei ha-shalom malachei elyon,
mi-melech malchei ha-melachim Ha-Kadosh Baruch Hu.

Barchuni le-shalom malachei ha-shalom malachei elyon,
mi-melech malchei ha-melachim Ha-Kadosh Baruch Hu.

Tzeit'chem le-shalom malachei ha-shalom malachei elyon,
mi-melech malchei ha-melachim Hu-Kadosh Baruch Hu.

I videotape the children singing, and a woman looks at me and smiles. From her pride at the group I realize that she must be their mother.

Soon afterward, I'm surprised to find that some of the adults, even a few of the women, have gathered in the back of the tent, where they are drinking small pegs of whiskey with Thums Up. The whiskey must be expensive, but this is clearly a special occasion, cause for celebration. I take a seat next to the father of the singing children, who introduces himself as Solomon.

"You are from U.S.A.?" he asks.

"Yes, from New York."

"Ah, New York." He raises both eyebrows. "There are many Jews there."

"Yes."

"Tell me, do they know about us?" he asks.

"I think some do," I say tentatively. "But many do not."

I compliment him on his children's singing, and he tells me that he and his wife are very proud. All of their children are learning Hebrew, and both of his sons are learning to blow the shofar, the traditional ram's horn that is sounded in synagogues on Rosh Hashanah, the Jewish New Year.

"How many people worship in your synagogue in New York?" he asks. "Five hundred? A thousand?"

"I'm not part of a synagogue . . ." I hesitate.

"Not part of a synagogue?" he asks, looking alarmed. "But where do you spend your High Holidays?"

I feel slightly reluctant to tell Nana's story in this context. I realize that I have enjoyed, for a short while, the assumption that I am Jewish, that I belong here. As I tell it, people start to listen in, gathering around me, translating the story into Marathi, and I become a greater source of curiosity. Those who missed the beginning ask me to tell it again, how my grandmother grew up in Castle Rock, Thane, Pune, and Bombay, how she eloped with my grandfather in the 1930s, how she moved to Pakistan. I look up and catch Rekhev's eye. He is standing in the doorway of the tent and watching me, and he looks attentive, protective almost.

"But how were you raised? With what religion?" Solomon asks me.

"I was raised with three religions."

"Three religions? In one house?" he says, translating for the group. "But that's not possible!"

"It is possible." I try not to sound defensive. "Now I've come here to learn about Judaism."

"You've come here to learn about Judaism, or about our Bene Israel Judaism?" he asks pointedly. I think for a moment about his question.

"I've come here to find out about Bene Israel Judaism. About the life that my grandmother left behind."

"You are doing this thing for her, then."

"Yes," I say.

AS THE EVENING PROGRESSES, the tent gets more and more crowded. Rekhev tells me that people are arriving from all over the area, making trips as long as two hours to join David's party after the celebrations at their own synagogues are over. Solomon's children beg him for the chance to stay another day in Revdanda. They are camping out in a house on the Waskars' property and enjoying the holiday atmosphere.

Solomon laughs, turning to me.

"My children are from the city, but they feel at home here," he says. "Everyone feels at home in David's house. Everyone is welcome."

At well past midnight, Rekhev and I catch a ride to Revdanda with one of the departing cars and slip quietly up the stairs of the Sea Side Holiday Home.

"Tonight was fascinating," Rekhev says as we walk up the stairs.

"You thought so?" I'm pleased to hear him say it. "You had a good time?"

"Think of it. They live this story, each week, in chapters. Then they come together on this night and they celebrate this story—then they begin it again, they start to read it again with new eyes. Some stories, they will seem the same to them, perhaps. But others, others will change. The stories will grow with them as they grow, as they age."

"It's a beautiful idea," I say.

"I saw how you told your story tonight," he says. "I saw how you told that story to explain who you are. And I think all of this"—he makes a quick wave of his hand, indicating everything around us—"all of this will be part of it."

We stand for a moment in silence, in the flickering light of a night-light that dispenses mosquito repellent.

"I don't travel, Sadia," he says. "Never. But with you, I'm a traveler here as well."

I put my arms around him.

"Don't do that," he says softly, pulling away from me. "I don't want to be a chapter in your book." He turns around and reaches for his key. The key turns in the lock. "Good night."

"Good night, Rekhev," I say, watching him enter his room and shut the door.

I get into bed fully dressed. I watch the silhouette of palm-tree leaves moving back and forth across my window. I try for hours to fall asleep. I wake up, exhausted, at dawn, still in my borrowed sari.

The next morning, Rekhev and I pretend that nothing unusual has happened between us. We walk in silence to catch a rickshaw to the Waskars' house, where we begin to shoot the everyday goings-on of the house. We do this for a week, folding ourselves into the daily rhythms of the place. The children come to visit with us, pushing their small faces into the lens and asking to look through the camera at one another. But mostly we fade into the background, becoming a part of the yard, like the swing or the water pump. Rekhev and I build separate relationships within the Waskar compound: he with the Buddhist carpenters in the Waskars' woodshop, and I with Benjamin's and Ellis's wives, Shoshanna and Noorit.

I sit cross-legged on the kitchen floor and videotape Shoshanna and Noorit peeling ginger and garlic, chopping vegetables for the midday meal. I watch as the local Koli fisherwomen, their saris tucked between their legs to create a functional pair of shorts, come to the doorway with baskets of fish for sale, which they carry on their heads. I am reminded of the Bene Israel folktale I have read about a man named Rahabi, a Jewish traveler, who visited the Bene Israel in the Konkan hundreds of years ago. During that visit, he gave the women of the community a test, to make him a meal of fish. He watched them sort through a basket for the fish with fins and scales and discard the rest, according to the kosher laws, and decided then that they were really Jewish. Shoshanna and Noorit tell me about the other ways that they keep kosher, how if they are having lamb in the evening they will not take milk in their tea in the morning. How did you learn these things? I ask them, but they have no answers. It's always been this way, they tell me.

I ask if they plan to migrate to Israel. If they can live like this, they tell me, together in one house, then they'd like to go. If they would have to live separately, then they want to stay here.

IN THE AFTERNOONS, David sits on the porch and entertains a string of male visitors, his Hindu friends and business partners, acquaintances from other towns. He serves them tea, coconut water, and melons from his farm, and they tell him the latest news of the crops, who is selling and buying which properties in the area, who has stolen from whom. These visits are how David gets his news, how he stays on top of what is happening locally.

"These two are putting us on the movie camera and taking it back to Bombay!" he tells his friends.

"What for?" they ask.

"Oh, they want to know everything about how to be a Jew," David explains. "What we eat, how we pray, what the old stories are, how we came here in a ship . . ."

We conduct long and rambling interviews with David, who tells us stories from his life and his impressions of Bene Israel history. He tells us that, in the old days, his grandparents' grandparents did not have a synagogue. He explains that on Passover his ancestors sacrificed a lamb and placed a handprint of blood on each doorway of their home, in memory of the sacrifice that the Israelites offered at the command of God the night before their Exodus from Egypt. The blood of this sacrifice sprinkled on the doorposts of the Israelites was to be a sign to the angel of death to pass over the homes of the

Jews. David takes us around his compound and shows us the handprints that can be seen in every Bene Israel home in the region, even now.

Each Yom Kippur, his ancestors would whitewash their homes, dress all in white, and pray. On this day, their neighbors knew, the Bene Israel would do no work, and so neighbors offered to tend their livestock for them. They offered similar help on the Sabbath. Out of respect, the Bene Israel abstained from eating beef, taboo to the Hindu population, even though it was not against their own dietary laws.

"Have the Bene Israel always enjoyed such good relations with the other communities?" Rekhev asks.

"India has been good to us Jews. Elsewhere, the Jews have had many problems. But not here," he says. "The problems between the Hindus and the Muslims are not our problems, though in the city it is not always so easy. Sometimes we have been caught in the middle; we are neither one nor the other. . . ."

"What do you mean?" Rekhev asks.

"I'll tell you," David begins, pulling up a stump and sitting down. "I was working in Bombay when the Hindu-Muslim riots broke out at Partition time, in 1947. My brother had taken me to Bombay to work, but the riot was at its peak, and there was a curfew order. We used to work in the daytime, and at night we would hide underneath the building. Then, one day, I was very hungry and I went to buy *pav bhaji* to eat, after curfew. What could I do? I was very hungry. A crowd of people caught me." David straightens his spine and impersonates someone from the crowd. "'Who are you?' they said. 'Tell! Are you Hindu or Muslim?' Now what could I do? I am an Israel Jew. I didn't know what to say, which was the right answer that would save me. They picked me up in a Muslim locality, and I began to realize that they thought I was a Hindu. I was worried that they might kill me. So then I dropped my pants!" David makes a quick motion to pantomime dropping his pants, and laughs, a sharp exhalation of breath. "And I was naked! And I was circumcised! And everyone started saying, 'He's a Mohammedan! He's one of us!' and they embraced me and let me go. One of them even dropped me home." David laughs at the memory. "What

to do? I am an Israel Jew!" he says. "But one has to adapt to the country one
is in. . . ."

IT'S OUR LAST DAY in Revdanda, and I ask Rekhev if he'll accompany me
to shoot some street scenes in the Revdanda market. After we finish, we run
into Sangeeta, who asks us to come to her home for tea. Inside her apartment, Rekhev sits on a chair and I sit on the bed while Sangeeta boils water
in the kitchen. I look around the tidy room, ready and waiting for Sangeeta's
husband to arrive. Her young daughter, Neena, returns from school, and
Sangeeta asks the child to practice her English with me. Neena is shy, almost
engulfed by her mother's large personality, but tries to converse with me. I
ask her about school, if she gets along with the other children. She's learning
Marathi, and she tells me that she's almost fluent. When our tea is ready,
Sangeeta hands us each a cup and saucer and sits cross-legged on the floor as
she hooks up her camera to her television and searches through the pile of
tapes. She wants to show us her films.

Most of the tapes are Sangeeta and her husband traveling around Maharashtra and visiting local temples, set to popular Hindi film music. In almost
all of them, Sangeeta can be seen popping behind and out of small groves of
trees and smiling at the camera like a Bollywood heroine. True to her word,
she has made extensive use of the special effects on her camera. We watch,
mesmerized, as Sangeeta and her husband can be seen in mirrored images
on either side of the frame, doing dance moves, waving to us as if they are
performing in a fun-house mirror. Sangeeta's husband is tall, with a carefully
groomed mustache, and it is clear that he plays the romantic lead to Sangeeta's heroine. In the later tapes, a small Neena can be seen loping along amiably behind her parents, waving to the camera and gamely inspecting the
temples and picnic spots of their family outings. The music swells, and there
is a dramatic shot of Sangeeta's husband in a black leather jacket and dark
sunglasses, standing at the top of a small cliff.

I ask Rekhev to ask Sangeeta when she thinks her husband will return
home from the Gulf.

"Soon," she says dreamily, looking at the screen. "He is coming back very soon."

On the journey home, Rekhev and I cram ourselves into a crowded six-seater rickshaw bound for Alibag. My entire left side borders on his right, and I have a heightened sense of our proximity, like a line of current from shoulder to knee. When some of the other passengers disembark, making more room in the cab, I don't peel away from him, and we sit like that, fitted like a puzzle, for more than an hour. I don't know where he'll go when we get back to Bombay. Perhaps he'll take a bus back to Pune, or stay with a friend in the city. I'm not sure and I don't ask, afraid of breaking the spell that binds us together for this one moment.

When we reach my house, he helps me bring the equipment inside, and we begin to unpack it, counting the tapes we have shot, separating the rolls of film that need to be processed.

"So what's the story of the Bene Israel?" Rekhev asks me when we have finished. I think it over for a minute, considering my response.

"It's about being caught between these two places, I think—India and Israel—and between two identities—Indian and Jewish. They all have a decision to make: whether they are going to stay here or move there."

"Your Nana would be proud of this hard work," he says. "Are you happy?"

"I am happy," I say, and find that I mean it.

We sit at my table in comfortable silence, Rekhev reading one of my books, I labeling tapes. When he leaves later that night, I shutter myself inside and comfort myself with the private rituals of a life alone, boiling water, chopping vegetables, pouring myself a drink. I'm curious to hear the sound of American English, and keep company with CNN. It's a year after the World Trade Center attacks, and the announcer says that 52 percent of Americans say that things are not at all back to normal in the United States. When they are asked if things will ever be back to normal, 54 percent say no. I watch a report about the IT industry in India; it shows a handsome announcer walking around a crowded bazaar as he comments on his surprise at Indians' efficiency with computers. I see New York from two vantages: the eyes I traveled here with, and the eyes that I see with now. I understand for the first time why some people leave home and never come back. I wonder if I could do the same.

I watch the middle part of the evening stretch out before me. I think of all the things I will tell Rekhev the next time we meet.

The next morning, my mother calls, worried that she has not heard from me in two weeks.

"Where have you been?" she asks, and I explain about the holidays, that I've been staying in Revdanda. "Where did you sleep?" she asks, trying to imagine it.

"In a hotel," I say, vaguely.

My mother is calling with bad news. She has heard from one of her cousins that Uncle Moses, the curmudgeonly relative whom I first met in India, is in ill health and may have only a matter of weeks, or days, to live. She asks me to go see him and pay my respects. Apparently, he is now living in Bombay with his daughter. I promise my mother that I will find him.

IT IS ONLY A YEAR since I first met him, but I find Uncle Moses very much changed, his feisty spirit cloaked underneath what seems like a tremendous amount of pain. I don't know what he is dying of, and I don't ask. Whereas before he seemed likely to chase me out of the room with his cane, now he seems weary, almost too tired to raise his head.

I have brought with me some of my photographs, large color prints that I've had blown up at a professional lab in Bombay. I thought perhaps I could show Uncle Moses my work, show him what I've been doing this last year. His daughter tells me that she doesn't think that he will have energy for such activity, that his eyesight is going, but I take them out of their box anyway, bringing my chair up close to his, and lay them in my lap.

"These are Bene Israel families in Bombay," I tell him. "Here is Magen Hassidim, and the Gate of Mercy Synagogue. . . ." I say, "This is a wedding. . . . This is a *mehndi* ceremony. . . ."

Uncle Moses looks barely cognizant of what I am saying. He has trouble focusing on me and closes his eyes from time to time.

"This is a family in the village of Chorde," I say, pointing to a portrait. "I think that your wife Lily Auntie was also a Chordekar, if I'm not mistaken. . . ."

He doesn't seem to be listening to my running commentary.

"This is a photograph of the Jewish cemetery in Bombay; this is a photograph of a young boy learning to blow *shofar*. . . ."

Uncle Moses clears his throat as if to speak, and I lean in to hear him.

"These . . . look . . . *expensive*," he says, with difficulty.

"The prints?" I ask. "They are a little expensive. . . ."

"Waste . . . of money!" Uncle Moses says, and I'm relieved that he hasn't lost his persnickety spirit.

"This is the synagogue in Revdanda," I continue. "I have just spent Sukkot and Simchat Torah there, and this is I think my favorite place in India. For some reason, I feel very at home there in that synagogue. I don't know why."

I haven't articulated this thought until now, but as soon as I say it I know that it is true. Uncle Moses looks at me. I see a glint of recognition slip through the milkiness in his eyes.

"I know why," he says. "Your great-grandparents were from this place." He raises his eyes very slowly to meet mine. "They grew up near here. They were members of this synagogue."

I feel a prickling sense of having known this already—though how could I? With a flash, I remember the large, mossy stone wall that circles the perimeter of Revdanda. The village inside a fort that my grandmother spoke of. Of course.

I hug Uncle Moses. He feels impossibly fragile between my arms, like a stack of bones held together with cloth. There is a palpable feeling of imminent death in the apartment, as if he has already made peace with the idea of leaving and is holding on simply to give those around him a chance to say goodbye.

The more I think about what Uncle Moses told me, the more remarkable I find it. If my grandmother's mother and father were members of this synagogue, then Revdanda is my native place. So I do have one, after all.

23

LEAH AND DANIEL

BOMBAY, JANUARY–MARCH 2003

"Miss Sadia!"

I hear a young woman's voice, and then I look up and see a head emerge over the top of the ORT school stairwell. I see a young woman in her early twenties, in a mauve-colored salwar kameez made of shiny polyester. "Miss Sadia, it's time for my marriage!" she says, coming down the stairs, and hands me a white card, embossed with gold letters in a flowing, ornate script.

Leah marries Daniel

Of course. Leah. She was one of my students who performed the play. A girl so shy she could barely utter her lines onstage; the one who was embarrassed to talk about her engagement.

"Is it time for your wedding now?" I say, reading the date, two months away.

"You will come?" she asks.

"Of course, I'd be honored," I say. "So who is Daniel?"

Leah blushes and shrugs, not sure how to answer the question.

"He's Daniel."

"He's a Bene Israel from Bombay?" I ask.

"His family stays in Thane. An hour outside. He stays in Israel."

"So after you marry . . ."

"We're going to Israel the day after the marriage."

"Have you been there before?" I feel oddly protective. I try to imagine shy Leah navigating Israel.

"No, but I've been wanting to go. Miss Sadia, first you come for my *malida* ceremony." I have read about the *malida,* a Bene Israel ritual to ask Prophet Elijah for his blessing, or to show thanks.

"You'll do the *malida* to bless your marriage?"

"We do the *malida* before we start the preparations for marriage. We will have it at my place on Sunday at seven. Please come."

THAT SUNDAY, I make my way to the east side of the city, where I find Leah's apartment, one small room, about eight feet by twelve, in a large building of identical rooms stacked on top of one another—a *chawl.* I've visited Bene Israel families in other similar buildings, and I'm struck again by how each room in the building is a different, private world, packed with multiple members of different families and all of their belongings. As I walk up the stairs, I peek into other people's spaces. I see small Hindu shrines, calendars, televisions, women chopping vegetables on the floor. The doorway to Leah's family's apartment is hung with a mezuzah and a tile containing a Hebrew prayer, and inside I see eight women squatting on their heels washing and cutting fruit, beating rice, and grating coconut to make the *malida,* a sweet mixture which will be eaten after the recitation of prayers to honor the Prophet Elijah. Leah greets me enthusiastically, and introduces me to her mother. I say hello to Leah's best friend, Judith, who smiles affectionately when she sees me, and sit down next to the two young women, where I start to help wash and peel fruit.

Leah lives with her mother, father, and younger brother, Joseph. I can't imagine how they all fit here. There's a system, Leah explains to me matter-of-factly, which makes it all work. In the morning, the room is a kitchen, where Leah's mother prepares food for her family. In the afternoon, the room is a social space, when friends drop by and sit on a bench perched in the bay window overlooking the street. In the evening, it becomes a kitchen again, when Leah and her mother prepare dinner; after dark, it becomes a bedroom, when sheets and pillows are pulled out of the trunk and the family rests side by side on the floor.

"Would you like some water, Sadia?" Leah asks, offering me a bottle of mineral water, which I realize with equal parts guilt and gratitude has been purchased especially for me, the foreign guest. I look around, trying to ascertain who is related to whom. Everyone sits on the floor except for a slightly more affluent-looking guest in a silk sari with a gold border, who sits on a plastic chair in the corner, amiably watching the proceedings.

Leah and Judith have grown up together. They are neighbors, and their parents are close. Judith points out her mother, who is busy grating coconut on the other side of the room.

"Judith is like my sister," Leah tells me. "We have done everything together since we were babies."

"You'll miss each other when Leah moves to Israel . . ." I say to Judith, pointing out the obvious.

"We were going to move there together last year," Leah says. "But then my mother said, Don't go there single. Marry, and then go. Judith will get engaged soon, and then we'll both be in Israel."

Judith smiles at the thought. "Soon," she sighs.

"So what is the significance of the *malida*?" I ask.

"The *malida* is a very old Bene Israel tradition, an offering to Prophet Elijah, our Eliyahoo Hanabee," Leah tells me. "When you do the *malida*, you make a mixture of beaten rice and coconut, and you decorate it with five fruits. The person seeking a wish to be granted asks the Prophet Elijah for his help. Then you distribute the mixture, to be eaten. When the wish is granted, again you do *malida*, to thank him."

"Without this *malida* we cannot do anything," Judith adds.

For this evening's festivities, the adjacent apartment has been borrowed from Leah's neighbor to make room for the thirty or so guests who have gathered to join in the ritual and prayers, and when the *malida* mixture is complete, we assemble in the other room, where we cover our heads and face the street. The room is crowded with guests, mostly men, who sing the prayers aloud in Hebrew. I help Leah's mother to distribute the *malida* mixture in small paper plates, placing a small portion of the beaten rice and coconut on each plate, followed by a section of each of five fruits. At certain moments in the prayers, we eat the pieces of fruit in succession, and finally the *malida* mixture itself, praying for Prophet Elijah's help to ensure that Leah's marriage to Daniel will proceed smoothly.

The next day, I return to Leah's apartment for another ritual, one that I have found in no book on the Bene Israel. Leah's mother takes two new copper vessels and fills one with jaggery, a kind of unrefined sugar, and the other with a paste made of turmeric. She ties them together with brightly colored strings, and she says a prayer, stacking one on top of the other and placing them on a high shelf. She explains that this jaggery and turmeric will be used in a ritual to bless Leah before her wedding. Then she and Leah and I go around their building and gather five happily married women. One of them is a Bene Israel, but the rest of the women are Hindu—whoever happen to be at home preparing lunch or dinner for their husbands. In each of their hands, Leah's mother places a leaf, and on that leaf two pieces of jaggery, like nuggets of concentrated sugar. Next to the jaggery she places a piece of *paan* and a one-rupee coin. Each of the women is instructed to eat one piece of jaggery so that her mouth is sweet, and then to feed Leah the other piece. Each wishes for Leah that the coming years of her marriage be sweet, and that she may have a successful life.

When the ritual is complete, each woman kisses Leah and wishes her well, and returns to her own apartment. Leah's mother looks relieved.

"Now we can start buying things for the wedding," she explains. "I have to buy saris for the groom's family, a green sari for the reception, so many things . . ."

I ask Leah's mother how she feels about her daughter's going to Israel, and Leah translates my questions into Marathi. Her mother explains that before, when Leah wanted to move to Israel with Judith, she was very worried. "I was thinking, Who will take care of her? Now she has a partner to take care of her, so I am no longer tense. I am feeling happy as well as sad that she is going to Israel."

I ask her how she feels about the political tensions in Israel, and she thinks for a moment. "God is one, and he will help," she says. "Hashem will help her."

Leah and I sit in the bay window of her apartment, facing the busy street, and I ask her about Daniel. What is he like? She asks me if I'd like to see his photograph.

She pulls two snapshots out of an envelope, giggling. These are the pictures that Daniel sent in order to be considered a possible match for Leah, and she did the same.

Both of his photos were taken at wedding functions; the clothes are ornate, and the people are covered in garlands of roses. In one, Daniel has both arms around his mother; in the other he poses with his mother and brother. I note with a little surprise that he is completely handsome, with sharply defined features and a thoughtful look. I think about how a girl like Leah, strong and dependable but not known as a beauty, can benefit from the system of arranged marriages. She is clearly ecstatic at the match. In a word, Leah *scored.* I hope that he's excited, too.

"What did you think when you first saw these pictures?" I ask Leah.

"I was thinking that he must be a very angry person!" she says, laughing. "Looking at these photos I was thinking, Baba, he's looking hot-tempered!"

I look at the pictures again, trying to see it. I suppose his serious look could be considered stern, in a certain light.

"And now?" I ask, and Leah blushes deeply. I realize that she is in love.

REKHEV BEGINS VISITING BOMBAY once or twice a week for meetings about a short film that he's directing, a 35mm narrative film based on Indian

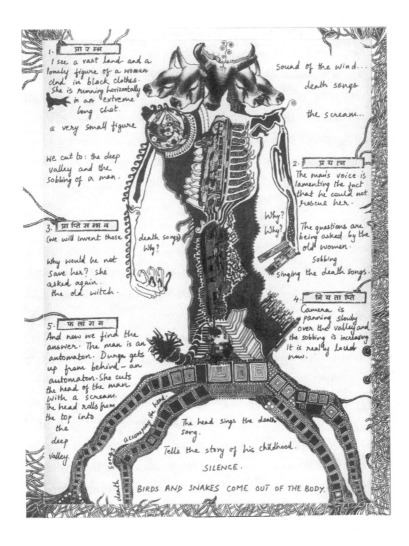

storytelling traditions. When he is in town he comes by my apartment for tea, sometimes staying for dinner. He shows me pages and pages of drawings from his notebooks, lists of images and storyboards for his upcoming projects: a village shaped like a fish, a disappearing book, a mysterious figure who reveals himself to be an automaton, his body filled with birds and snakes. There's a magic to Rekhev's work, informed by his understanding of Indian history and mythology. It's nothing like my interest in the everyday.

Time slips forward, and I experience it in a way that I never have before, without calendars. I notice the rising heat as January becomes February and February becomes March, but this, too, feels familiar. Bombay is a kind of home to me now. Nana is a part of my present. I spend my days photographing and videotaping Bene Israel families and celebrations, and now people know me. I'm the teacher from ORT India, the American girl with the camera, the one whose grandmother was a Bene Israel.

"Why don't you take up a job here?" Rekhev asks me one afternoon, echoing my own thoughts. "You could teach full-time at the Jewish school, or work for a filmmaker."

"And what about my life in the U.S.?"

"Is it asking for your return?"

It's true that I have nothing concrete pulling me back to New York—no job, no relationship, no apartment. What would be the harm of staying here, I wonder, for another year, perhaps two?

One day, I see a white woman, presumably American, dressed like myself, in a modest beige salwar kameez with a printed dupatta thrown over one shoulder, her brown hair in a ponytail. I can see that she's not a tourist, here for a yoga retreat, or on her way to an ashram. Something about the way she walks, adeptly dodging men on the street, keeping her eyes straight ahead, tells me that she lives here, and I wonder what her life is like—if she's married to an Indian, if she has children, if her center has shifted from wherever she was from before to here. I wonder if I could do the same thing, if someday my friends in New York will say to one another, "Whatever happened to Sadia?" and the answer will be that I went to India and never came back.

NOW, ONE OR TWO afternoons a week, I accompany Leah or her mother on one of their shopping errands, and learn how a Bene Israel wedding is put together. Meanwhile, Leah is preparing for her IATA exam at ORT India, which will certify her to work in a travel agency in Israel if she so chooses. Leah's reasons for wanting to migrate are not spiritual. Her concerns are more practical, economic. One afternoon, Leah and I go in a taxi to pick up the wedding invitations, up a long flight of stairs to a dusty old print shop. There are sample cards in Hindi, Marathi, and English script, with icons of birds, wedding bells, and flowers. Leah pays for several boxes of formal wedding cards, separating them into two piles, one for her family and one for Daniel's.

I see how efficient Leah is at getting around Bombay, the only place she has ever lived, and I admire her impulse to move to Israel, as much as I don't quite understand it.

"Basically, taking my education here, the jobs I was getting, I was not satisfied," she explains during the taxi ride home. "Then I thought, 'Going to Israel and getting a good job is good.' So I was planning for career only to go to Israel. Then . . ." She laughs nervously, her practical nature dissolving at the thought of her fiancé.

"And then what happened?" I ask her, poking her in the shoulder to tease her.

"Then I saw Daniel. . . ."

BACK IN LEAH'S APARTMENT, her mother looks agitated, crisscrossing the imaginary quadrants between living and cooking spaces.

"We have a lot to do. Leah, Joseph, you have to help me. . . . We have to deliver half the invitations to Daniel's family in Thane. . . ."

I offer to take the invitations to Daniel's family. Leah's eyes light up at the idea.

"Then you can meet him, Sadia," she says, with a smile. "You can talk with him, find out what he's thinking."

DANIEL MEETS ME at Thane Station in a rickshaw, and he seems much different from my students at ORT India. He seems more confident, and more comfortable talking to an unfamiliar Western woman. On the way back to his house, Daniel tells me that he has been living on his own in Israel for the last two years. I wonder how he feels about his upcoming marriage, if this is something that he chose, or something that his family wanted. I hope, for Leah's sake, that he wants to get married.

I deliver the wedding invitations to Daniel's mother, a jolly woman with glasses and curly dark hair. She kisses me on both cheeks and tells me how happy she is to meet me. Their apartment is located in a relatively new stucco complex with a courtyard. The place is quite large, a marked contrast from Leah's apartment, with two bedrooms and a large living room. I notice a tiny Hindu maidservant scurrying in and out of the kitchen with a broom. Daniel translates his mother's Marathi into English for me, and over tea I learn that Daniel's mother is a widow who lost her husband several years ago. She tells me that her older son and his wife and baby son live nearby, and Daniel, of course, lives in Israel. Her two sons are her greatest joy in life. She was not supportive of the idea of Daniel's moving to Israel when he first broached the subject, three years ago; she didn't want him to be so far away from her. But now she is proud that he has relocated there and is doing well. With the addition of an Indian Jewish wife, she will consider him settled, and she will be content. Has she been looking for a long time for his wife? Not long, she says, with a shake of her head. She announces that she is going to the market to buy groceries, and instructs Daniel to host me properly and offer me some cake.

"So, Sadia," he begins, as he sits down and pours me more tea, "you're the famous American photographer. . . ."

"Hardly," I say, laughing.

"But really," he says, "everyone is talking about you these days. About how you've come to take photos and do interviews with the Bene Israel. You are doing a kind of study, is that right?"

"A personal kind of study, I suppose."

I tell Daniel about Nana, and about why I came to India, which intrigues him. "So she was a very important person for you, then," he says, and I nod. "May I ask you a personal question?" I say yes. "Do you think your grandmother wanted you to marry a Jewish person?"

In this way, Daniel and I fall into an instant friendship, talking frankly about life and family and his plans for the future. I tell him that I think it might have made Nana happy if I were to end up with a Jewish person, but that she wasn't one to insist on her opinion, or even always make it known.

"And have you ever considered marrying?" he asks. "If you don't mind my asking, that is."

"Once," I say. "I considered it. But then I realized that I had more traveling that I needed to do, more work."

"Ah, you're a dreamer, I can tell," Daniel says. "This is my trouble, too." He sighs and looks out the window. "But this is why Leah is a good match for me."

I feel suddenly as if I am a spy, sent from the other side, but I'm thrilled to find myself in such a position.

"Did you want to have an arranged marriage?" I ask, casually.

"Arranged marriage is the best thing, I think," he says, nodding. "Somebody my mummy selects for me. Because she knows me better than anybody else. So she knows my . . . with what sort of girl I can spend the rest of my life. She's the best judge. So I left it on her to decide."

Did he ever consider any Bene Israel girls living in Israel? I ask him.

"I met some Bene Israel girls who were born in Israel," Daniel tells me. "But basically I found them to be more Israeli than Indian. . . . I'm not saying that I think Indians are better, but . . . there are certain values. I feel more comfortable with the idea of having an Indian Jewish wife."

Daniel begins to tell me what led him to move to Israel, how through the study of the Torah he began to learn about the importance of the Holy Land.

"In the Torah, so much importance is given to a Jew going to Jerusalem." He taps his heart three times with his right hand. "I started to feel that, although I liked India, I was meant to wrestle with the questions of the Torah there, not here."

"I've noticed that sometimes people don't distinguish between the Israel of the Torah and the modern nation-state of Israel. Are they different?"

"But it's not something you can separate, Sadia. Ever since the destruction of the Second Temple and the dispersal of the twelve tribes of Israel, we have been longing to go back there, to be reunited in Jerusalem. Even at weddings—even at my wedding—we will crush a glass. Why? To remember the destruction of the Second Temple, even in a time of great happiness to remember that sadness. We pray facing Jerusalem, even now. Israel now—it's a redemption, it's a renewal."

"Do you worry about the violence there? Do you worry about raising your children in a place of such uncertainty?"

"I want to raise my children in a Jewish country, with Jewish schools, where they will learn to speak Hebrew, not like I do, but as a mother tongue, alongside Jewish children from all over the world. I want that for them."

"Was it difficult to make the adjustment from India to Israel?"

"Actually, Sadia, this was the second time that I migrated."

"The second time?"

"The first time I tried was three years ago," he explains. "I went with one suitcase, with hardly anything in it. I found a place to live and a job, and at night I used to sit in my room and cry, missing my mother and India."

After a month, he came back home to Thane, feeling defeated. He worked in Bombay for another year, saving up money, learning Hebrew, and studying the Torah. At the end of that year, he was resolved to try again, and this time he made a success of things. He found work in a hotel, and shared an apartment with several other men about his age. But something was missing. His mother began to send him photographs of young women in the Bene Israel community.

"This is Leah," he says, showing me the two photographs of Leah and her family in Magen Hassidim Synagogue that served as his introduction. Leah is wearing makeup in the pictures and looks happy and attractive. He smiles as he looks at them, and I realize that they hold the same power for him as his photographs did for her.

"What happens after the exchange of pictures?" I ask. Daniel explains that if both families are amenable to the match, a visit is arranged. The prospective bride and groom are given a few minutes alone.

"When we met for the first time, I could tell that she was very much tense and all. She asked me, 'How is your nature?' I told her that I'm a cool guy; there are no dos and don'ts in my house."

"You could tell that Leah wasn't sure?" I ask him.

"Generally, you go to see a girl, a girl sees a boy, and you don't immediately give the answer, yes or no. The bride's family says, Okay, we'll tell you afterwards. . . ."

"But with Leah?"

Daniel blushes deeply. "At that time I felt that it was . . . it was *on*. Very much on." He smiles. "And *then* . . . I was on the top of the world!"

Daniel sings this last part and actually giggles. The spirit of his excitement is infectious.

I RETURN ONCE A WEEK or so for lunch with Daniel and his mother. I shoot interviews with each of them, and volunteer to help Daniel memorize his wedding song, the traditional Bene Israel hymn that all bridegrooms sing as their brides walk into the synagogue. It's a gorgeous, lilting song about the beauty of the bride as she walks toward the *bimah* to meet her future husband and recite the marriage vows. Daniel has trouble mastering the difficult tune in conjunction with the words, but by my fourth visit to Thane he's making progress.

"I think I've got it." He stands, closes his eyes, and sings the words with affection. When he's finished, I clap to show my enthusiasm.

"You've done it, Daniel! Leah will be really impressed."

"I hope so," he says. "Sadia, do you think that she'll like Israel?"

"I haven't been there, Daniel," I say. "I don't know."

"I worry that she will miss India a lot," he says. "Her mother and her friends and everything. But for me, now, Israel is home. I hope someday that it will be for her, too."

24

WHICH WAY IS EAST

L ately, I wake up with the same thought, as if I am trapped in a specific moment that I have lived through. It's not quite a dream; more the feeling of inhabiting a memory.

Though I know I'm in Bombay, for the first few moments that I am awake I feel convinced that I am in Nana's room on Aragon Avenue in Coral Gables. I can remember the sense of her nearness, and I stay there for a few moments, unwilling to wake up. I recall her small frame next to me in the bed, the sound of her knitting needles clicking by my ear. In this reminiscence, it is March 2000. My parents have left the Boston area to teach architecture at the University of Miami.

Nana can no longer stand the cold Boston winters and wants to be closer to her sons, now living in other parts of Florida. My mother, father, and grandmother are living in an apartment for the first time. It is a place my father took sight unseen: an L-shaped apartment in a four-hundred-unit pink stucco building, with a steak house on the ground floor and palm trees all around. Miami seems like a foreign country after Boston, and I can't quite make sense of my family's creating a life here. My father's mahogany colonial furniture looks ridiculous, too large and old-fashioned for this place. My mother's miniature paintings from Pakistan look out of place, relics from another reality.

I have flown home for a visit from graduate school in California. I'm in a master's program at Stanford, learning how to make photographs and documentary films. I am twenty-four, Nana is eighty-two. I am trying to record Nana's stories, prodding her to talk into my little tape recorder. There never seems to be enough time. There are doctors' appointments, my mother needs help with the laundry, dinner needs to be made, and Nana can do very little now without resting. Her knees seize up, and her back bends over her cane. Her soft, tiny body is becoming smaller. She is stubborn as always and doesn't like to admit it, but she is in pain, and I can see it.

This afternoon, I am determined to stay home with Nana in her bedroom and coax her to tell me about her life. In her bedroom she keeps the old wooden dresser with five drawers. They are hard to pull out now, filled with Nana's treasures: postcards, balls of yarn, gifts not given, safety pins, greeting cards, birth certificates, old photos, recipes. In this new apartment, this piece of furniture is the only site of her history, the only place with sedimentary layers of objects. Nana is pushing the top drawer closed when I enter, and she looks up at me quizzically while she brushes her hair with a small brush. My mother has told me that Nana has always worried that if I know the truth about her life and the mistakes she made as a young person, I won't respect her. I want her to know that I am anxious to know everything, that nothing she can say would ever affect what I think of her. Sometimes I am able to coax her into talking—and she will speak firmly and fluidly—but this happens rarely and with little warning. I stand there at the mirror watching her while she brushes her hair, wondering what kind of mood she is in.

"Nana, I want to interview you."

"Me? What for? I have nothing to say."

"That's not true, Nana, you have quite a lot to say."

She puts down the brush and looks at her hands, thinking. Then she opens the bottom drawer and pulls out three sets of knitted woolen baby clothes. One is white, one is pale green, and one is pink.

"Do you like them?" she asks me softly, placing them on the bed carefully. "I am almost done with them."

"They're beautiful, Nana. Who are they for?"

"They're for your baby."

The idea of my producing a child hovers over the abstract of my future like a remote mirage—something I hope for someday, when I am grown up. I realize suddenly that Nana knows she will not be there when the time comes for me to have a baby, that these baby clothes are Nana's last project, and when she finishes them she will leave us. My eyes sting with this new knowledge.

I have been preparing myself to lose Nana as long as I can remember; to know her is to be acutely aware of the fragility of her body and the strength of her will. One of her doctors told me on my last visit that the fact she is alive in the face of such extreme pain—in her knees, in her back, in her legs, which are swelling at the indignity of too many drugs to regulate too many ailments—shows just how strong her determination is. Recently we learned that she has tiny tears on the inside of her kidney, a hereditary illness that she was born with. It's her resolve that I now see changing, the decision of a person who believes that the work she was put on this earth to do is done.

"Nana, tell me a story," I say, trying to change the subject, lifting her legs, heavy with swelling, one at a time, and placing bolster pillows underneath each one. I rub her legs in long motions, from thigh to ankle, trying to draw out what hurts her.

"Tell me the story of how your ancestors came to India. Tell me about the shipwreck."

"What for, sweetheart?" she asks, folding up the baby clothes. "Why do you want to hear that story again?"

"I want to hear you tell it," I say. "Like you used to tell it in Chestnut Hill."

She lets out a small sigh and begins her story. She tells me that her ancestors left the land of Israel and were shipwrecked off the coast of India. Seven women and seven men survived; they lived in coastal villages, pressing seeds into oil for their livelihood, and remembered only one Jewish prayer.

"There was once a ship, a ship that left Israel after the destruction of the Second Temple, two thousand years ago. A ship that sailed for forty days and forty nights, until it crashed on the Konkan Coast, near Bombay. . . ."

Shema Israel: Hear, O Israel, the Lord our God, the Lord is One.

This story: my inheritance and my mystery.

That week, we spent several afternoons pasting stacks of small black-and-white photographs into plastic albums.

"Don't worry about this," she chided me. "Never mind."

I wrote in pencil on the back of each photograph whatever she remembered about the image, the year it was taken perhaps, or a place, a person's name. I was most fascinated by the earliest images, the ones taken in India, candid windows into her youth that came before the formal portraits from weddings and birthdays in Pakistan. In one picture, Nana appears as a very young girl, swinging on a swing with a friend or cousin, her braid swinging; she's in motion and laughing. In another, she and her husband are sitting on a hillside and smiling, posing with another couple. My grandfather rests a dapper-looking hat jauntily on his knee.

The later pictures were color snapshots of Nana from the 1980s and 1990s, taken when she was living in my uncles' various homes in Florida, Texas, and New Jersey. It is not the custom for a woman to live with her daughter and son-in-law, and each extended stay was an attempt to live with one of her sons. Inevitably, she came back to us in Chestnut Hill, to her room at the top of the staircase. Cassim and I were her special projects, the two children she was given free rein to spoil and discipline as she saw fit, and when she returned she fussed about the kitchen, making breakfast and clipping coupons as if she had never left. To us she was more than a grandparent, she was our constant source of support; and I hated to think that she didn't think we were enough.

In the two years after my parents relocated to Miami, Nana did more of this shuffling from place to place, spending months at a time in her sons' homes. I visited her in each of these places, and I saw how her other grand-children respected her from a distance but saw her as old, something separate from their present lives. They didn't engage her in conversation or ask her advice, and she didn't have authority in those households the way she did in ours. No one wanted to hear her stories. The subject of Nana's Judaism raised too many unanswered questions: if she was Jewish, what were they? She retreated more and more into her bedroom, into an interior world of television and memory.

But more and more, Judaism was on Nana's mind. She began to confide in my mother that she worried constantly about death—not the physical pain of dying, but the prospect of meeting her parents in heaven. She was terrified to face her mother and father with the decision she had made to leave the religion of her birth.

My mother took her to the library to borrow books on Judaism, to a lo-cal synagogue to meet with a young rabbi.

"My husband promised me a Jewish funeral," Nana told her one after-noon, driving back from the synagogue in the car. "He promised me that if I raised you children as Muslims I could die as a Jew."

It made my mother upset to hear her mother talk about dying.

"Shhh, now, Amma. Don't talk about that."

THE LAST TIME I saw Nana was in Miami, and I took her to an appointment with a physical therapist who was helping her to strengthen her back and unlock her knees. The therapist's office was a generic-looking place in a strip mall, but the man was kind and patient with her, showing her how to do the exercises. He took me aside when Nana was changing back into her street clothes at the end of the session, looking concerned.

"I can tell that you two are close," he said.

"Yes," I said, nodding. "It's nice to see her."

"Listen, I need your help. She comes here, but she doesn't do the exercises at home. She's giving up, giving in to the pain."

"I see."

We took a taxi back to my parents' apartment, and I looped my arm around Nana's small back, holding her close as we rode, something I had never done before.

"The physical therapist says that you don't do your exercises, Nana."

"Never mind," she said stubbornly, looking out the window. "What's the use?"

"Don't say that." I felt myself getting upset. "I need you to be well for my graduation, to come to California." My graduation from Stanford was in three months, and we had spoken about her making the trip. I knew that she didn't quite understand what I was studying, but it seemed like an event that she would appreciate, with red robes and flags, a football stadium filled with relatives, the kind of America that she aspired to for her grandchildren.

"I'll try," she said absentmindedly, patting my knee. "Let's see." We rode along in silence.

That night, I tiptoed into Nana's bedroom. Nana had asked if, this visit, I could stay with her in her room, instead of sleeping on the couch, and I was touched that she wanted to be near me. I entered her room and heard the quiet, raspy sound of her breathing; I was afraid of disturbing her fragile body. She smelled like comfort and rose talc. As I slipped into the bed I woke her, and I held my body still, hopeful that she might fall back asleep.

"I could have stayed," she said.

I let her words hover in the dark for a moment, wondering what she meant.

"Stayed where, Nana?"

"Bombay," she said. "I owned my house, Rahat Villa, and my brothers were there, my mother was there. It was 1948, and I could have stayed. As Rachel Jacobs, I wouldn't have had to go to Pakistan. I could have lived my life in Bombay."

"Do you mean that you wish you had never left India?" I was shocked to hear her express regret for her life in Pakistan with my grandfather, the decades that had come after Partition.

"I should have stayed."

MY LAST DAY IN MIAMI, Nana found me writing down notes from one of our conversations in one of my notebooks and stood next to me, quietly, not wanting to disturb me.

"Do you need something?" I asked her, and she shook her head to say no. Then she said, "Come, let's have a cookie."

I followed her to the kitchen, curious about what she meant. She had never volunteered such an activity before.

We each took a cookie from the kitchen cupboard, and then she motioned for me to sit next to her on the couch.

"So," she said formally, once we were both seated, "what are your plans?"

"For my life?"

She nodded.

"Well, soon I will finish graduate school . . ." I began. "And then I'd like to get a job, perhaps in New York."

"What will you do there?"

"I will make films," I told her. "Documentary films."

"Will you write books? Like your mother?"

"Yes, I hope so."

"Promise me one thing," she said, placing a hand on my arm, her voice suddenly serious. "Go to India, study your ancestors."

Nana had never asked me to do anything before, nothing more than to set the table, or to call when I arrived somewhere. But the idea opened up before me, curious and unfolding, persistent and asking for recognition.

"I will, Nana," I said, clearing my throat. "I promise that I will."

I returned to California with pieces of Nana's stories scribbled in notebooks, recorded on tiny tapes, and I called her and told her that I would be back in Miami for the summer. I told her that I wanted to do more interviews. I asked her if she would teach me how to knit, and she scoffed.

"You and your mother, you have no patience!" she said, but I assured her that I wanted to try.

"And to cook," I told her. "Nana, you never taught me how to cook."

"Studies are more important."

"But my studies are almost finished," I told her. "Now I want to learn."

TWO MONTHS LATER, Nana went to the hospital for a series of routine tests on her kidney, and ended up staying there for more tests, then for monitoring. Once she was inside the hospital, it was difficult for her to come out. She had contracted an infection that necessitated that she stay. I spoke to my mother frequently. Is she all right? I asked. Do you need my help? No, no, Mama said, sounding distracted. It should be fine.

SHORTLY AFTER THAT, my mother came to San Francisco for some meetings at Berkeley. Tony and I met her in a restaurant on Sunday morning for brunch. It was a sunny place, the walls painted a bright yellow and decorated with paintings of sunflowers. I wanted her to like the place I had chosen; I wanted her to like Tony.

She seemed anxious. "It's very nice," she said, looking at the menu. "I'm sorry, I can barely concentrate, I'm thinking about Nana."

"How was Berkeley?" I asked her, trying to keep my voice level. We were both worried that Nana wouldn't be there when Mama returned, that she should not have come on this trip.

"Good," my mother replied.

I wanted to say, Take me with you—but I didn't. I was one month from graduation, wading through the last weeks of my thesis. We both understood that if Nana took a turn for the worse I would fly to Miami, but we didn't discuss what the criteria would be for me to leave school early.

"You have a big week coming up?" my mother asked.

"I do," I said. I didn't ask myself until later if this was true.

Tony squeezed my hand under the table and turned his chin toward me, smiling, his light brown hair falling in his eyes. He was always so comforting, even when I couldn't express quite what was wrong. I smiled back, quickly, grateful for his company, and we returned to talk of books and films and weather.

For the rest of the day, I couldn't work. My thesis was a 16mm film about the small town of Stewart, Mississippi, which was being demolished to make room for a four-lane highway. I had spent weeks interviewing the older residents of the town about the fact that the buildings they had grown up in were about to be razed. That afternoon, I watched the footage slide back and forth over the wheels of my editing machine. The words didn't make much sense to me. I had interviewed other people's grandmothers, I realized.

I forgot to eat dinner. Late at night, I took a handful of Nana's *sev puri* mix out of a carton she had sent me and leaned my head back, tipping it into my mouth, the way I had seen her do. I decided that I would eat it in tiny handfuls until it was gone. I need to concentrate, I told myself. Nana would want me to work. My mother's cell phone didn't always ring in the hospital, but I tried her late that night. She told me that Nana was okay, that Nana had been awake to see Mama when she reached the hospital. Then I slept, knowing that Mama was there to take care of her.

On Monday, I called again and didn't get any answer. I went to the library and tried to read; in conjunction with my film, I was writing a paper about the residents of Stewart and how they had lost their town. I was reading books about the theory of landscape, about how we are formed by the buildings, the trees, the slope of the hills that surround us. I lost myself in these books. When I walked out of the library, the bulk of the day was behind me, and I felt sad, disoriented, betrayed by the sunlight. What time is it? I wondered. It was three hours later in Miami. Three more hours into evening. I called my mother, suddenly terrified. She picked up. I was so worried, I said. But Mama made everything all right.

"Nana's okay," she said. "We were having some tests done—did you call?"

"I called earlier today, in the morning," I said. I should have called again in the afternoon, I thought. But Nana was all right.

"Should I come there?" I asked. "I can come there."

Mama hesitated. "No," she said. "You stay there. It's so expensive. Do your work."

"But you'll tell me if I should come?"

"I will," she said. "I'll ask Nana if she wants you to come."

A week went by. I found some pictures of Tony and me dressed up, from a Viennese ball we had gone to at Stanford. Tony was wearing a rented tuxedo and a dark pink bouttoniere that matched my long dress, his hair cut short for the occasion, making him look more like the pictures I had seen of his dad in the navy. Standing next to me, he looked tall; not as tall as my father, but lanky and WASPy like him, his posture erect and his gaze straightforward. Nana will like these, I thought. I found a card, and I wrote to her about Tony and school and the film I was making. Just this once, I didn't simplify. I wrote in my own handwriting, my small scribbled lines, instead of the large rounded letters I normally wrote to her in. A few days later, I asked Mama if Nana had looked at the card. "We will have a Ph.D. in the family," she had said to Mama, proudly. "Do *you* have a Ph.D.?" Mama had said no, smiling. "See?" Nana had said, shaking her head and raising her eyebrows, impressed.

That spring, I had started to ride an old used bicycle to get from my room in graduate student housing to my department on the Old Quad. My friends found it quaint, my late start on the bicycle. Didn't you ride one as a kid? they asked me, laughing. Sure, I said. Just not between then and now.

One morning, on my way to school, I thought about Nana, about all of the things I wanted to tell her. I pushed very hard on the pedals to go faster, to feel the wind whip through me; I wanted to see everything go by faster than I could make it go. I saw my route down the path, and I took it. I saw my turn, left through the arch. I saw a tiny rock, nothing really, out of the corner of my eye. I should avoid it, I thought. I should call Nana, I thought. Suddenly I felt myself slipping, the bike coming down with me, my hands hitting the gravel. The rocks on the ground sliced through my jeans, scraped through the skin of my knees and shins. Tiny rocks were embedded in my palms, in my knuckles, caked and sealed with dirt and blood. I was covered in dirt, the way I never had been as a kid, when I was too timid to go so fast. I threw my bike to one side and walked to my department, holding my arms around myself. I called Nana's hospital room from the phone in the basement of the building. Her voice was strange, crackling into the line.

"Sweetie," she said.

"I fell, Nana."

"What's that?"

"I fell. On my bike, on the ground. I cut up my hands."

"Oh, sweetie, you must take care," she said, sounding concerned. "You must take alcohol and wash it, take some iodine and apply it. It will sting, but it will make it better." She was attached to tubes in a hospital, but she was still a nurse.

"I will, Nana. I will." I was crying, but I didn't want her to hear me. "It's not that bad. I miss you."

"Does it hurt?"

"No, it's fine, Nana. I shouldn't have mentioned it."

"When are you coming?"

"Next week," I said, making it up.

"When are you coming?" she said again. I couldn't tell if she couldn't hear me, or if her drugs were making her foggy.

"Next week."

"Tomorrow?" she asked.

"Next week."

"I'll see you tomorrow," she said. "I'm waiting for you." I leaned my head against the wall of the phone booth and tried not to cry. "You are my sunshine," she said, before she hung up.

MY PHONE RANG AT SIX the next morning. I was dreaming about Karachi. Nana was in the garden of Siddiqi House, hanging up clothes to dry on the clothesline. Nana is fine, someone said. What were we so worried about? We were being silly, my dream self said. In my sleep, I picked up the telephone receiver, knowing somehow that it was my mother. I will tell my mother the good news, that Nana is fine, I thought. Then I heard a rustling, my mother's voice, and I was instantly awake.

"Mama?" Suddenly the 6 a.m. light was seeping into my room, and I couldn't make it stop. I felt myself pushing at the air around me.

"She's gone." Mama's voice was like the voice of someone being strangled. "Take this," I heard her say, and she passed the phone to my cousin Salim. I let Salim hear the sounds I was making before I could register what I was doing. He listened to me until he couldn't bear it any longer.

"She was my grandmother, too, you know," he said curtly, and handed the phone to my uncle Salman.

I should have stayed. I should have stayed. I should have stayed.

ON THE PLANE TO MIAMI, I ran my fingers across my knuckles, feeling the embedded sand still trapped in the surface of my skin. The last time I talked to her, imprinted in my fist. I crossed the country on a last-minute ticket, a trip I might have taken just as easily the week before. I stared out the oval of my window and let the hum of the airplane match the one I heard in my chest. My father picked me up at the airport, looking worn and hollow. We didn't know what to say, what to talk about on the way home. He told me that Cassim was arriving later in the day, that my mother was not doing well, that he was worried about her. I felt swollen, as if the slightest knock would render me liquid.

When I saw Mama, I was startled. She seemed so much younger, like a little girl. She was lost; seeing her like that terrified me. I hugged her and tried to comfort her, but I didn't know how.

"It was a test," she said, over and over again. "But the resident didn't check her chart. He didn't see that she was allergic to heparin. Her blood got too thin. She wasn't supposed to go now," she kept saying, over and over. "It wasn't her time. She didn't have a dream."

I sat on Mama's bed, then lay next to her, as I did when I was small. She read the Qur'an, laying a dupatta over her head and closing her eyes.

She told me that tomorrow we would drive to West Palm Beach, where two of my uncles were living, that Nana would receive a Muslim burial.

"But she wanted a Jewish burial," I said, alarmed. "Your father promised her."

Mama shook her head. "My brothers were in charge. It is the way she would have wanted it, for her sons to arrange it."

"But she wanted to die as a Jew."

"I know," Mama said quietly, and explained what happened that last morning, while I slept in California. A week previous, Mama had arranged for the young rabbi from the local synagogue to come and visit Nana, to talk to her about Judaism's view of the afterlife. Their appointment was for 11 a.m., and when he arrived, he found my mother, my father, and two of my uncles at Nana's bedside, Nana attached to a life-support machine. My mother asked the rabbi if he would read Nana her last rites in Hebrew, which he did.

"We tried to figure out how to give her a Jewish funeral, but the rules here in Florida were so hard to understand, so different for us. We wanted to bury her the way we know how, with women that she was close to washing her body, preparing her. We wanted to bury her in a pine casket, the way we would have done at home. The way her mother was buried."

"But we should do something, something Jewish," I insisted.

"In Judaism, there's something called an eleven-month ceremony," Mama said. "We unveil the tombstone eleven months from now, and convert the resting place from a place of mourning to a place of reflection. We can do that."

I spent hours in Nana's room. I opened up her bureau, slowly, as if she might still catch me. I didn't know what I was looking for, but the idea of her burying secret things into the folds of these drawers gave me comfort, the idea that there were still layers to uncover even though she was gone. In a tea tin, the red paint cracked with age, I found a curious-looking key; it was three-cornered and made of brass. I slipped its chain around my neck, feeling its coolness and wondering what it was for. In the bottom drawer of her bureau I found the baby clothes, now complete. White, pale green, pink. I lay on her bed, her sheets still smelling of her, and covered my head with her pillows. So this is grief, then. This is what it means.

THE NEXT DAY, we drove to West Palm Beach for Nana's funeral. I tried to get used to the idea that I would be one of the five women elected to wash Nana's body. I was frightened to see her in death. In the gathering hall of the cemetery, my uncles' wives had laid the floor with white sheets. According to custom, we were all dressed in white kurta pajamas, save the Western guests, who stood out awkwardly in black. People, familiar and unfamiliar both, rose to greet my mother, who could barely look at them. All around me was the sound of weeping, discomfort. A tiny Pakistani woman walked deliberately with a cane to embrace my mother. She spoke in Urdu, pulling my mother's face close to hers with both hands. She had bright blue eyes; they were streaming with tears. I couldn't make out what she was saying, but I saw my mother's gratitude, how hungrily she embraced her in return.

Mama told me that this was Ruko Apa, a cousin of her father's and a friend of my grandmother's from Karachi. She had been living in Chicago for the last several months, with her son. When she heard the news of Nana's death, two days previous, she implored her son to start driving. They had driven eighteen hours to be here today. Ruko Apa knew the rite of washing the body. She had come here to lead us in the ritual. She had brought sweet *attar* from Mecca for Nana's body. Come, she said. It's time.

I followed two of my aunts, my mother, and Ruko Apa into a separate space, cold and white, where I saw Nana's body laid on a piece of marble, her tiny frame covered in a sheet.

Ruko Apa instructed us, but I couldn't understand her Urdu. I followed the motions of her arm, the way she soaped a cloth and ran it over Nana's shoulders, her back, but I was always the last to complete my part of the task. As we navigated the details of the ritual, the prayers, the careful execution of each step, I felt afraid to touch her, but I kept my hand on Nana's shoulder, not wanting her to feel left behind. I closed my eyes and said a small prayer; I told her how much I missed her.

When the washing was complete, I stayed in the room. I kissed Nana on her forehead, the way I always had before I left for school. I told her how wrong I was, that I should have come earlier.

In the hall, we waited, sitting on the floor, for the grave to be dug. Then we heard the sounds of disorder, men talking, disagreeing with one another. My father and brother went to offer their help and see what the trouble was. The grave had been dug, but my cousin Sartaj felt that it had been dug in the wrong direction, that it did not face Mecca, the way it should. Which way is east? I heard them asking each other. Which way is east? Who has a compass?

I could feel the women around me getting impatient.

"Such a shame," I heard someone say.

It took another hour to redig the grave facing the right way. We waited, and prayed, and I felt Nana looking down at us, watching our confusion. My father, my brother, my uncles and cousins carried her casket above their heads, walking Nana's body to her grave site. The imam recited the prayers and we bowed our covered heads.

When it was all over, Nana was covered with a pile of earth.

"I don't want to leave her here," my mother said, looking up at my tall father, her voice rising and breaking. "How do I leave her here?"

My father folded my mother into his chest. They stayed there for a few moments. I felt the same sense of panic.

We walked to our car and drove back to Miami. There were four of us now, once and for all, not five.

25

DEPARTURES

BOMBAY, MAY 2003

I change the date of my return ticket to New York. Once, twice, then a third time. March becomes April, and I feel the heat of Bombay's streets rising to almost unbearable temperatures once again. I wipe sweat from the back of my neck with a handkerchief that I now carry with me for this purpose. I am staying to shoot Leah and Daniel's wedding. I watch them shop for their new life in Israel, filling out Leah's paperwork at the Israeli Consulate, lining their suitcases with spices. I hear both of them talk excitedly about their new life ahead, stories that hint at the titillating prospect of unfettered time together. Two nights before their wedding, I shuttle between their *mehndi* ceremonies, held in neighboring synagogues, blessing the bride, then the groom, by placing a morsel of jaggery in each of their mouths and throwing rice over their shoulders, accompanied by the pulsing beat of the latest Bollywood hit songs. On the day of their wedding, I dress up in a pale green silk salwar kameez and stand at the front of the synagogue, greeting guests and videotaping the ceremony like a relative. I'm amazed at how many people in the community I now know—how many people I have photographed, how many know me. I watch as Leah approaches the *bimah,* shyly but deliberately, and Daniel serenades her. She is dressed in the ornate white lace gown Judith and I helped her choose at the Catholic bridal shop, and swathed in a large veil that cascades from an ambitious topknot at the top of her head. I watch as Leah and Daniel recite their prayers, as Daniel places a ring on Leah's henna-covered hand, and as they sign the marriage contract and walk around the synagogue, thanking their well-wishers. At the reception, in a nearby marriage hall, an emcee enthusiastically narrates the proceedings, shouting *"Mazel tov! Mazel tov!"* as Leah and Daniel enter the brightly lit tent and sit on red-and-gold thrones decorated with garlands of roses. Their first kiss takes place in the middle of a raucous chair dance, both hoisted up high above their guests' heads in red plastic chairs. Daniel places his lips over Leah's for a brief and awkward moment, and the crowd cheers. The next day, they fly to Israel.

Later in April, at Passover, I photograph over a hundred Bene Israel women sitting cross-legged inside a tent in the yard of Magen David Synagogue, beating balls of unleavened dough into wide, circular sheets of bread. Tip-tap, go the balls of dough as they hit the backs of the pans before they are rolled flat, in a syncopated rhythm through the large tent. Tip-tap. Tip-tap. "Matzah!" one woman calls out once her bread is flat and ready to be brought to the oven. "Matzah!" another woman echoes, and a boy comes running with a plate on which he places the flattened dough, taking it quickly to the back oven to be baked and prayed over.

In this way, winter becomes spring. The rains will come soon. I missed them last year, while I was in Massachusetts, and Julie tells me that on certain days in July you will be barely able to walk down the street for the water rushing past your feet. I think about the fall, High Holidays once more, followed by the temperate winter, those rare months when it's possible to go out in Bombay in the middle of the day. Then the cycle will repeat. The inevitability of my return to the United States is an idea now making itself felt, but by May I'm still not ready to go back. Not yet, I think, pushing the thought out of my mind, making lists of photographs I need to take, interviews that I hope to record. But when? I hear another voice ask. When will my work here be finished?

"Come home, Sadia," my mother says on the phone. My father doesn't say it, but I can hear in his voice that wants me home too. Stubbornly, I hang on.

REKHEV RINGS MY DOORBELL one afternoon, and when I go to the gate to let him in, I see that he looks distracted, strange.

"Are you all right?" I ask him, and he tells me he was up all night working with an editor on a new short film. It's an adaptation of a folktale, he tells me, based on a story he grew up with. He hooks up my video camera to the television and shows me a rough video copy of the film. I watch, mesmerized, as images from Rekhev's notebooks come to life—a book whose pages fall upward into the air, a girl who becomes a tree. Even in this rough state, I can tell that the film is going to be beautiful, and I get very excited, asking him how he did certain things, telling him what I think he should do next.

"I'm happy to show this to you," he says. "It's just an exercise, but I'm starting." He gets up and lights a cigarette. He sits by the window, and I watch as he blows long plumes of white smoke between the iron bars of the grate. The room is quiet except for the tinkling recorded signal of a truck in reverse. Something about his silence makes me sit up straighter. "Sadia," he says, "I have something to tell you."

He turns and faces me, and I feel a strange sensation at the base of my skull, something like vertigo. "I think you should stay in India," he says finally. "Don't go. Stay in India for a year and live with me."

"Live with you?" I ask. I want to make sure that I heard him correctly.

"We could go to the Konkan and rent a small house. Like Sangeeta's place in Revdanda. Or Bombay, the Himalayas, anywhere you like. You can work on your projects and I will work on mine, and it will be a good life. I will teach you many things. I'm not asking you to marry me. I'm asking you to stay for one year."

I think about the shape of that imaginary year and its inevitable complications, what it would look and feel like. I feel slightly taken aback by the boldness of his offer, but also by his intuition that I might be drawn to such a plan. We have read the same novels.

"And at the end of that year? What then?"

"At the end of that year, you can go home and return to your plans, to your life in America. That's all I ask. A year."

I feel a crushing sense of regret at the consequences of calling out what we are, and what we are not, into the open air of this room; I would have happily lived longer in our unnamed state.

"Don't say anything now," he says, rising to go. "Think it over."

I WALK THROUGH BOMBAY, thinking over Rekhev's idea. I find myself retracing my steps, the paths that I first walked in Bombay when I arrived eighteen months earlier. I walk along Marine Drive to Cama Hospital, where Nana served as head matron, across the dirty sand of Chowpatty Beach. I walk to the Gateway of India, along the quiet lanes of Colaba near the Taj Mahal Hotel, and think about how Nana longed for this city, its crowds, its elegant streets. I came here trying to find the paths that Nana didn't choose, but now I wonder if, in leaving her city, in missing this place, I will come to understand her in yet another way.

Crossing my street to the tea shop one afternoon, I see a woman who looks familiar, the American-looking woman I've seen before, dressed in a salwar kameez. Upon closer inspection, she appears to be older than I by about ten or fifteen years, and I see what I imagine to be the marks of her life here, the way she has adapted her facial expressions to make herself understood, the fact that she has traded the bright colors of the recently arrived for the muted browns and beiges she wears now. I notice how expertly she wends her way through the crowd, motioning to her driver that he should meet her at the end of the block. I see how nearly invisible she makes herself. Perhaps she has an apartment near here. A membership at one of the former British clubs. An

Indian husband. Indian children. I wonder when her parents stopped asking her when she was coming home, when this became her home. She registers my watching her and turns to look back at me—a sort of mirror. She takes in my appearance, my similar clothing, my American sandals, and she waits, standing perfectly still, asking to be considered. For a moment, as I look at her, I see a path opening up in front of me, the chill of recognition, and then, as quickly as it arrived, the feeling fades. Her driver waves to her from his parking space. "Madam!" he calls, and she climbs into the car and speeds away.

I CHOOSE THE DATE of my departure to coincide with the anniversary of Nana's death, which my mother celebrates each year with prayers and by making my grandmother's favorite foods. It's been three years since she died, half of which I have spent here, in her city.

I call Rekhev and tell him that I have chosen a date for my departure.

"Are you there?" I ask. "Did I lose you?"

There's another long silence, and then I hear him breathing.

"I have to go home, Rekhev," I say.

I ask him if he will come to Bombay to see me, but he doesn't answer. We end the conversation in a series of small, terrible silences, with no certainty of a plan to meet again.

I START THE ROUNDS of goodbyes. I begin easily, with the grocer, the vegetable man, the shops that I frequent regularly. Then I say a series of farewells to favorite places: to my train station, at Grant Road; to B. Merwan, the local Irani café; to Magen Hassidim Synagogue; to my bus stop; to the slide in the park shaped like an elephant. At ORT India, Benny Isaacs asks me when I'll return, and I tell him that I don't know when but that, now that I've lived here, I have a sense that I'll always be coming back.

"You'll get some kind of diploma, I hope? For all of this work you've been doing? Or a grade of some kind?"

I don't know how to explain.

"Well, I hope you get an A," he says, and I thank him for making me feel so welcome.

In Sharon's office, I find him sitting with a group of high school students discussing the weekly Torah portion, and I'm impressed at the strength of debate that the boys bring to the endeavor.

When the boys finish and say goodbye to Sharon, I join him at his desk and tell him that I've decided it's time for me to return home. Sharon tells me that he's now making monthly trips to the Konkan Coast to give Hebrew lessons, and that he's been teaching Benjamin and Ellis Waskar's children. I ask him if he'll help me write a letter to the Waskars, and he happily obliges, translating my dictation from English into Marathi. In my letter, I tell them that I am leaving soon for America, and that I will miss them. I tell them that I have discovered that Revdanda is my native place.

When Sharon finishes with the letter, he turns to me. "Have you made your decision yet? About your religion?" He smiles amiably, and I consider how to respond. "Okay, so tell me something," he says, leaning forward in his chair. "Let's say you're home in New York and you want to pray, and in front of you are a church, a mosque, and a synagogue. Which one makes you want to go inside?"

I try to picture it. I think of myself in Manhattan, peering into the doorways of different religious buildings. Every way I can imagine it, I'm standing outside, looking in.

"I feel sometimes that I am expected to choose, that my parents have laid out these options for me and that I should choose. Living in India has made me very aware of the choice. But, truthfully, Sharon, I feel disloyal picking one over another. The truth is that I feel emotionally connected to all three."

"Ah," Sharon says. "So you have more work to do, then."

"Yes, I think I do."

"I wish you all the best for your journey, Sadia." Sharon stands up and extends his hand. "May it be a happy one."

. . .

ON THE NIGHT that I am set to leave, my apartment suddenly becomes a social space, with all sorts of people dropping by to say goodbye: Julie, my students, the man who printed my photographs of the Bene Israel. Mangoes are in season, and I serve them to my string of guests, who sit on my floor devouring the fruit and watching as I distribute the items that I have no room for in my suitcases—books, small appliances, extra clothes. I look hopefully out the door each time the bell rings, hoping it's Rekhev, but there's no sign of him.

Julie instructs me not to clean up anything, just to leave it to her to take care of. "Sadia, you are not finished with the packing up! Stop this cleaning and finish the suitcases!" she scolds me, taking a broom out of my hand.

She tells me that when I go I should just leave the key on the shelf where I always leave it. She will come the next day to clean up and will return the key to my landlord.

By about 11 p.m., my guests have gone, and I take one final look around the small room that has been my world these last fourteen months, at the maps on the wall, the remaining books and clothes I have left for Julie, presents for her children. I place the key on the shelf, as Julie instructed me, and I walk out the door, rolling my suitcases behind me. I hear the iron gate clang shut. There's no way back in, I think.

I don't see Rekhev until I am at the end of the driveway, trying to figure out how I will roll each suitcase into the street so I can hail a taxi without leaving any of them unattended. I see his shadowy form in the light of the streetlamp, the shape of his familiar satchel over one shoulder.

"How long have you been here?" I ask.

"Just a few minutes. I wasn't sure if I was going to stay."

"I'm going to the airport now."

He nods. "I will come also."

Together, we hail a cab and find room for my overloaded suitcases. The driver and Rekhev have to tie the boot of the trunk to the bumper with rope and a series of knots, so that nothing falls out. We drive the hour to the airport in a tentative silence, but I'm infinitely glad for Rekhev's presence.

Rekhev buys a sixty-rupee ticket so that he can come inside the airport to see me off, and we walk past the queue of waiting families and chauffeurs in tasseled jackets with signboards.

"I didn't think you would really go," Rekhev says. "Not now, anyway."

We walk through the fluorescent light of the airport and toward the ticket counters, where I check in and pay exorbitant fees for my excess baggage. There are hours to go until my flight, which departs at nearly 3 a.m., and I tell Rekhev that he should go.

"How can I go," he says, "when there's so little time left?"

I nod, and we find two seats and two tiny plastic cups of tea.

We sit there in silence for what seems like an hour but is perhaps less. I'm not sure what to say.

"Tell me something, Sadia," Rekhev says finally, looking at me. "Is this reality for you, or is this fantasy?"

"What do you mean?"

"When I first came to Pune from Jammu, the whole place felt like fantasy to me. What was real, what I understood, was my father's house, eating my meals in my mother's kitchen, getting a job. Pune, all of this talk of ideas, of becoming an artist, of meeting new people, all of this was fantasy. I used to take rickshaw rides at night and just look around me and marvel at all of it, at how all of it could be happening to me. It was all so new. In time, it has become more comprehensible, but I still think sometimes that I will wake up and I will be at home, daydreaming. Now I wonder if this is the same for you. When you go back to New York, will it be reality for you, or will it be fantasy? And what, then, will Bombay be?"

I pause to think it over. "Right now, Bombay feels very real. But part of me thinks that it will always be fantasy for me, especially when I return home."

"Is home New York?"

"Yes."

"Will you think about this moment, here in the airport, when you go back to New York?"

"Of course I will," I say, and look at him. I put a hand on my throat, trying not to cry.

"Go now," he says, and laughs, running his hand over his face. "Before this thing kills me."

"Yes," I say.

We embrace, awkwardly, and I walk quickly toward the guards without looking back. I hand over my Foreigners Residence Permit, the last emblem of my temporary citizenship here, and I walk, as fast as I can, toward the security checkpoint.

IN THE PLANE, I push my face against the small oval of the window and watch the millions of lights of my adopted city recede from view.

RETURN

WEST PALM BEACH, MAY 2003

When I got back from India, I went to visit Nana's grave. I flew to Miami and drove a rental car to West Palm Beach. Southern Florida, with its wide roads and low banks of horizontal shops, its ever-present air-conditioning, seemed peculiar to me now. It struck me as strange and arbitrary that Nana was buried here. When I reached the cemetery, I found a large plot of unusually flat, artificially green grass flanked by a four-lane road. I drove in slowly, registering the ornate white arch at the entrance and the orderly rows of graves decorated with plastic flowers in a way I didn't before, when I felt cloaked in the newness of losing her. The cemetery was divided into sections according to religious denomination, marked with signposts shaped like old-fashioned road signs, black block letters on white backgrounds that read "Hope," "Faith," and "Devotion." I found Nana's plot near the intersection of two interior roads and pulled the car to one side, getting out slowly and feeling the oppressive heat of the day, cloudless and overly bright.

I thought of the last time I was here. Eleven months after Nana's death, as Mama had promised, we gathered for an unveiling ceremony. Mama had arranged for two of my grandmother's relatives—her niece Lena and her youngest brother, Nissim—to come from Israel and India. They were the only ones present who were already familiar with the Jewish prayers. The rest of us—my mother, father, brother, and two of my uncles—listened carefully to the rabbi as he guided us through the ritual, bowing our heads as he recited verses from the Torah. He explained that, on this day in the Jewish tradition, the period of mourning comes to a close and the burial site is transformed into a place of remembrance.

The tombstone, designed by my parents, had been set the day before and lay swathed in a dark purple velvet shroud with Hebrew characters, on loan from the local synagogue. When the cloth was pulled back, we saw that my mother and father had placed Nana's two names, "Rachel" and "Rahat," in Hebrew, Arabic, and English script, and I heard sounds of surprise around me when the stone was revealed. One of my uncles said: "Our father's name isn't on the stone. He should be there, too." But my mother simply shrugged, acknowledging the thought yet secure in her decision. I wished that more of our relatives had been there to see it. I imagined how much Nana would have enjoyed the moment, the chance to be recognized, in death, for the plurality of who she was.

Rachel Jacobs
June 17, 1917

Rahat Siddiqi
May 16, 2000

Later that day, Uncle Nissim told me that a few months before she died Nana had called him up in India and asked him to look into how she might be buried in Israel. She told him she would call him back after she had thought it over, but she never did. At the time, his story made me think about how conflicted Nana was in her choices, how much of her I didn't understand. Four months passed, and then I left for India.

Now, two years later, I sat cross-legged on the ground and placed a small white rock that I had brought with me from Bombay's Chowpatty Beach on top of her headstone. I stayed there for the rest of the afternoon, listening to the sound of cars speeding by and the low, empty buzz of a nearby streetlamp left perpetually switched on. I thought about how Nana had always assured us that she would warn us before she died. I realized, as if acknowledging something that I had known all along, that she must have had a dream; she just decided to keep this last one to herself, to save us the hurt of knowing too soon. As I sat there, I made a list of all the things that I wished I could tell her. I felt grateful for the tree that my father had planted nearby the year before. When it grew dark, I got up and walked to my car. That night, I would drive back the way I came, and then head home. To New York.

AUTHOR'S NOTE

Some people who appear in this book do so under different names, either at their request or in an effort to protect their privacy. In a few cases, I have also changed identifying characteristics and collapsed or expanded time. Some conversations that appear in the book were recorded on videotape, others in my journals; most have been reconstructed from memory. Much of this book is based on the time line of my life and my grandmother's life. In some instances, I have taken liberties for the purposes of the narrative. My account of events that took place in Siddiqi House is told from my perspective alone—were my relatives to serve as narrators, I am sure they would do so differently.

It was Bombay, not Mumbai, that my grandmother missed deeply, and for this reason I have chosen to use the older spelling.

Heartfelt thanks go to my editor, Jane Fleming, whose dedication and friendship have made this process a delight from start to finish. Ann Godoff provided a home for this book at The Penguin Press, and made it possible for me to tell this story. Thank you to Tracy Locke, Maggie Sivon, Liz Calamari, and their ace publicity team for their hard work and vision, and to Bruce Giffords, who expertly guided this book's editorial production.

Carin Besser offered her insights and her keen sense of pace and structure, and showed me how text can be shaped and trimmed like footage. I am indebted to her for her active attention to tense and time in this narrative and for teaching me so much along the way. I thank her for her unfailing serenity and her continued pursuit of a better book.

My agent, Fredrica S. Friedman, convinced me that I could write this book, patiently nurtured and firmly guided a glimmer of an idea into a proposal, and encouraged me to keep pushing forward when I doubted the course.

I am profoundly grateful to all those who have shared their stories with me and allowed me to retell them, especially to those who welcomed me to participate in and photograph Bene Israel rituals, celebrations, and aspects of daily life. In particular I would like to thank: Benjamin Isaacs and ORT India, Elijah Jacob and The American Jewish Joint Distribution Committee (Mumbai), Sharon and Sharona Galsurkar, Bunny and Krishna Reuben, Samson Massil and family, Abraham Moses, Abraham Samson Mhedeker, Samson Solomon Korlekar and family, Jonathan and Ruth Solomon, Shoshanna Nagavkar, Hannah Kurulkar and Ronen Solomon, and David, Erusha, Ellis, Benjamin, Shoshanna, and Noorit Waskar.

Rekhev Bharadwaj introduced me to ideas and worlds that I could not have imagined previously, only a few of which appear here. So many journeys—on paper, in person, and in mind—would not have been possible without him, and his point of view and collaboration continue to inspire me.

Pheroza, Jamshyd, Navroze, and Raika Godrej created a haven for me in their home and have become my second family in Bombay. The compassionate attention of Dr. Rati Godrej made it possible for me to stay healthy in India. Rachel Reuben welcomed me as a long-lost "cousin-sister."

A Fulbright Scholarship, administered by the Institute for International Education and the United States Educational Foundation in India, created the opportunity for me to begin this project in 2001. My subsequent work in Bombay was made possible through the thoughtful mentorship of Ann Kaplan and by a grant from the Jeremiah Kaplan Foundation. I am grateful to Nathan Katz for his advice at the start of my research, and to Joan C. Roland, whose scholarship on the Bene Israel illuminated my understanding of their history. The Foundation for Jewish Culture provided fiscal sponsorship and support through the Lynn and Jules Kroll Fund for Jewish

Documentary Filmmaking. Anne Greene and a Wesleyan Scholarship to the Wesleyan Writers Workshop gave me the opportunity to return to Middletown at the start of my writing process. John Taylor "Ike" Williams gave wise counsel with panache. Suketu Mehta offered new ways to think about Bombay and about book covers. Richard Nash Gould, my self-appointed godfather, let me monopolize his time and his office at pivotal moments in this project, and painstakingly restored and improved the images that appear in this book. Andreas Burgess helped me develop many aspects of this book's public face and has been a sounding board, equal parts enthusiasm and wisdom, throughout its final stages.

Hope Hall and Purcell Carson have been companions in this journey from distances as far as New York to Bombay and as close as Second Street to the Bowery; my life is enriched by their guidance, companionship, and constant support. William Elison's careful, repeated readings produced invaluable insights and corrected numerous errors in the text—those that remain are mine alone. Adam Chandler shared his thoughts on the importance of wrestling with notions of personal faith. Lucas Bessire taught me the meaning of fieldwork.

My parents, Richard Shepard and Samina Quraeshi, intrepid travelers, seekers, and teachers, have shadowed and strengthened every phase of this project from start to finish in thousands of uncountable ways. They are an inexhaustible source of wisdom, humor, and direction, and I am blessed to be their daughter. I thank my family in Karachi for teaching me the laws of hospitality and for continuing to welcome me as both relative and friend across distances of opinion and geography. Lastly, I thank my brother, Cassim Shepard: comrade, collaborator, and witness. Not only are his instincts and grammar without parallel; he remembers everything better than I do.

ILLUSTRATIONS

A NOTE ON TYPE

The text of this book is set in Adobe Garamond,
based on designs by
Claude Garamond
in the early sixteenth century.

This book was designed by
Nicole LaRoche.

This book was printed and bound
by R. R. Donnelley
at Bloomsburg, Pennsylvania.